Scota,
Egyptian Queen
of the Scots

Scota,
Egyptian Queen
of the Scots

Ireland and Scotland were first settled by the descendants
of an Egyptian pharaoh and his queen.

by
Ralph Ellis

Edfu Books

...

Scota, Egyptian Queen of the Scots
First published in 2006 by Edfu Books

Published in the U.K. by:
Edfu Books
PO Box 165, Cheshire
CW8 4WF, UK
info@edfu-books.com

First edition July 2006
Revised
Second edition March 2009
Third edition March 2014

V 6.1

PoD edition
ISBN 978-1508499824

Muse

Now that is the time when Gaedel Glas,
From whom are the Gaedil born,
Of Scota daughter of Pharao.
From her are the Scots named,
Ut dictum est,
Feni are named from Feinius,
A meaning without secretiveness:
Gaedil from comely Gaedel Glas,
Scots from Scota.

Lebor Gabala Erenn,
(Book of the Invasions of Ireland)

Acknowledgments

To the morning star, who often rose above the eastern horizon to greet me, and to remind me that it was time I descended into the west and the land of slumber. My thanks also to Andy Power, who assisted in my tour of the monuments at Newgrange and pointed out the strange mummified head in St Peter's Church, Drogheda.

Ralph Ellis
Cheshire
July 2006

www.edfu-books.com

Contents

Intro

The Scottish Chronicles

Long, long ago in a faraway land, it is recorded that a prince and princess were enthroned, amongst great pomp and ceremony, as king and queen of their people. But fate was not looking kindly upon either them or the assembled throng of courtiers and officials who supported them, because many of these people would shortly be forced to flee their homes in search of less turbulent lands beyond the 'Great Sea'. The political turmoil that surrounded this marriage, and its theological implications, took nearly four years to fester and ulcerate. Finally, there was a popular uprising of some kind that forced the abdication of the king and queen; but the revolution was peaceful enough that they were allowed to depart with the majority of their administration and followers.

Hundreds of people were forced to take to the sea in small, precarious vessels, and boldly set off towards the setting Sun and great uncertainty. This was an era in which many of these waters were completely uncharted, but since returning to their homes would mean instant death, they sailed on regardless of the dangers. Eventually, after many trials and tribulations, the royal couple and their small flotilla discovered a new land which seemed to hold great promise. Like the Pilgrim Fathers in a much later age, these émigrés set about creating a new nation, a new Jerusalem, far away from the political and religious strife of their former homeland in Egypt.

The prince and princess in this Scottish chronicle were called Gaythelos and Scota, and it is from these appellations that the <u>Gae</u>lic and <u>Sco</u>ttish people are reputed to have been named. And while this harmony in terminology may seem a little convenient, and possibly even contrived, it should be pointed out that this connection was not derived from modern New Age romanticism, nor was it from a Victorian fairy-tale. In fact, the chronicle of Gaythelos and Scotia was recorded in the *Instructions* and the *Pleading of Baldred Biset,* two documents drawn up by the Scottish nobles and intended for submission to the Papal court to demonstrate the great antiquity of the Scottish people. A small element of this history was then appended to the more famous *Declaration of Arbroath,* a document that was drawn up on 6th April 1320 AD, possibly by Abbot Bernard de Linton. This famous document, which is comparable in many respects to the American Declaration of Independence, was likewise signed by numerous earls and barons of Scotland and then sent on its long journey to Pope John XXII. The declaration was made in the wake of Robert the Bruce's victory at Bannockburn in 1314, and like the later American document it sought to legitimise Scotland's independance from England.

Abbot Linton may have been drawing on material written six centuries earlier by Nennius, the eighth century bishop of Bangor, Gwynedd, N Wales, whose *Historia Brittonum* contains a similar history of Ireland and Scotland. Even earlier still is the *Lebor Gabála Érenn,* a collection of Irish poems and mythology thought to date from the 6th century, although the earliest surviving copy is from the 12th century. The main feature of interest in the *Lebor Gabála* being its narration of the first immigration to Ireland by Queen Scota. The one or two paragraphs mentioning the travels of Queen Scota and King Gaythelos in the *Lebor Gabála* and the *Historia Brittonum* demonstrate that this entire semi-mythological story predates the *Pleading of Baldred Biset* and the *Declaration of Arbroath* by a considerable margin.

A later fourteenth and fifteenth century version of this history, by John of Fordun and Walter Bower, is called *Scotichronicon.* This more comprehensive chronicle demonstrates that this popular tale had been told and retold for generation after generation, with little in the way of corruption. As many as half a dozen different sources are cited in Book I of *Scotichronicon,* which all follow a similar story-line about the origins and fate of the royal couple, Gaythelos and Scota. So yes, incredible as it may seem, it has been seriously suggested by the ancient chroniclers that both Ireland and Scotland were first settled by the descendants of an Egyptian pharaoh, his queen and their various courtiers and followers.

Previous authors throughout the generations have investigated this legend, and yet the deductions they have made have been inconclusive to say the least. Many have consigned the story to mythology, and the need for a small nation to have a dramatic and well-connected past. Others have speculated that some aspects of the story are possibly based upon historical events, and suggest that these might belong to the fifth century BC. The author Lorraine Evans saw a possible connection with the Egyptian pharaoh Akhenaton, but did not pursue the matter in nearly enough detail; indeed, her book *Kingdom of the Ark* was not much more than an introduction to the legend. The task was therefore quite clear – I had to thoroughly research the legends of Scota and Gaythelos to see if there was any historical foundation to this ancient story. For if there was, it would greatly impact not only upon the ancient history of the greater British Isles, but also upon some of its more recent trials and tribulations.

The author has already written four books on revisionary Egyptology, and has already come to the conclusion that much of biblical history and many of the biblical characters were actually based upon Egyptian history and personalities. But since the royal families of Europe were founded by the descendants of biblical families and bloodlines, it seemed entirely plausible that European history was linked to Egyptian history in some respects.

Having researched the subject in more detail, it was apparent that Egyptian and Irish histories met and meshed with uncanny symmetry. This easy synchronicity demonstrated that this was a real history, and not the figment of an ancient scribe's fevered imagination (nor, indeed, mine). Not only did the general thesis of *Scotichronicon* appear to be verifiable, but it would seem that real, historical names can be matched with most of the characters too. The history of Ireland, Scotland and the British Isles will never be quite the same again.

Note:

Before we start this adventure, perhaps I should point out that there is no evidence of a link between the Egyptian pleated kilt and its sporran-like flap (sometimes a triangular apron)* and the equivalent Irish and Scottish pleated kilts and sporrans – for all the evidence points towards the Celtic kilt being a relatively recent fashion.[1] It is entirely possible that a link does exist, which may have been passed down through the ages via the covert medium of the masonic apron, which may be why the late seventeenth and early eighteenth centuries witnessed the dual emergence into popular culture of the kilt and Scottish Rite Freemasonry. If readers have any information that places the Celtic kilt back into the pre-Christian era, I would be more than happy to be enlightened. (See the book *Eden* for an analysis of the links between Masonry and ancient Egypt.)

---

* For an illustration of this style of dress, see the many statues and illustrations among the treasures of Tutankhamen. Tutankhamen was, of course, effectively an Amarna prince and pharaoh.

Notes to the reader

a.   This book represents a sequel to six previous titles by Ralph Ellis. While it can be read as a stand-alone title without reference to the previous works, there will inevitably be occasions when it is assumed that the reader has already read, digested and understood certain concepts – primarily that there are innumerable pieces of evidence that point towards an Egyptian heritage for the Israelites, and that their leaders were actually the Hyksos pharaohs of Egypt.

To have read the other titles in advance will prepare the reader for some of the more difficult sections that lie ahead. This is not a hard sell, just a well-intended warning that the history of the greater British Isles becomes rather convoluted at times, and readers need to arm themselves with as much information as possible to understand the full implications of this research.

b.   Because of the radical nature of this book, it has been necessary to highlight the difference between standard orthodox assumptions and those generated by my lateral view of theology. Throughout this book, therefore, I have used curved brackets ( ) to denote orthodox assumptions and square brackets [ ] to denote my radical new assumptions. I hope that this serves to clarify the text.

c.   As readers of the book *Jesus, Last of the Pharaohs* will have noticed, the history of the biblical exodus is not quite as it seems. Not only were the circumstances and nations involved not quite as advertised in the Bible, but, in fact, there were two exoduses from Egypt. Because there is no longer one definitive Exodus to refer to, the term 'exodus' has been left in lower case.

d.   The references in the text are numerous. To ease the problem of continuously referring to the reference section at the back of the book, some references have been prefixed. Prefixes are as follows:

B = Bible, K = Koran, J = Josephus, T = Talmud, S = Strabo
M = Manetho, N = Nag Hammadi, SC = Scotichronicon.

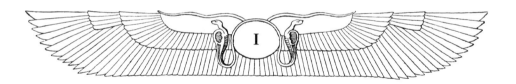

Scotichronicon

Scotichronicon is a vast work set out in sixteen books. It was nominally written by Walter Bower, an Augustinian abbot of Inchcolm monastery in about 1430. Although it was largely his work, he drew extensively on John of Fordun's earlier chronicle of 1360, and quoted extensively from a host of other venerable historians and chroniclers, as was mentioned in the introduction. Of this vast work, only Book I deals with the saga of Gaythelos and Scota, and so the entire chronicle of their and their descendants' exploits are set out in about 80 or so pages.

The interesting part about the story, which has generated so much heated debate and speculation, is that the founding royal couple of both Ireland and Scotland were a Greek prince and an Egyptian princess, who became king and queen of Egypt for a short while. Such fantastic accounts are thought to be the stuff of legend, not historical reality, and so much of the early sections of *Scotichronicon* have been consigned to the fantasy or mythology shelf. It is neither probable nor possible that a royal couple from the eastern Mediterranean could or would embark on an epic journey all the way to the damp, emerald-green coastline of Ireland – especially if this story is supposed to be recalling events from the fourteenth century BC. They simply did not have the technology for such a journey, nor the imperatives to make it. Donald Watt, the translator of *Scotichronicon*, summed up the story in this fashion:

> The story begins with the mythical voyage of Scota, the pharaoh's daughter, from Egypt ... The land that her sons discovered in the Western Ocean was named after her: Scotland.

> It scarcely needs saying that none of this is history in the proper sense ... the name Scota is a back-formation from the name of the people ... She nevertheless

incorporates some features of the mythological sovereignty who figures in Irish and other traditions – the divine partner of the king in a sacred marriage, the successful consummation which confirms his kingship. [SC1]

Here is the usual explanation for the opening chapters in *Scotichronicon* – that it is all mythology. In addition, Watt is making the argument that the Scots have donated their name to their mythological founding princess, rather than her name being the true origin of the Scots' name. In fact, the point being laboured throughout the notes in Watt's translation is that the whole story is a Middle Ages fabrication, designed to impress on readers the great antiquity and cosmopolitan origins of the Scots. However, the evidence that will be presented in this book will conclusively demonstrate that the story is actually a true history, and we shall eventually uncover the identities of all the major players in this ancient tale.

The story itself centers on the royal couple called Gaythelos and Scota, and it is from these two individuals that the Gaelic and Scots people are said to be named. Gaythelos is said to have been a wayward Greek prince who had a dispute with either his father or his brother and so left Greece to look for new opportunities. Being a precocious and fortunate individual, he is supposed to have arrived in Egypt and ingratiated himself with the royal family there. Against all the known customs of Egypt he is said to have married the daughter of the pharaoh, with a view to inheriting the throne of Egypt. However, his successful bid for the throne was not welcomed by the Egyptian proletariat and so he and his wife, princess Scota, were expelled from Egypt and embarked upon an epic voyage across the Mediterranean.

After many short stays and exploits, they are said to have landed on the river Ebro in Spain, where they set up a small fortified town called Brigantia. But, being constantly plagued with attacks by the natives, the new proto-nation looked again for less populated lands to emigrate to. The first of these islands was discovered relatively quickly, and may well have been Mallorca. Finally, after four generations or so, another island home was discovered, and this is more positively identified as being Ireland. It is recorded that both the son and great, great grandson of Gaythelos were called Hiber, and it is from this name that the countries of Iberia (Spain) and Hibernia (Scotland) are said to have been named.

Many of the, by now much larger, population of Brigantia then emigrated to Ireland, which was called Scotia after the name of the people's founding queen. That Ireland was originally called Scotia before the third century AD is fairly well known. Amongst others, Claudian, Orosius, Marianus Scotus, Isidore and Bede all mention that Ireland was called Scotia:

I Scotichronicon

Surelie very much, for Scotland and Ireland are one and the same ... Therefore
yt cometh of some wryters, that Ireland is called Scotia-major, and that which
nowe is named Scotland, is called Scotia-minor.[2]

The name 'Scota', like the parallel name Hiber, obviously had a habit of
moving on to new lands as the people moved to new pastures, and so it
is not so surprising that when the Scots settled in Canada they called their
new homeland Nova Scotia, or New Scotia. This is compelling evidence that
the names of countries do move to new lands, as significant portions of the
population emigrate.

Fig 1. Map demonstrating that Ireland was called Scotia.
Waddell, The makers of Civilisation, 1929.

The people stayed many generations in Ireland, and it is possible that their
primary necropolis, or burial ground, was either at the megalithic site at
Newgrange or the sacred site of Tara; both of which reside on the river Boyne
to the north of Dublin. After many generations, probably in the sixth century
BC, the Picts came to Ireland from an unknown location. The venerable Bede
has them coming from Scythia (Ukraine and towards the Caspian Sea), a
location which has been amended in recent times to Scandinavia. However,
Scotichronicon variously places the Picts in either Aquitaine (southwestern

3

France) or the Basque country. In fact, the southern portion of Aquitaine lies in the Basque region, and an old dialect of Easkal, the Basque language, was called Aquitaine; so it is likely that both of these accounts were referring to the Basques.

The chronicles indicate that the Scotian people were not impressed with these unwelcome (but possibly related) newcomers to their shores; and that the Basques had come with no (or too few) women. A deal was therefore struck whereby the Scotian people of Ireland gave the Basques (the Picts) some of their women and advised them to go to Scotland instead. This they did, and the new Scotian/Pictish colony there became rather successful – so much so that many of the Scotians later emigrated to that region by choice. It was through this process that the name Scotia became transferred from Ireland to what we now call Scotland. Likewise, Iberia, the name for Spain that had been derived from the son of Gaythelos called Hiber, was also donated to Scotland, which became known as Hibernia.*

Lebor Gabala

This is the story of Gaythelos and Scota, as given by the ancient Scottish chronicles. The task now is to sift through the evidence and try to discover how much of this is a true history and how much is mere fable. However, we might initially start with a few broad-brush assumptions. Firstly, one might observe that the Scots did not exactly have much reason to trace their history back to an obscure Greek prince and an equally obscure Egyptian princess.

Had the Scottish chronicles related that the Scottish people were directly related to Moses of the Torah, Jason of the Odyssey, or Ramesses the Great from Egyptian history, one might have immediately dismissed the story as a complete fabrication. The fact that the proposed Scottish ancestors are so obscure, and the fact that evidence for the pharaoh mentioned in these texts was only rediscovered in the nineteenth century AD, suggests that there is likely to be an element of truth in this ancient history. The only trouble with this suggestion being that none of the other characters involved in the story are easily identifiable within the historical records of Egypt or Greece.

In regard to Prince Gaythelos, it might seem unlikely that we could ever find evidence for this character, as the fourteenth century BC lies in prehistoric times so far as Greece is concerned. We know next to nothing about this pre-Iliad era of Mycenaean Greece, and even the events detailed

---

* It is said that the name 'Hibernia' stems from the Latin *hibernus* meaning 'winter', but this hardly explains this name's application to Spain as well as Ireland and Scotland.

in the later accounts of Homer are far from certain. With regard to Princess Scota, the records of ancient Egypt do, of course, stretch back much further than in Greece. Unfortunately, however, the name 'Scota' is not known from any Egyptian history, nor is there anything remotely similar. What, then, can be done about this situation? By what method can we start to investigate the traditions of the *Scotichronicon* account?

The first avenue of research might be the origin of the text. *Scotichronicon* is a Scottish chronicle, based upon much older texts that have come from many locations including Ireland (the *Lebor Gabala* from the *Book of Leinster*) and Wales (the *Historia Brittonum*). But this diverse range of chronicles is obviously not the original source, so where did the story originate?

One possibility is given to us by Nennius, the monk who penned the *Historia Brittonum*. He indicates that he used Roman and Ecclesiastical documents to compose his history of Britain, and this seems likely as some of his work appears to be taken from the *World Chronicle*, by Bishop Eusebius. It will be demonstrated in a later chapter that the chronology of Egypt used in *Scotichronicon* was also taken directly from Eusebius, so he is definitely a likely source for the Scota story. But, as ever, Eusebius was only quoting others, and it would appear that some of his inspiration was taken from Euhemerus, a Greek historian who wrote a philosophical romance called *Sacred Scripture*. Although it embedded features of the Scota story, Euhemerus' story was largely fictional and what we are really looking for is a true history. So from where and from whom did Eusebius and Euhemerus obtain these details? Since the Gaythelos and Scota story is deeply embedded in Egyptian history, it is there that we must look for the original sources.

It is said that the trail goes cold at this point, but actually there is a very good candidate for the next link in this literary chain back into history. Since Euhemerus lived around 300 BC, there is a very likely candidate for the Egyptian end of this story, and he is the Egypto-Greek historian known as Manetho. Not that much is known about the life of Manetho, but it is thought that he was a priest of Heliopolis, Egypt, who lived around 300 BC and wrote a long history and chronology of the nation called *The History of Egypt*. The original text has unfortunately been lost to us, but snippets of his history were copied by other historians and one of those happened to be Eusebius. Furthermore, since we know for certain that Eusebius' chronology of Egypt was taken directly from Manetho, perhaps the other details about Scota and Gaythelos and their flight from Egypt were copied from the same text. Again this is likely, as a close similarity between the Scota story and Manetho's *The History of Egypt* will be shown later in this book.

The possibility that Manetho was the original source of the Scota and Gaythelos legend is interesting, because it gives the whole story much greater credence. It is known, from comparisons with the archaeological record, that Manetho's history of Egypt was quite factual; indeed, his royal chronology of Egypt, and the dynastic separations that he indicated, are still the basis for the modern chronology of Egypt. If the ultimate source for *Scotichronicon* had been Herodotus, one might have been justified in being highly skeptical about its authenticity, but with the originator being Manetho, there is every possibility that there is a great deal of truth in the story.

This hope is considerably bolstered by the constant discovery of small, obscure details from *Scotichronicon* that are known to be correct. Even aspects that are generally unknown today, let alone in a cold and drafty monastery in fifteenth century Scotland, can be shown to be correct. Take, for instance, the general history of Egypt. This is described as:

> The kingdom of Egypt (the name of which was originally Etheria) is the most ancient of all kingdoms except for the kingdom Scythia ... SC3

Egypt is indeed a very ancient kingdom, as we all know, but that is not the interesting element here. The fascinating aspect of this quote is the unusual name that was given to Egypt – Etheria. Surprisingly enough, Egypt was indeed known as Etheria, and the true spelling of the name in the Egyptian was actually Aturti or Eturti ⌐◌𓂝𓈖⌐ . The name relates to water and to the flooding of the Nile, and the 'ia' on the end of Walter Bower's version is simply a typical Greek rendering of an Egyptian name.* In addition, Geoffrey Keating, the venerable historian of Ireland, indicates that this name for Egypt was reduced down to the name 'Aeria' in later generations, and used for the island of Ireland. It is from Aeria that the modern name of Eire was derived. Thus the current name for Ireland is actually a corruption of an original name for Egypt. Interestingly, Keating states that this was also the original name for Crete, and we shall be looking at some Cretan connections both with Egypt and Ireland in later chapters.

---

* It is also probably worth mentioning that Jesus was called the 'Egyptian False Prophet' in both Acts and Josephus' *Antiquities* and, in addition, I have independently demonstrated that he was a prince of Egypt. However, by using this ancient name for Egypt, Jesus would then become known as the Aturti Prophet (Arthur Prophet) and, since I have already identified Jesus as the leader of 600 rebel soldiers (rebel fishermen according to Josephus), the New Testament accounts seem to have many similarities to Arthurian legend. In other words, 'Arthur' may simply have been a Templar name for Jesus, derived from information that these warrior knights had gathered during the long years of the crusades. See the book *King Jesus* for further details.

Perhaps the most important element of this potted history is the fact that the ancient Scottish chronicle is correct, and it accurately records a little-used and very ancient name for Egypt. If this small detail, which is only mentioned in passing, can be seen to be correct, how many other names and events within this ancient chronicle may also be historically correct?

If Gaythelos and Scota came from Egypt, as Walter Bower and others maintain, then much of Celtic mythology may have once had an Egyptian flavour. Was this what happened all those millennia ago? Did an Egyptian queen and her consort arrive in the greater British Isles some thirteen centuries before the Common Era, and establish a society based upon Egyptian culture and principles. If this did occur, one might initially suppose that this would manifest itself in an overtly 'foreign' culture being present in Ireland during the Bronze Age. However, this is not necessarily so.

I have already demonstrated that Judaism was based upon the creed and culture of the Amarna regime of Pharaoh Akhenaton, and that many of the Old Testament verses have been copied verbatim from ancient Egyptian texts – including large segments of Genesis, Exodus, Psalms, Proverbs, the Song of Solomon and the Lord's Prayer. We tend to think of our present culture as being a mix of Celtic, Roman and Anglo-Saxon societies that have been heavily influenced by a later blanket of Judaism (Christianity). However, had early Celtic culture been founded upon Egyptian principles (Amarna principles), we would hardly notice the difference, because the Amarna culture of Pharaoh Akhenaton *is* our Judaeo-Christian culture – whether this was derived directly from Egypt or via the indirect transmission route of Israel and Rome.

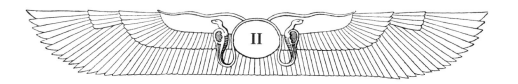

Scota and Gaythelos

This brings us to the nub of this investigation, for if Princess Scota was the daughter of a pharaoh, then evidence for her existence should be available in the relatively well-recorded history of Egypt. Some of the previous research and speculation into her origins has casually identified her as a daughter of Pharaoh Akhenaton, of the Amarna dynasty, but not shown any convincing reason why this should be so. In contrast, this chapter will not only positively identify the pharaoh and his daughter (Princess Scota), but also positively identify her husband, Prince Gaythelos, in the historical record.

This will represent a fundamental turning point in Irish-Scots history, not simply because it will be shown that both Scota and Gaythelos are relatively well known, but also because their discovery turns fiction into fact. The ancient history of these lands and people, as detailed in the great chronicle of *Scotichronicon*, has long been sidelined and dismissed as being unreliable mythology. However, if we are able to show that the names used in these ancient chronicles equate with the known history of Egypt, then these chronicles must be closer to real life than fable. Suddenly, there is the very real prospect that the ancient history of the greater British Isles was conceived and nurtured within the advanced culture of ancient Egypt. And since modern Judaism and Christianity were both born from Egyptian theology, the long-held notion that Ireland originally harboured the secrets of what has become known as the 'Old Church' of Christianity, may not be so far wide of the mark.

So who was this fabled prince of Greece (who briefly became pharaoh of Egypt), who is said to have fled towards Spain and Ireland? And which pharaoh from these ancient lands would have dared give his daughter away to a renegade prince from a foreign land? The ancient texts of Egypt clearly state that Egypt never gave its princesses away to foreigners, so how and why would this have happened?

> At the height of the New Kingdom, pharaohs regularly took to wife the daughters of Near East princes, but refused to permit their own daughters to be married off to foreign rulers.[1]

Biblical scholars might point towards the marriage of King Solomon and an Egyptian princess, and indicate that the ancient texts were obviously wrong in their boasting. This did indeed remain a bit of a problem, until I deduced, in the book *Solomon*, that King Solomon was also a Lower Egyptian pharaoh himself. In other words, the princess in the biblical accounts had not been given away to a foreigner at all, as King Solomon [Pharaoh Sheshonq] was resident in Tanis in the Nile Delta. But if Egyptian princesses were never given to foreign princes, then the *Scotichronicon* story is already looking suspect, unless we can reinterpret it in some manner.

The name of the royal father of Scota, and the era in which he reigned are debatable too. Some researchers have been led astray by the biblical chronology because of the frequent references to the biblical exodus within *Scotichronicon*, and so they place the era as being just after Ramesses II, the supposed pharaoh of the biblical exodus. One interpretation of *Scotichronicon* even places the era in the sixth century BC, because of a mention of the Persian pharaoh of Egypt, Xerxes. Even the translator of *Scotichronicon*, Donald Watt, is slightly confused. He placed the father of Scota in the Amarna era, which is correct, but he could not deduce exactly which pharaoh he should be. Lorraine Evans said the pharaoh concerned was Akhenaton; she was right, of course, but there was no real explanation as to how she came to that conclusion.

In actual fact, the truth about the era and the precise pharaoh concerned is fairly plain and simple. The pharaonic chronology is given in Book I chapter 10 of Walter Bower's *Scotichronicon*, and here the author is plainly following the records of the Greco-Egyptian historian, Manetho. If we list the two chronicles together, readers will clearly see the comparison:

Bower chronology		Manetho chronology	
Amosis	25	Ahmosis	25
Chebron	13	Chebron	13
Amenophis	21	Amenophis	21
Mephres (Joseph died)	12	Miphres	12
Mispharmatosis	9	Mispharmuthosis	26
		Tuthmosis	9

Amenophis	31		Amenophis	31
(Moses born)			(Memnon statue)	
Horus	38		Orus	28
Acencris	12		Achencheres	12
			(Moses and biblical exodus)	
Achorisis	7		Acherres	8
Chencres	18		Cherres	15
(biblical exodus and Scota exodus)				
			Armais (Dannus)	5
			Ramesses	68

Numbers represent the reign lengths for each pharaoh.

Now this list of pharaohs from Egypt is rather interesting, for at the very least it demonstrates that Walter Bower had a copy of Manetho's work with him in his monastery at Inchcolm. Indeed, to be more precise, this is a copy of Manetho's history of Egypt that arrived into the Medieval era via the Armenian version of the Christian chronographer Eusebius. Bower has not only faithfully copied this text, minus one pharaoh, he has also added some other interesting details, which might suggest that he had access to other documents long since lost to us.

The mention of Moses' birth in Bower's account is one of these interesting additional interpolations, and the position in which this has been placed ties in very nicely with the revised history of Egypt that I have already outlined in the book *Jesus Last of the Pharaohs* - the notion that Moses was actually TuthMoses, the brother of Pharaoh Akhenaton. If this were so, then the biblical Moses would have been a son of Amenhotep III (Amenophis in Manetho's chronology), which is what Bower appears to indicate. Thus Moses [TuthMoses] and Akhenaton would have been brothers, which is exactly what I have previously demonstrated from other evidence and sources. Bower and Manetho also state that the biblical exodus took place just after the reign of Acencris (Achencheres), which is again perfectly correct according to this same revised 'Amarna' history of Judaism, as we shall see shortly.

However, to tie all of this into classical Egyptian history, we now need to make a comparison between Manetho's chronology the standard historical chronology, to see how accurate the histories of Manetho and Bower really were. The following chronological table does just that:

II Scota and Gaythelos

Manetho's chronology	Classical chronology
Amos	
(Amoses) (Tethmoses) - 25	Ahmose I - 24
(Moses, first biblical exodus)	(agreed, first exodus)
Chebron (Chebros) - 13	(see Tuthmoses II below)
Amenophis	
(Amophis) - 21 (24)	Amenhotep I - 27
(Tethmosis?)*	Tuthmoses I - 6
(see Chebron above)	Tuthmoses II - 14
Amensis (Amesse)	
(Amersis) (f) - 22	Hatshepsut (f) - 15
Memphres	
(Misaphris) (Miphres) - 12 (13)	(Amenhotep II ?? see below)
Mephrammuthosis	
(Misaphris) - 26	Tuthmoses III - 54
	Amenhotep II - 34
Tuthmoses - 9	Tuthmoses IV - 33
Amenophis - 31	Amenhotep III - 37
(speaking statue of Memnon)	
Orus - 28 (37)	(see Horemheb below)**
Achenchres	
(Acherres) (f) - 12 (16) (32)	Nefertiti (f) - 14 (all as co-regent)
Rathotis (Achencheres)	
(Rathoris) (Rathos) - 6 (9) (39)	Akhenaton - 17
(Moses, second biblical exodus)	(12 as co-regent with father)
	(agreed, second exodus)
Acencheres	
(Chebres) (Acherres) - 8 (12)	Smenkhkare - 3
Acencheres	
(Cherres) (Acherres) - 12 (15)	Tutankhamen - 9
Armais (Armesis)***	
(Harmais) (Dannus) - 4 (5)	Aye (Armait) - 4
(see Orus above) **	Horemheb - 14 (28) (see Orus)
Ramesses (Aegyptus) - 1	Ramesses I - 2

Sethosis - 51 (55)	Seti I - 11 (15)
Ramesses (Rhampses) - 66 (68)	Ramesses II (The Great) - 67
Amenophath (Ammenophis) - 19 (40)	??

Numbers after the pharaoh's name are reign lengths.
Names in brackets are alternative names
(f) = a female pharaoh.

The accounts of Manetho have arrived via a number of ancient historians: Josephus, Theophilus, Syncellus, Eusebius, and the Armenian version of Eusebius. It is the variations between these different versions that give the differing titles, the additional pharaohs that were not included in the previous list, and the alternative reign lengths.

*   This extra Tethmosis is reported by Wallis Budge, but it is uncertain where he derived this name from.

**   The names <u>Or</u>us and <u>Hor</u>emheb were both derived from Horus (Heru), the hawk-headed god of Egypt.

***   Manetho says of Armais: "Armais, also called Danaus, at the end of his reign he was banished from the land of Egypt. Fleeing from his brother (Ramesses) Aegyptus he escaped to Greece, and after capturing Argos he held sway over the Argives." Note that Argos is on the southeastern side of Peloponnese, while the Argives are the people of Argos.

This list demonstrates the problems involved in equating the known archaeology of the region with the historical accounts of Manetho, for many of the names do not appear to match. Some of the names are obvious equivalents: like Tuthmoses being Tuthmoses IV, and the two Amenophis kings being Amenhotep I and III - although the reign lengths differ slightly. Some of the other pharaonic names are not so obvious, but many of them can nevertheless be resurrected from Manetho's distorted Greek renderings by using a little common sense.

     For instance, Pharaoh Amoses is obviously Ahmose I, while the alternative name for this same pharaoh, Tethmosis, is merely the result of a scribe reading the Moon glyph as being the god Thoth. Thus Ah-moses becomes Tuth-moses or Tethmoses. The reign-length for Amoses in Manetho's record also agrees well with the modern king-list, but this may be due to the well-known artifact of Egyptologists simply copying Manetho where they have no alternative information.

     Looking further down the list, Amensis must be Hatchepsut, as she is pointedly said to be a woman: the sister of Amenhotep I according to Manetho. This family connection conflicts with modern Egyptology somewhat, but since Tuthmoses I is missing from Manetho's list this may well create some confusion. The name Amensis or Amersis for Hatchepsut may come from the prominent glyphs for 'Amen' in her cartouche, and the perennial difficulty of reading her birth name, as the glyphs used in her cartouche are hardly common or well-known.

Another interesting Greek translation is Chebron for Tuthmoses II. One needs quite an in-depth knowledge of the 18th dynasty and a fertile mind to discover the roots of this strange translation, but the truth can be seen in this king's praenomen which is Aakheperenre. And while Aakheperenre may not sound much like Chebron, the *kheper* component of this name happens to be derived from the glyph of a fat dung-beetle, which translates as *karub* כרוב in the Aramaic, as *karabos* καραβος in the Greek, as *scarabaeus* in the Latin, and scarab in the English. What has happened here is that the Egyptian 'p' in *khe̱per* has become a 'b', resulting in *khe̱ber* or *kara̱bos*. And on the translation of this same word by the obfuscative ecclesiastic scribes a softer 'ch' has replaced the harder 'k', resulting in the Greek *cheroubim* χερουβιμ and the English cherub. Yes, the chubby winged angelic beings in ecclesiastical artwork are actually chubby and winged dung-beetles! Readers will never see Michelangelo's work in the same light again!

And as we saw in the book *Eden in Egypt*, the *kheper* dung-beetle was also identified with the constellation of Cancer, the crab. It was for this reason that a humble-dung-beetle became closely identified with the Sun-god, because it was one of the zodiacal constellations that the Sun-god traversed during the Great Month of Cancer. But if this is so, then we might well see here a much more ancient etymological ancestry for the Anglo-Germanic word 'crab'. The *kheper* dung-beetle had become a *karub* or a *karobos* in the Aramaic and Greek, and from *karub* it is but one step to a *krub* or a *krab* (a crab). So the chubby crab-like dung-beetle not only became an chubby angelic cherub, it also became a water-loving crab. It is always interesting to see how symbology can change and mutate over the millennia, when it is transferred to different cultures and societies.

Anyway, if we take another look at the praenomen cartouche for Tuthmoses II, the original translation for this name was Aakheperenre or Aa-kheper-en-re, with *kheper* referring to the dung-beetle. But if we delete the 'aa' and 're' glyphs we are left with Kheper-en. And if we transliterate this shortened name into Aramaic or Greek we derive Karub-en, Cheroub-en, Cherub-en or Chebron. Thus Manetho's pharaoh called Chebron was actually Pharaoh Aakheperenre Tuthmoses II. And so this novel translation gives us two addition details to ponder: firstly, that Manetho is more often right than he is wrong; and secondly, that Manetho was often using Greco-Aramaic translations of these royal names. This obvious detail has been vehemently denied by academia, but it is undeniably true.

Fig 1. Cartouches of Aakheperenre Tuthmoses II. Note the large beetle in the cartouche, which is called a kheper or a cherub (identified with the constellation of Cancer, the crab).

If we look further down Manetho's king-list, Pharaoh Orus is obviously Horemheb, as both of these names are derived from the god Horus. The misplacing of Horemheb in Manetho's version of the king-list was probably due to the Amarna regime being deleted from most Egyptian records. Having been presented with an entire new dynasty, which was missing from all the other records, it was probably difficult for Manetho to decide where to place that dynasty. He chose after Horemheb, whereas the historical evidence seems to conclusively show that the Amarna era came before Horemheb. There is also an amount of confusion over the names of the Amarna dynasty, who all appear to have inherited the generic names Cherres, Acherres or Achencheres. The meaning of this name will be explored shortly.

Within Manetho's differing accounts (derived from the multitude of transmission routes for his original king-list) the era of Moses and the Exodus is given two possible locations or eras: either at the time of Tethmosis (Amoses) at the beginning of the 18th dynasty, or at the time of Achencheres (and Rathotis) during the Amarna era. This equates very well with Manetho's other accounts and with the conclusions drawn in my previous works. In short, there were two exoduses out of Egypt involving the Judaic peoples: the first being the great Hyksos Exodus during the reign of Ahmose I, and the second being the smaller Amarna Exodus of Akhenaton and Nefertiti (or Akhenaton and Khiya) at the end of the Amarna era. And so although the translators of Manetho are confused by this apparent duplication of the Exodus, the differing accounts are perfectly correct.

However, the central point of interest in the present discussion is Pharaoh Chencres, the king who Bower and Fordun *et al* indicate was the father of Princess Scota. Just who was this particular pharaoh? In Manetho's king list this pharaoh (the pharaoh of the exodus during the Amarna era) is called either Achencheres or Rathotis, and we can ustilise both of these names in order to decipher the true identity of this pharaoh. Readers will note that this particular pharaoh comes after a female pharaoh, called Achencherses or Acherres, and that gives us a good clue to the next pharaoh's identity. There was only one female who could be considered a pharaoh during the Amarna era (directly after Amenhotep III) and that was Nefertiti. In fact, Manetho says that Rathotis-Achencheres and Achencherses-Acherres were brother and sister, which may be correct. Queen Nefertiti was indeed closely related to Akhenaton, although most modern Egyptologists would say that she was the daughter of (Pharaoh) Aye rather than Amenhotep III. Because of all these helpful indicators, Pharaoh Rathotis-Achencheres has been placed opposite Pharaoh Akhenaton in the table above, and for two very good reasons.

Let us first compare the names Achencheres and Akhenaton. The first syllable in each of these names is the same: 'Akhen' in the historical texts versus 'Achen' in the records of Manetho. The former of these being a syllable derived from the ibis glyph 𓅜 , which can be pronounced as 'Aakh'. The Greek version of 'Achen' uses either a hard 'k' or a soft 'kh' ('ch'), in the differing accounts of Manetho, and so there is a direct correspondence between these two words or syllables.

The next syllable(s) in these names are merely two variants of a title for the Sun-god, with one version using god-name 'Aton' and the other using the Hebrew 'Cheres' חרם meaning 'Sun'. Several Egyptologists have challenged my interpretation of Cheres, indicating that the Hebrew for 'Sun' is actually Shemesh שמש. This may be so, but the biblical Mt Heres חרם (ie: Cheres - Kheres) was known as the 'Mountain of the Sun', and so Heres (or Cheres - Kheres) does indeed refer to the Sun.

Another challenge to this interpretation, which has been made on numerous occasions in academic circles, is that the Egypto-Greek world of Manetho would not have been influenced by an Aramaic word like Cheres חרם. However, it has been demonstrates in *Eden in Egypt* that much of the Aramaic language was derived from Egyptian. In addition, it is a recorded fact that Manetho uses the term Cheres in many pharaonic names that include a reference to the Sun-god; be that Aton, Amun or Ra. A good example of this alternative Aramaic name for the Sun-god can be found in the titles for Pharaoh Neferkare Amenemnisu, who reigned for four years during the 21st dynasty. Manetho calls this pharaoh Nephercheres and again assigns him a four year reign. So why the different pronunciation? What Manetho has done, of course, is to translate the Ra glyph in Nefer-Ka-Re as Cheres, and has therefore derived Nepher(ka)cheres or Nephercheres.

Thus academia is wrong yet again. The deans and dons appear to suffer from NIH syndrome - the inability to accept an idea or argument if it is Not Invented Here. In reality, it is abundantly clear that Manetho was using the term Cheres for the Sun-god, and during the Amarna era this term would have denoted the Aton rather than Amen or Ra. The result of all this deliberation is that Manetho's pharaoh called Achen-Cheres was actually the historical Amarna pharaoh called Akhen-Aton (Akhenaton), and since Bower's pharaoh called Chencres is the direct equivalent of this Acencheres, then the father of Princess Scota must also have been Pharaoh Akhenaton.

However, this does not explain why this same pharaoh was also called Rathotis, in some of the king-lists that have been derived from Manetho. How did this translation come about? Now this is an equally interesting name and it rather confirms the translation that has just been made. It so happens that the ibis glyph  in Akhenaton's name can also be pronounced as Thoth in the Greek (Thoth being a Greek pronunciation of Djehut). So the Thotis in Ra-Thotis is simply the god-name Thoth. Meanwhile, the Ra in Ra-Thotis is obviously a manifestation of the Sun-god. Thus the names Akhen-Cheres and Thoth-Ra are direct equivalents of each other; and if we reverse the syllables in Thoth-Ra we derive Ra-Thoth, or Manetho's Rathotis. Here is a tabular comparison of these names, for clarification:

Akhenaton		**Akhenaton**	
Akhen	Aten	Akhen	Aten
(Ibis)	(Sun-god)	(Ibis)	(Sun-god)
Achen	Cheres	Thoth	Ra
Achen-cheres		Ra	Thoth
		Ra-thotis	

Thus it would appear to be abundantly clear that Pharaoh Achencheres-Rathotis, the father Princess Scota, was actually Pharaoh Akhenaton. And so we have narrowed the era of the Scota Exodus down considerably, for we now know where and approximately when this princess was born, and we may even know a great deal about her life and her disappearance from Egypt.

Fig 2. Cartouches of Akhenaton Neferkheperura Uinra.

Finally, it should be noted that of all the Amarna pharaohs (including Smenkhkare, Tutankhamen and Aye), only Akhenaton had children during his reign, and so the only pharaoh from this era that could be the father of Scota is again Akhenaton. Here, then, we appear to have a definitive resolution to the question of which pharaoh fathered Princess Scota. Whatever the level of truth and fact that resides within the rest of the *Scotichronicon* story, it is fairly certain that the pharaoh it speaks of is a real historical character – he was Pharaoh Akhenaton and, just as the Scottish tale implies, he presided over a pretty unstable regime.

Scota

Having identified the actual pharaoh mentioned in the ancient chronicle, it is worth noting that it is very fortunate that the story it relates takes place during this precise era in Egyptian history. At almost any other time in Egyptian history one might pronounce that it would have been impossible for an Egyptian princess to have been allowed to sail away from her country on such a perilous journey, and so the Scottish chronicle would have to be based upon fantasy. Egypt was the world's superpower, and while foreign princesses may have made perilous journeys to Egypt, the opposite was never true.

However, the Scota story happens to take place during a period of unprecedented social turmoil within Egypt, an era during which even a mighty pharaoh (Akhenaton himself) may have been forced into exile. Of all the dynasties in Egypt's long history, the fact that *Scotichronicon* should focus on this precise period of instability strengthens its claim towards historical veracity. How would Bower, Fordun or any of the previous chroniclers who have handled this history, have known that it was entirely possible that an Egyptian princess may well have escaped from the crumbling Amarna regime of Akhenaton by boat?

If the discovery of Akhenaton being the father of Scota greatly strengthens the chronicle's story, then which of Akhenaton's six daughters could have been called Scota? Unfortunately, this is unlikely to be a true name for an Amarna princess and so what we probably have here is a hypocorism: a nickname. Like many a prince or princess before and after, Scota became known for her deeds rather than her birth name. What she managed to do, together with her husband, was take a whole community out of their comfortable homeland in Egypt and steer them westwards, in a flotilla of small boats, towards the setting Sun.

> So Gaythelos gathered together all his followers and left Egypt with his wife Scota. Because he was afraid to return to the regions from which he had come (Greece), because of old feuds, he directed his course westwards. [SC2]

Thus the heroine princess became known as Skoti ⌐⌐⌐ or, when using a Sean Connery accent, Shkoti ⏀ ; a name which refers to the boat of the setting Sun, the boat on which the Sun-god rowed towards the western horizon. A more fitting name for this queen would be hard to find.

This reasoning is similar to the name given in mythology to Mary Magdalene. She too was exiled from her homeland and she too is reputed to have sailed westwards from the eastern Mediterranean towards France, in a boat with no oars or crew. So, in the legends that describe this journey, the Magdalene is called Mari Stella, or Sea Star. And since this legend was so important to the Illuminati, it went on to spawn Sir Arthur Conan Doyle's more modern legend of the Mari Celeste (Mary Celeste), a name that can be translated as Sea Heaven or perhaps Sea Star.

Negra

This voyage of the Magdalene also spawned the cult of the Black Madonna. It is said that several of the New Testament Marys, including Mary Magdalene, were on this voyage to Provence in France. Whether Mary the Virgin was on this small boat or not, she was later portrayed as being black; both in France and across the wider continent. Some enterprising minorities have jumped upon this mention of blackness, as they often do, and argued that Mary was of an African phenotype – which is plain and simple nonsense born of desperation. That respected authors like Lynn Picknett should follow their lead just goes to show how far this political correctness has spread. There are even some overly zealous types who inhabit archaeological discussion sites on the web, and try to convince all and sundry that the beautiful bust of Nefertiti demonstrates that she was a Negress. Such a strategy again smacks of desperation.[3]

The truth of the matter is slightly more cryptic. For a start, the identity of this dusky Mary is not entirely certain, for while she is often assumed to be the Virgin (Jesus' mother), this could well be a subtle portrayal of the Magdalene. In addition, the Church authorities were not allowed to say, for doctrinal reasons, what the true ancestry of Mary Magdalene and Jesus really was. To the common people Jesus was a carpenter and Mary was a prostitute and that was that, with no questions asked. And if anyone got a little too inquisitive, the overpowering threat of the Inquisition, at the slightest hint of heresy, was a powerful motivation for caution. But, as we are slowly finding out in our more enlightened times, the truth was and is much more complex.

As I have already explained in the books *Jesus* and *Solomon*, Mary Magdalene was not a street prostitute but a temple prostitute, or God's Wife, which was a highly exalted position within Egyptian theology. Similarly, Jesus was not a simple carpenter, but God's Carpenter (Setepenre), which was an old pharaonic title used by many of the royal dynasties in Egypt.

Furthermore, Mary and Jesus were not simply husband and wife, as has been publicly exposed recently in *The Da Vinci Code*; they were also brother and sister, with sibling marriage again being a long-established tradition within the royal dynasties of Egypt. The book *Cleopatra to Christ* also demonstrates that Jesus and Mary were descended from the royal dynasties of Egypt and Parthia (Persia).

As one might imagine, supreme Christian heresies such as these were difficult to discuss back in the Middle Ages, with the ever-present threat of being burned alive hanging over any such deliberations. Accordingly, a masonic-type initiatory system was devised, so that only the true and trusted at the core of this particular secret society were told the real truth about Western history and religion. But to place that truth into public view, perhaps as a calculated snub to the Catholic authorities, the Illuminati used a series of secret codes that only the initiated would be able to decipher. In this particular case, they simply painted Mary black. While the Illuminati may have given a host of banal reasons for this choice, from the black colour denoting death to the original statues being made of ebony, the truth is that this colour actually revealed Mary's true ancestry.

The simple answer to this cryptic code is that in the Egyptian language 'black' is called *kam* 🔲🐦𓏤, and at the same time the proper name Kam 🔲🐦⊗ happens to refer to Egypt herself. So the blackness of these Madonnas simply means that Mary (in fact, both Marys) were of Egyptian heritage; which is exactly what I relate in the book *Cleopatra*. This is why Mary and the infant Jesus were said to have fled to Egypt when there was a threat to his life. Mary's family was of Egyptian heritage and so it was natural enough for Mary to go to her homeland for safety, and where the young Jesus could complete his education at Heliopolis.

This is why there is also the strange tradition of Saint Mary of Egypt. She was supposed to have been a reformed fifth century AD prostitute who turned to Christianity, but she shares so many similarities with Mary Magdalene that many think she is a secret code for her. But this is a code that again deliberately places Mary Magdalene's heritage back into Egypt. Once again, the Illuminati within the Catholic Church wanted the evidence out there within the public domain, even if it is only obliquely hinted at.

Also on board this small boat, heading towards France, was a young 'servant' called Sarah, who was again said to be black. But the Hebrew name Sarah שׂרה simply means 'princess' and so the true parentage of this young 'servant' should be obvious – she was Mary Magdalene's daughter, fathered by Jesus. This young Sarah, or princess, is especially venerated by the Gypsy community at Saintes-Maries-de-la-Mer in Provence, France, where the small boat is supposed to have come ashore. The Gypsies re-enact Sarah's arrival on these shores every 24th and 25th May, and hold a festival there. This again demonstrates the possible links between this story and Egypt, as the name for the Gypsies themselves is also supposed to have been derived from the name 'Egypt'.

One other point worth clarifying is the peculiar references to Mary's boat having no sails or oars. This lack of propulsive power sounds decidedly odd and so it has to be, as one might expect, an allegorical allusion of some nature. The answer to this little riddle lies in the alternative meaning for a ship's mast. Just as the blade (Λ) and chalice (V) that form the outline of the Star of David are representative of the male and female reproductive organs, so too are the ship and its phallic mast – which is why all ships are said to be female. In a typical piece of Egyptian humanist duality, the ship is the vessel that holds humanity, but it is the mast that propels it along; and so both are required to make a functional vessel or society. Thus the curious reference to a ship with no mast merely implies that Mary Magdalene arrived in France without Jesus and most probably without her sons too. The legends seem to confirm this when they speak of Mary arriving with just her 'Egyptian slave'; that is, her daughter Sarah.

As this explanation clearly demonstrates, many inconvenient facts have been lost from general knowledge and history. This was the fate of the truth during the Middle Ages, to be driven underground and passed on in hushed whispers by the initiated few of the Illuminati. But so strong was the oppression, and so complete was the obliteration of the truth, that much of this information still remains hidden. And yet, just as it would appear that much of this information will resurface and be understood by the general public, another calamity is about to descend upon us.

Unfortunately, if the British government's new Incitement to Religious Hatred law is eventually passed, the truth will once again be made to suffer from the traditional forms of censorship, obfuscation and persecution – even during our supposedly enlightened twenty-first century. We have already arrived at the point where to criticise a religion results in your throat being cut and a message of love and affection from the 'Compassionate and Merciful' deity being pinned to your chest with a dagger; but now the government wishes us to be put in jail too. The repercussions of this new ill-advised law (or any of its pernicious descendants) are all too predictable, for in the eyes of the rabid few it will legitimise their campaign of terrorism against their critics.

Our cherished freedom to question or belittle a peculiar religious proclamation or belief will soon be severely curtailed, and since faith is not based upon rational truth and hard evidence, both the truth and the inconvenient facts that support it will be buried once more within the inner cores of secret societies. Fanaticism and bigotry will become the Liberal Left's victors, and a new Dark Age of repression will spread across Europe and the entire Western world. Today this repression manifests itself in book burnings, fatwas, murders, death threats paraded openly through the streets of London and widespread religious terrorism in Western capitals; tomorrow the ignorant masses will be building funerary pyres for the infidel unbelievers.

Gaythelos

While it might be satisfying to see that Princess Scota's name was based upon a real Egyptian title, which again indicates that the *Scotichronicon* chronicle is familiar with Egyptian traditions and language, it is disappointing not to find an actual name that can positively identify Scota as a daughter of Akhenaton. Nevertheless, her true identity can be discovered, but the method of deciphering which daughter she was will have to be indirect; through the identity of her husband, Gaythelos.

The information about Gaythelos is sketchy; however, there is enough information in the chronicle to allow us to come to a surprising deduction. It is worth noting that the *Scotichronicon* account is not simply the invention of one scribe, priest or historian, for Walter Bower quotes five or six different chronicles that all relate the same kind of information. Using these different sources, a consistent picture begins to emerge about turbulent times and a royal marriage that occurred at about the time of the biblical exodus:

> In the time of Moses there was a certain king of one of the kingdoms of Greece called Neolas. He had a son who was good looking but mentally unstable, Gaythelos by name. Since he had not been permitted to hold any position of power in the kingdom he was provoked to anger, and with the support of a large number of friends he inflicted many disasters on his father's kingdom. He greatly outraged both his father and the inhabitants (of the country) with his violent behaviour. So he was driven out of his native land and sailed off to Egypt: and there, since he was outstandingly brave and daring and of royal descent, he was united in marriage with Scota the daughter of Pharaoh Chencres. [SC4]

Note here the comment about the prince being mentally unstable, which is an obvious comment about the Amarna dynasty. Akhenaton was known as the 'unstable one', the 'criminal of Akhetaton' (Amarna), or the 'heretic pharaoh'. But while this mental instability was a particular comment about Akhenaton himself, from the Theban Amun priesthood's point of view, it is likely that it also applied to the whole of the Amarna dynasty, and in particular to any of the administration and royal family who publicly supported the god Aten. Professor Watt, the translator of *Scotichronicon*, sees this royal instability as being an unusual feature of the text. He says of this:

> It is curious that (Gaythelos') early life is portrayed in such hostile terms, which have no parallel in the Irish tradition. [SC5]

Having already asserted that *Scotichronicon* is only a local Irish myth, it would now appear that this presumed 'Celtic' mythology does not conform to local literary traditions. However, it does correspond very closely with the literary tradition of the Egyptian late eighteenth dynasty, and the bitter aftermath of the failed Amarna regime. Slowly but surely, we shall see that many of the more unusual aspects of the Scottish chronicle jar with local Celtic traditions, but dovetail nicely with Egyptian history.

There are some differences between the various chronicles that comprise Bower's story, and one says that Gaythelos went to Egypt with an army to help the pharaoh. While it is known that Greece sent mercenary soldiers to help Egypt in later eras, not much is known of such exploits during the Amarna era; and although the Pendlebury papyrus may show Greek mercenaries with traditional 'boar-tusk helmets' fighting in Egypt in this era, this evidence is far from conclusive. The Amarna era was two or three hundred years prior to the Iliad's account of the invasion of Troy, and so Mycenaean Greece may not even have been able to muster an army at that time.

Another account in Bower's story says that Gaythelos married his Egyptian princess before he was exiled to Egypt. Yet another indicates that Gaythelos and his army were assisting pharaoh to eject the Israelites [the Hyksos] from Egypt. Finally, one last chronicle indicates that Gaythelos (now called Aegialeus) was actually battling with his brother Apis, rather than his father.

All in all, it would seem that Gaythelos was an Egypto-Greek prince of dubious character who had fought with his father/brother and been exiled to Egypt for his crimes, where he rather fortuitously married a princess with the hope of becoming king of Egypt. However, as has already been explained the latter point is nigh on impossible, as pharaohs of Egypt never gave their daughters to foreign princes. So who was Gaythelos, and where did he really come from? Well, compare the previous quote from *Scotichronicon* with the following quote from the Greco-Egyptian historian, Manetho:

> This king appointed his brother Harmais (as) viceroy of Egypt, and invested him with the royal prerogative ... He then set out on an expedition against Cyprus and Phoenicia ... (but) Harmais who had been left behind in Egypt, recklessly contravened all his brother's injunctions. He outraged the queen and proceeded to make free with the concubines; then, following the advice of his friends, he began to wear the diadem (crown) and rose in revolt of his

brother .... thereafter Harmais was banished from Egypt and, fleeing from his brother, he arrived in Greece, and, seizing Argos, he ruled over the Argives. ᴹ⁶

While the tale of a wayward prince plotting a revolt against his father/brother the king is as old as time itself, how many of these stories result in an exile from Greece to Egypt, or *vice versa*? Indeed, apart from the switching of the departure and arrival points, these two stories appear to be exactly the same. But this is not all, for there are yet more similarities to come.

Firstly, it should be noted that it is entirely possible that Manetho was the original source for *Scotichronicon*. If this is so, then it should be expected that there will be areas of agreement between these two histories of ancient Egypt, and the differences may simply be due to the number and variety of historians and scribes through which these chronicles have passed. Thus these two quotes may be from the same history of Egypt.

Secondly, both of these stories occurred at substantially the same time. The Gaythelos story relates to the era of Pharaoh Akhenaton, as we have seen; while the Harmais story relates to the time of Akhenaton's uncle, Aye, as we shall see later.

Thirdly, the story of Gaythelos eventually ends up in Ireland, where some of the newcomers to that island were known as the Tuatha de Dannen, or the Tribe of Dannen. If this is true, then some of the exiles who left Egypt with King Gaythelos must have been of the tribe of Dannen. However, in a similar fashion, the prince of Egypt called Harmais, in the previous quote from Manetho, was also called Dannus. Indeed, on his arrival in Greece he donated his name to the Athenians, and so Homer's *Iliad* says that it was the Danaoi (the Greeks) who went into battle against Troy. (The book *Eden* demonstrates that Troy was actually the city of Tanis in Egypt, and the great armada of ships in the Greek confederation was actually the great armada of the Sea People alliance that attacked Egypt.)

Caesar

The two quotes just given demonstrate that there is a possibility of a direct connection between Gaythelos and this prince called Harmais (Armais), who was also called Dannus. So could they have been one and the same person? Was Gaythelos a prince of Egypt who went to Greece, rather than a Greek prince who went to Egypt? This would certainly make more sense of his marriage to an Egyptian princess, and it would also make more sense of the degree of prestige that is being given to a minor princeling from an otherwise unimportant land.

The method of discovering the true identity of Gaythelos partly lies in the meaning of his name. What, then, does the name Gaythelos really mean? Actually, the rather astounding answer to this question is that 'Gaythelos' most probably means 'Caesar' – yes, Caesar, as in the Roman emperor. While this suggestion may initially seem a little peculiar, bear with me a while longer.

The name Caesar is the family name for Gaius Julius Caesar. His birth name was Gaius, his family name was Caesar and his clan name was Julius; so his name should really be given as Gaius Caesar, rather than Julius Caesar. But the more important aspect of his full name, in regard to Gaythelos, is the family name of Caesar – what is the origin of this name?

As with many areas of this research, the etymology of the name 'Caesar' is not known. It is said that it could have been derived from *caesar*

meaning 'hairy', hence the jesting and carping about Julius Caesar going a little bald. Alternatively, it could have been derived from *caesar* meaning 'seizure', since some of Caesar's family are said to have suffered from epilepsy. While the name Caesar may have been derived from either of these terms, there is actually a much more satisfactory origin to this famous name.

Firstly, it should be noted that the name Caesar was adopted as a title for subsequent emperors, many of whom were not of the Caesar family at all. So why was this name thought to be so important that it would be used as a title that was almost akin to 'king'? The answer is that the title did refer to a king, but this was not a king of Rome. Instead, the name Caesar was also held by a pharaoh of Egypt and in the Egyptian original the name is given as Kaisares ⬭𓏤𓈖𓏏𓊃 , which is the spelling given for Ptolemy Caesarion, Caesar's son. Another

Fig 3. Julius Caesar.

spelling of this name is Gaysares 𓊨𓅓𓈖𓏲𓏭 , with an initial 'g', while the equivalent Greek is translated as Kiasaros Κιασαρος.

It is thought by some hardy historians, who don't mind going out on an academic limb, that it is from the Greek title *Kaisaros* that the Latin name and title of 'Caesar' was derived (and not *vice versa*). So Julius Caesar may have derived his family name from an alternative source, rather than his name initiating the common Roman title for 'emperor'. But in what way does this name relate to Gaythelos?

Well, the Egyptian 'r' was invariably transliterated into the Hebrew and Greek as an 'l', as the Egyptians did not have the 'l' consonant. This would mean that an alternative pronunciation for Kaisares, in the Egyptian, might be Kaisales or Gaysales. There is also the problem of missing vowels, as these were never written in Egyptian, and so the positioning of the correct vowels is always a problem with these transliterations. If we are allowed to make these two common alterations to the Egyptian cartouche given above, we can then derive either the title Caesar (Kaisaros) or the name Gayselos:

Egyptian to Roman	Egyptian to Greek	Egyptian to Celtic
G a y s a r e s	K a y s a r e s	G a y s a r e s
C a e s a r	K a i s a r o s	G a y s a l o s

In addition, the 's' to 'th' alteration is fairly common to many languages, especially among the Catalonian Spanish, who seem to place a 'th' in every word possible. (Note also the problems that German speakers have with the 'th', which is invariably converted into an 's'.) This final alteration would then make the full transition of this name into the Celtic:

Egyptian to Celtic
G a y s   a l o s
G a y th a l o s

Here we seem to have a direct association between the titles for a Roman and a Greco-Egyptian leader; but the question remains as to which of these names was the formative. Was the name for Prince Gaythelos influenced by the tradition of Roman emperors who bore the name Caesar, or was his name taken directly from the Egyptian title Gaysares?

Fig 4. Egyptian title of Gaythelos (Gaisalos / Gaisaros).

There are many strands to this question, and the first element is the widespread use of this term or title. As was mentioned in the book *Jesus*, the term Caesar and its equivalents are by no means restricted to Rome. The Germanic tribes used Kaiser, while the Persians used Kasra. The former of these titles was probably derived from Roman usage, but the latter was certainly not, as it was used by successive Persian kings over many generations. Thus, the Persian usage of this title predates the known Roman and Egyptian examples by many centuries.

One Persian example of this royal name is the Persian pharaoh of Egypt called Xerxes, a name which is actually an extremely poor Greek (and English) transliteration of his original name. In the Persian cuneiform, and in the Egyptian hieroglyphs (Xerxes became an Egyptian pharaoh), this king was actually called <u>Khashiarsha</u> . By picking out the letters 'Kh', 'a', 'sh', 'r' and 'a' from this name, we can derive the Persian title Kh-a-s-r-a (Kasra), meaning 'king'. As an Arabic dictionary says of this word:

> **Kasra** pl. *Akasirah*. The Khosroes, a name given to almost every king of Persia of Sassanian dynasty. The name is similar to that of Caesar among the Romans and Pharaoh among the Egyptians.[7]

Remember that if Kasra (Kaisars) was a Persian title, then the hieroglyphs in the cartouche for Xerxes may well represent an Egyptian transliteration of this. This, plus the many varied spellings for Kaisars, may point towards this being a foreign title, with no intrinsic meaning within the Egyptian language.

Fig 5. Cartouche of Khashiarsha (Xerxes).

This gives us an interesting new possibility; the suggestion that Gaythelos was actually a Persian prince, rather than a Greek or an Egyptian. If the royal title 'Kasra' originated in Persia, then was Gaythelos Persian? This is a possibility, but on balance perhaps not. The chronology given in *Scotichronicon* places these events squarely within the Amarna era, and the Persians simply did not exist at that time. The ruling empire in the east during this era was Hittite, and it is unlikely that 'Kasra' was a Nesa (Hittite) word. No, even if the term turns out to be Persian, it must be a more recent title applied to an earlier historical individual.

Instead, what may have happened here is that the term actually originated in Egypt, as many things appear to do. When Cambyses II and Darius I invaded Egypt in the sixth century BC, they naturally took this term back to Persia. There, it spread throughout the Persian Achaemenid dynasty and that is why Xerxes and many subsequent Persian kings were called Kasra (Khashiarsha or Xerxes) meaning 'caesar' or 'king'.

This would mean that the original 'royal' title was the Egyptian Gaysares (Kaysares), and the Persian Khashiarsha was a corruption of this. But these new alternatives mean that the table of transliterations just given can be greatly expanded upon:

Egyptian - Persian I	**Egyptian - Roman**	**Egyptian - Celtic**
K ays ares	G ays ares	G ays ares
Kha s ar s	Ga ys ar	Ga y th a l e s
Kha shi ar sha	C a es ar	Ga y th e l o s
Khasiarsha	Caesar	Gaythelos

Egyptian - Persian II	**Egyptian - Greek**
K ays ares	K ays ares
Ka s ares	Ka i sares
Ka s ra	Ka i saros
Kasra	Kaisaros

As can be seen, the transpositions required from the Egyptian to the other languages are relatively simple, which would strongly suggest that the Egyptian term was indeed the original. And, although it is a slightly circular argument, the evidence linking Gaythelos to the Amarna regime would also lend support to Gaysars being the original form of this title. In other words, the name adopted by the Caesar family in Rome was probably an Egyptian title that may already have been in use for over a millennium by a diverse range of nations; including the Persians.

Perhaps it is also worth noting that some versions of the Gaythelos and Scota saga give the prince's name as Gaedel. The 'th' to 'd' transliteration is well known within the Egyptian language, and so an Egyptian Gaythelos could readily be transposed into Gaydelos and thence Gaedelos or Gaedel. Another factor to bear in mind is the meaning of Kaisares / Gaysares. I have not seen a reasonable meaning in the Persian. Various translations have been proffered, from 'Rule of Heroes', 'Mighty One', 'House of the King' and an interesting derivation in the biblical Concordance of 'I Will Be Silent and Poor', which sounds highly unlikely. However, none of these offerings come with any explanations, and should be dismissed as guestimations.

In the Egyptian, the title Gaysares (▨▨||◁◁◌||) may well have been derived from *gaiy-sar(s)* ▨▨||◌ ||◁◌◌ . This phrase simply means 'anointed prince' and since a prince is only anointed upon becoming king, this term effectively means 'king'. This is the same meaning as is given for the titles 'messiah' מָשִׁיחַ and 'christ' Χριστος, which also mean 'anointed one'.

However, if an alternative spelling for this word is used, a similar derivation can be found. The Roman pharaohs of Egypt after Caesarion preferred the title Kaysares (◁▨||◁◌||), which was formed from *kaiy-sar(s)* ◁▨||◌ ||◁◌◌ meaning 'exalted prince'. But the Egyptian term for 'exalted' also has strong connotations of a high place or a pyramid, from which we might derive *kaiy-sar(s)* ◁▨||◌◌ ||◁◌◌ meaning King of the Mountains. While this final derivation might sound unlikely, it is exactly the same as has been previously obtained for the title of the Hyksos pharaohs, who ruled much of Egypt during the 13th to 17th dynasties (see the book *Tempest* for details). Both of these terms would, of course, be referring to the pyramids of Giza rather than a barren hill in the wilds of the Sinai Peninsular. Thus, the Persians and Greeks may have been following in the footsteps of the Hyksos-Israelite pharaohs of Lower Egypt, and using the same symbolism and titles.

In some respects, all of these translations are related. The exalted individual represents a king or high priest who officiated at the Giza 'cathedral' complex; the anointing refers to the ritual anointing of stone pillars or pyramids, as recorded in Genesis 28:18 (as well as the anointing of the king); while the sacred 'mountain' refers to the Giza pyramids themselves. Since the cartouche of Nero Caesar uses this exact same 'exalt' determinative glyph, of a man with his arms held high, this is likely to have been the exact translation for this name. Determinative glyphs are not often used in cartouches, so this anomaly is very useful (his cartouche uses the short form of the word 'exalt', which is *ka* ◁𓀀).

Fig 6. Nuariu Kasars (Nero Caesar), using the 'exalt' glyph.

Further evidence for this link with the Hyksos-Israelites may also be seen in the name of Xerxes himself. The spelling of his name in the Egyptian is Khashiarsha (𓈖𓏤||◁◌◌𓈖𓈖), and there is only one suitable derivation for the first syllables of this name, which is *khasut* 𓈎𓆼𓈉 meaning 'foreign lands'. But this is the very same word that is used for the Hyksos themselves, who were known as the Hyka Khasut 𓋾𓈎𓄿𓏏 𓈎𓆼𓈉 , meaning 'Kings of the Foreign Lands', or perhaps more accurately, 'Kings of the Pyramids'. (The three-hills glyph being a reference to the three pyramids of Giza rather than a line of foreign hills, as is explained in the book *Tempest*.)

While it may be true that a Persian king might not want to utilise a purely Egyptian title, to be honoured with a name that invoked the greatest wonder of the ancient world, and the largest and most sacred temple complex in the ancient world, might well be appealing. But there is another reason for Xerxes to be influenced by Hyksos-Israelite traditions, as we shall see.

Esther

The fact that the title Gay Sars (Kay Sars) has such a satisfactory meaning in the Egyptian, strongly suggests that the word may have originally been coined in Egypt. Also, the Egyptian word *kaiy* 𓈎𓄿𓏭𓀠 meaning 'exalted' or 'mountain' is very ancient, so it is unlikely that this is a term that has been borrowed from Persia in the sixth century BC. So the kings of Persia and the emperors of Rome may have been honoured with an Egyptian title meaning 'Anointed Prince', 'Exalted Prince' or even 'King of the Pyramids'.

While this translation is all very interesting, just why should a Persian king use an Egyptian name or title? The reasoning for this has already been given in my books *Solomon* and *Eden*, and the explanation hinges on one of the greatest biblical and historical events in Judaeo-Egypt – the Babylonian exile. In the sixth century BC, the Babylonian king Nebuchadnezzar sacked the city of Jerusalem (wherever that city actually resided), and also raided some parts of Lower Egypt. Following the fall of the Israelite capital city, its royalty and leaders were deported to Babylon as slaves, in what has become known as the Babylonian captivity. But somehow, instead of being incarcerated and subjugated, at least some elements of the Hyksos-Israelite royalty gained high office in Babylon.

Just four decades later the Persians, under Cyrus I, invaded Babylon and, quite incidentally, set the Israelites free. But many of the Hyksos-Israelites had done so well in Babylon that they did not want to return to Egypt/Israel. The Persians, under Cambyses II and Darius I, then went on to invade Egypt proper and became Persian pharaohs of Egypt. Herodotus maintains that the Persian kings waged this second campaign from the Arabias against Egypt because they had requested an Egyptian princess as a diplomatic bride, but had been fobbed off with a commoner. Determined to get a bloodline princess, they invaded Egypt to force the issue.

However, if many of the Egyptian royalty were actually the descendants of the Hyksos-Israelite pharaohs of Lower Egypt, as I have previously explained, then the Persians may well have been requesting a Jewish princess – and so a trace of this diplomatic wrangling may well be visible within the biblical accounts. Surprising as it may seem, this is exactly what we find. The Bible records that Xerxes' chief wife, Vashti, fell out of favour and was divorced. [B8] So Xerxes arranged to see a parade of young ladies and the damsel who caught his eye was a young Jewess called Hadassar הרסה, whose ancestors had been exiled in the Babylonian/Persian-controlled lands since the time of Nebuchadnezzar. Hadassar is better known as Esther אסתר, the heroine of the Book of Esther.

Who was this Esther, who rose from the position of lowly slave to be the queen of the most powerful nation in the world? The Bible tries to make out that Esther was a commoner, but this is simply the usual Cinderella-style fairy-tale for the faithful.* For a Persian king to divorce his wife in favour of this young Jewess strongly suggests that she was not only royal, but also of the ancient Egyptian bloodline (the Hyksos-Israelite bloodline) – which was admired and sought after by many of the nations that bordered Egypt. The name Esther means 'star', and after she married Xerxes she would have become the Queen of the Stars, or the Queen of Sheba (*sheba* means 'star' in Egyptian, and also in English). The book *Solomon* has already explored the long line of Egyptian 'God's Wives' who were known as Queens of the Stars; they formed a royal line who were honoured in Egypt as incarnations of Isis, who were descended all the way through history from Nefertari and Hatshepsut, through the era of King Solomon to the first century AD and Mary Magdalene.

The similarity between Herodotus' account in *The Histories* and the account of Esther in the Bible strongly suggests, once more, that the theory – that the Israelites were Hyksos Egyptians – is correct. However, the argument can be used in reverse to equal effect; for if Esther was an Egyptian princess, then surely her name or title should be Egyptian. Indeed it is, for the Persian

---

* The Cinderella story may again refer to this 'lost princess of Egypt' story. In reality, Cinderella may refer to Mary Magdalene, the Egypto-Judaic princess who was nearly lost to history because of the Catholic Church's insistence that Jesus was not married to her. But a strong faction within Judaeo-Christianity, who became known as the Illuminati, knew of her illustrious role and status, and preserved her name within the cult of the 'Black Madonna'. As mentioned previously, this title referred not to the Virgin Mary but to Mary Magdalene, and her strangely black complexion denoted that she was a princess of Egypt (Egypt was known as Kam 𓂓𓈖𓏏𓎼 , meaning 'black'). The Cinderella story is simply...

Continued overleaf...

spelling of her name is Aster, a name which was clearly based upon the Egyptian goddess, Ast (Isis) $\mathbb{J}\mathbb{R}$. The likelihood is, therefore, that as soon as the aggressively expanding Persian Empire began to come in contact with the Hyksos-Israelite exiles in Babylon and Egypt, the two royal lines began to assimilate. Thus the name for Xerxes, that of Khashiarsha, may well have been influenced by Hyksos-Egyptian custom and language. Indeed, it is entirely possible that Khashiarsha (Kaisares) was a Persian rendering of the Lower Egyptian title 'Hyksos' (Hy-Kasias).

Even if the royal title, Kaisares, had not been used in Egypt prior to the reign of Xerxes, the Scottish chronicle of Gaythelos was primarily based upon the writings of the third century BC historian Manetho, and Manetho would have been well aware of the Persian twenty-seventh dynasty of Egypt and its two kings called Kaisares (Khashiarsha).

Garland

How Julius Caesar's family managed to inherit this Egypto-Persian name is not known, but there are a few possibilities. The first of these is that the name came directly from Egypt in some manner; but the Egyptian dynasties prior to the Romans, that of the Macedonian Alexanders and Greek Ptolemys, did not use this title. Given this large break between the Persian usage and the Roman usage, it is unlikely that the title came to Rome directly from Egypt. But there is also an outside chance that the name Gaythelos (Kaisaros) had been used in Greece and around the western Mediterranean ever since Scota and Gaythelos departed on their exodus. Their descendants had spread throughout the Mediterranean, as we shall see, and so this name may have been used by the ancestors of Julius Caesar for over a thousand years before it regained the proper status it deserved. If so, then Julius would have been a descendant of this very ancient royal line that originally sprung from the Amarna dynasty of Egypt – as we shall see.

... another rendition of the story of the lost 'black princess', who thwarts the oppression of the ugly sisters (the Catholic and Orthodox Churches) and eventually finds her lost bloodline prince. This is why Cinderella is portrayed as being the rejected beauty sweeping the cinders from the fire, and getting very black in the process.

Significantly, Cinderella finds her royal prince through the traditional symbol of the lost slipper. Like Jason, of Argonauts fame, the symbol of the missing slipper is a symbol of special status, which is most probably linked to the royal bloodline. Masons use this same symbology in their initiation ceremonies to this day, and are presented before the WM 'slipshod'. See the book *Solomon* for more details of the Magdalene story.

It is also worth noting that the *sar* portion of this same title has been preserved in many languages around the globe to this day. It became Tsar in Russia, Shah in Persia, Sahib in India and Sire in Britain; with all of these titles originally denoting a prince or king. Since Gaythelos was supposed to have been the son of a king, and was later anointed as king himself, his having a title like Gaythelos (Kai-saros or Cae-sar) was only natural. Even today when we refer to events in ancient Rome, we still tend to say that "Caesar did this", without even mentioning the birth or family names of the emperor concerned.

Amarna prince

The etymological evidence we have just seen points towards Gaythelos being an Egyptian prince, or at least someone using an Egyptian title. Likewise, the historical evidence also points towards an Egyptian origin: for the Egyptian prince called Harmais (Dannus) in Manetho's accounts sounds very much

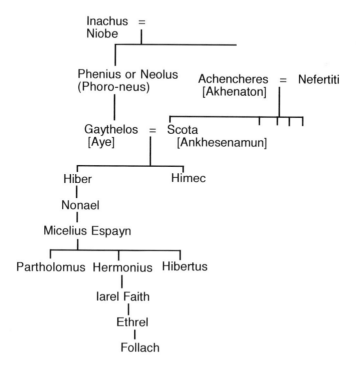

Fig 7. Family tree of Gaythelos.

like the Celtic character called Gaythelos in Bower's account. So could Gaythelos have been Dannus, an Egyptian prince of the Amarna dynasty?

Well, the genealogy that is given in *Scotichronicon* does not help that much in deciding if Gaythelos was an Egyptian royal, but perhaps it does serve to place him within an Egyptian context once more. In the family tree in fig 7, the father of Gaythelos is variously given as Neolas or perhaps Phenius. However, a third version of Phoro Neus probably gives a better idea of how this name was once pronounced. The Phar (Phor) forename was probably based upon the Egyptian *pa-aa* ⌑⌐ meaning 'Great House', a title that referred to the king or the royal family and has been translated into the English as 'pharaoh'. In a similar fashion, the last name of Neolas was probably based upon the Egyptian *neru* ⌇⌐⌐ meaning 'great'.

Thus, the full translation for the father of Gaythelos may well have been Pharo Neoru ⌑⌐ ⌇⌐⌐ , which translates as 'Pharaoh the Great' or 'Pharaoh Victorious'. No doubt all the pharaohs of Egypt professed themselves to be the greatest and so although this identification tells us that Gaythelos may well have been the son of an Egyptian king, it does not really settle the question as to who his father was.

The name of Gaythelos' grandfather is only mentioned once and it comes courtesy of the scribe who seems determined to place these events during the sixth century BC. He is said to have been called Inachus, and what we possibly have here is a corruption of Pharaoh Antiriuasha (Inetrush) ⌈⌐⌐⌐⌐⌐⌉ , otherwise known as Darius I. The familiar name for Darius is again a very poor Greek rendering of the original name for this Persio-Egyptian pharaoh.

Again, Gaythelos is highly unlikely to have been from the Persian dynasty of Egyptian pharaohs, as the general archaeology of the various sites we will shortly be looking at in the western Mediterranean date from the eighteenth dynasty of Egypt (c. 1300 BC). Likewise, the genealogy that is given in the chronicle, and the many references to the biblical exodus, again all point towards the eighteenth dynasty and more specifically to the Amarna regime of Akhenaton.

The confusion with the sixth century may have come about because some later emigrants came to Scotland in the sixth century. These were called

Fig 8. Pharaoh Antiriuasha (Darius I) of Persia and Egypt.

the Picts, as we shall see in a later chapter, but this event had nothing to do with the Gaythelos exodus.

Despite the odd side turning and dead ends, the general thrust of the evidence thus far points towards an unknown prince called Gaythelos (Caesar) marrying a daughter of Pharaoh Akhenaton, and yet this simple fact narrows down his true identity a great deal. It also places Gaythelos' life squarely within the Amarna era, and so there may well be a number of texts that detail such a royal marriage and allow us to positively identify this elusive prince.

One potential suitor might be Zannanza, a Hittite prince who was to marry Ankhesenamun (Ankhesenpaaten), the daughter of Akhenaton. After the death of Tutankhamen, Ankhesenamun found herself without a suitable royal suitor and so she wrote to Suppiluliumas I, the Hittite king, and asked if he had a son she could marry:

> My husband has died and I have no son. They say about you that you have many sons, You might give me one of your sons to become my husband. I would not wish to take one of my subjects as a husband.[9]

Now this request may seem to contradict the assertion that Egyptian princesses never married foreign princes. But not only was this an exceptional circumstance; more importantly, Ankhesenpaaten was not being sent away to marry a prince – rather, Suppiluliumas' son, Zannanza, was being invited into Egypt to become pharaoh. Since the royal line flowed through the female line in Egyptian tradition, this dynastic alliance ensured that no royal blood was being 'lost' to a foreign nation and the royal line in Egypt still remained Egyptian. So was Zannanza the prince called Gaythelos?

Unfortunately not. Zannanza was not Greek, nor was he Egyptian and, as far as we are aware, he never arrived in Egypt. It is thought that enemies within the administration, working either for Horemheb or Aye, assassinated the prince as he entered Egypt's borders, and so this fledgling diplomatic link with the Hittites abruptly ended. This is the only foreign suitor we know of who came to Egypt at this time and who had any chance of being close to a princess, and yet Zannanza could not be Gaythelos. So who was this mythical character who was mentioned so confidently within the Scottish chronicles?

Actually, the rather surprising identification for Gaythelos has already been inadvertently given in my book *Solomon*. The research in this chapter has closely identified Gaythelos with Manetho's Prince Armais (Harmais), and yet I have already demonstrated that Prince Armais was most probably the historical character called Pharaoh Armait. And while this identification may sound a little confusing at this stage, perhaps it should be explained that Armait is simply the throne name of Pharaoh Aye ⟨𓇳𓏤𓂋 𓇋𓏠𓈖𓀭⟩ , the pharaoh who followed Tutankhamen onto the throne of Egypt. Now while this suggestion might seem unlikely, it does have its merits – many of them.

We start with another look at the king-list of Manetho, where Pharaoh Armais is listed after the Amarna dynasty, and before Pharaoh Ramesses I. If we ignore Manetho's misplacement of Horemheb for the moment, the pharaoh who came before Ramesses I was actually Aye; and it was Aye who was named Armait. In addition, Manetho says that there were three royal brothers in this era: Sethosis, Ramesses, and Armais. Sethosis is obviously Seti I, as there is only one Seti who reigned at the end of the Amarna era. Ramesses is obviously Ramesses I because he only had a one-year reign, and the next Ramesses in the king-list is said to have had a very long reign-length of 66 or 68 years. This long-reigned Ramesses was obviously Ramesses II or Ramesses the Great. This leaves us with brother Armais who has now been identified as Pharaoh Aye Armait.

Manetho then says that Sethosis (Seti I) killed Ramesses (Ramasses I) very early in his rule as pharaoh, which may explain Ramesses I's short reign:

> After him came Sethosis and Ramesses, two brothers ... but Sethosis slew Ramesses in a short time afterwards, so he appointed another of his brothers (Armais-Danaus) to be his deputy over Egypt. (Against Apion 1:15)

The 'after him' in this quote refers to 'after Armesses Miammoun and Amenophis' (with Armesses Miammoun being Ramesses Meryamun II or Ramesses the Great). But this assertion is flatly contradicted in Against Apion 1:26, where this same long-reigned Rhampses (Ramesses the Great) is said to be the son of Sethosis (the son of the Sethosis mentioned in the quote above, or Seti I). It is likely that the latter assertion is more correct than the former. Thus the chronology of Manetho's king list, as given earlier in this chapter, maintains the succession according to the latter assertion; which happens to be the same as the chronology in the modern king-list, with Seti I being the father of Ramesses II.

There is also the small problem in this quote of Manetho apparently saying that Armais came after Ramesses I, and not before. However, this is again contradicted by Manetho's king lists. Thus the king-list given earlier in this chapter follows Manetho's king-list and modern Egyptology by placing Armais *after* the Amarna dynasty and *before* Ramesses I. Thus Pharaoh Armais was also called Dannus, and this Armais-Dannus just has to be Pharaoh Aye Armait. He can be no other pharaoh. Manetho's clarification note then goes on to say:

> Armais: also called Danaus. At the end of his (5-year) reign he was banished

from the land of Egypt. Fleeing from his brother (Ramasses) Aegyptus he escaped to Greece, and after capturing Argos he held sway over the Argives.

Bearing all of this in mind, the royal succession at the conjunction between the 18th and 19th dynasties, has to be:

Manetho king-list	Modern king-list
Orus (See Horemheb)	
Amarna dynasty	Amarna dynasty
Armais Dannus	Aye Armait
	Horemheb
Ramesses Egypt	Ramesses I
Sethosis	Seti I
Rhampses Miammoun	Ramesses Meryamun II

Modern Egyptology suggests that Seti I was the son of Ramesses I and not his brother, although the difference is of little consequence. Rhampses (Ramesses II or Ramesses the Great) is said to be the son of Sethosis (Seti I), which agrees with modern interpretations.

Then we come to the peculiar assertion that Armais-Dannus (Pharaoh Aye) was the brother of Sethosis; in other words, Aye was apparently having a royal dispute with his brother Seti I. But this is highly unlikely, as these two monarchs were from completely different generations. The answer to this conundrum is that there is some confusion in the accounts of Manetho as to who Pharaoh Aegyptus (Sethos-Ramesses) really was. In actual fact, he is most often identified as being a Ramesses (ie: Ramesses I), rather than a Sethosis. And so this peculiar assertion that Aegyptus was Sethosis is countered by the clarification that Ramesses (ie: Ramesses I) was sometimes called Sethos. Since it is virtually impossible for the young Pharaoh Seti I to have been in any royal dispute with Pharaoh Aye, the accounts that say Aegyptus-Sethos was Ramesses (ie: Ramesses I) are more likely to be correct. Aye (Dannus) and Ramesses I (Aegyptus) were almost of the same age, and could easily have been in a royal dispute when Aye took the throne in about 1325 BC. But whether Aye and Ramesses were brothers, is another matter entirely.

So while Manetho's claim to a sibling relationship between Aye and Ramesses I is not easy to verify, the very long reign-length that he gives to Seti is much easier to explain. Manetho claims that Sethosis (Seti I) ruled for 51 or 55 years, while modern Egyptology assigns him just 11 years. But if the royal chroniclers had deleted the entire Amarna era, as we know they tried to do, and therefore considered Seti to be the rightful pharaoh who followed on from Amenhotep III, then they would be obliged to add the reign-lengths of Akhenaton, Smenkhare, Tutankhamen, Armais (Aye), [perhaps Horemheb], and Ramesses I, onto Seti's own 11-year reign. The result of this, depending on the reign lengths given to Akhenaton and Horemheb, is a modified and greatly distorted reign-length for Seti I of either 46 or 59 years. (Much of Akhenaton's reign was in a co-regency with his father, while modern archaeology suggests Horemheb only reigned for 15 years.)

Thus there is no conflict here with the presumed age of Seti I's mummy, which is only middle aged, because much the huge reign-length Manetho ascribes to Sethos-Seti was artificial: created by the deletion of the Amarna dynasty. Conversely, the mummy of Ramesses-Aegyptus was definitely of a similar age and era to Aye-Dannus, and so these two pharaohs could easily have been brothers - although there is no historical evidence to support this assertion by Manetho. However, since Ramesses I was from Lower Egypt and came to the throne at a very late age, it is not impossible for him to have been a son of either Amenhotep III or Vizier Yuya, and the latter possibility would indeed make Aye and Ramesses I royal brothers

Having demonstrated that Pharaoh Armais-Dannus and Pharaoh Aye-Armait were the same person, what else do we know about Aye? Well, Aye is known to have been very close to the royal family at Amarna, and his name closely resembles that of Yuya (Aiuya or Yiuia), the influential noble whose daughters and granddaughters married into the royal family on several occasions. For these marriages to have proceeded, Yuya and his wife Tuyu must have been of the royal bloodline, and perhaps this was an even stronger branch of the bloodline than most of the royals themselves. For this and other reasons, it is presumed that Yuya was also the father of Aye (Armait or Armais). Thus Aye was not simply a usurper of the throne of Egypt, but a member of a parallel line within the royal family that was asserting its historical 'right' to rule.

Even before he became pharaoh, Aye had always been very influential at Amarna and bore the titles 'Commander of the Horse', 'God's Father', 'Vizier', and 'Creator of Laws or Justice'; these were prestigious ranks and titles, some of which were also held by his father Yuya. Aye's first wife Tey also held some impressive titles, being known as 'Favourite of the Good God', 'Nurse of the King's Wife Nefertiti', 'Nurse of the Goddess' and 'Ornament of the King'. Clearly, Aye and Tey were just as well-connected within the Amarna royal family as their parents had been.

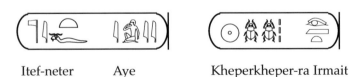

Itef-neter   Aye   Kheperkheper-ra Irmait

Fig 11. Cartouches of Pharaoh Aye.

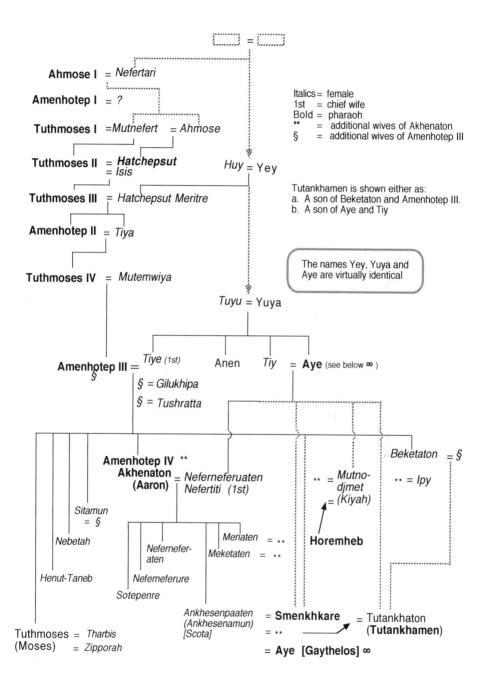

Fig 9.   Amarna family tree. The dotted lines show presumed and alternative ancestries for some of the Armarna royalty. Both Tutankhamen and Smenhhkare, for instance, are shown as being possible sons of Aye. Since Akhenaton never acknowledged a son, it is highly unlikely that Tutankhamen could have been his son.

For Yuya and Aye to have had so many prestigious titles marks them out as possible members of the Amarna royal family. But, as has been mentioned previously, this was not any old distant branch of the family, but a central trunk. Yuya's daughter, Tiye, married Pharaoh Amenhotep III to become his chief wife; and in turn Aye's own daughters are thought to have been Nefertiti and Mutnodjmet, the wives of the pharaohs Akhenaton and Horemheb respectfully. These marriages to three successive pharaohs virtually proves beyond doubt that Aye was of royal blood, so it is highly unlikely that there was anyone in the court of Amarna who was more influential than Aye. A more in-depth look at his life is presented in the next chapter.

It has to be remembered that nepotism was everything within these ancient cultures, because family members provided loyalty, and so all the important ranks and titles in the country were liberally distributed among the immediate members of the family. Tribal links were and are very strong bonds in this region and era, and at its very basic level this loyalty comes down to a question of 'us and them'.

Ankhesenamun

Whatever the political machinations and allegiances within the Amarna dynasty, it is certain that the vizier Aye was influential enough to work his way onto the throne of Egypt after Tutankhamen died – to become Pharaoh Aye (or Aii) Itef-neter Kheperkheper-ra Irmait. He then quickly married Tutankhamen's widow Ankhesenamun, an act which is sometimes said to demonstrate that Aye was not of the royal line and wanted to cement his claim to the throne by taking a royal princess as a wife. However, that argument completely fails to acknowledge that all pharaohs married a bloodline princess, who was often a sister or even a daughter (in the case of Akhenaton and Amenhotep III, amongst others). Thus the marriage between Aye and Ankhesenamun in no way invalidates the strong suspicion that Aye was a bloodline prince in his own right – even if that bloodline came through the parallel royal line of Yuya and Tuyu and not the queen herself.

Yuya and Tuyu, as we have seen, must have held the royal bloodline even if they were not royal themselves, and a son of theirs would, to all intents and purposes, have been a royal prince. This observation may give us another possible parentage for Tutankhamen, whose family history is currently uncertain. It has been suggested by many that Tutankhamen was a son of Akhenaton by Kiyah, his second and favourite wife; but that would not explain the complete lack of inscriptions about a son of Akhenaton being born at Amarna. Akhenaton had had six daughters and no sons, and surely the arrival of a cherished son, even if this was through a second wife, would have been mentioned somewhere.

The alternative scenario, which is beginning to look quite attractive, is that Tutankhamen was the son of Aye, who was of royal blood even if he and his parents were not on the throne. This is why Aye was able to claim the title 'God's Father', a title which is normally restricted to the father of a king rather than the father of a queen. Perhaps it is also why the name chosen for this child was Tutankhaton (later, Tutankhamen), which means 'Living Image of Aten', or 'Living Image of God'. Since the king was a god in his own right, did this name seek to impress on everyone how closely Tutankhaton resembled Akhenaton? In other words his title implied, 'this may not have been Akhenaton's son, but he is the living image of him and thus just like a royal son in all respects'. That there would have been a physical similarity between Akhenaton and Tutankhamen is not surprising. The line of Yuya and Aye had married into the royal line twice, with Tiye being Akhenaton's mother and Nefertiti being his wife, and so Aye's son (Tutankhamen?) may well have closely resembled the royal children.

This may also explain why it was Aye who was depicted performing the last rites in Tutankhamen's tomb. This has often been explained as Aye's way of increasing his power and prestige, in order to take the throne as the next king; but what if it were simply a portrayal of a father burying his son? The ritual of 'Opening of the Mouth' was a very important aspect of Egyptian funerary rituals, and this was normally carried out by the son and heir to the throne. But since Tutankhamen did not have a son, perhaps his father (and heir) was deemed the most suitable alternative.

Had Aye been the father of Tutankhamen, the ease with which he took the throne on the death of the young king is much more understandable. However, Aye's royal status and his marriage to Tutankhamen's widow, Ankhesenamun, greatly strengthens the growing links between Aye and Gaythelos [Caesar], because Ankhesenamun was a daughter of Akhenaton. Thus both Aye and Gaythelos are recorded as marrying a daughter of Akhenaton. But these links grow ever stronger when one realizes that very few men married into the family of Akhenaton.

Fig 12. Cartouche of Ankhesenamun.

II Scota and Gaythelos

Of Akhenaton's six daughters, two or three died at a young age, and Akhenaton married three himself.* That leaves us with Ankhesenamun, who had quite a chequered marital history. She began by marrying her father Akhenaton, then her cousin(?) Tutankhamen, then her uncle(?) Smenkhkare and finally her maternal grandfather, Aye. Out of the two or three marriage possibilities that are recorded for the daughters of Akhenaton, Aye stands out as a prime candidate to be the Celtic King Gaythelos.

Two further aspects of the various Scottish chronicles, as quoted by Walter Bower, are also pertinent to this identification. Firstly, Donald Watt, the translator of Bower, notes that:

> It is important that Scota is the wife, not only of Gaythelos (as here), but in other versions (of the chronicle, she is also the wife) of Gaythelos' father Neolas (and of his descendant and of his son). Her partners may at one time have been numerous. [SC10]

Donald Watt is implying that these other marriages of Scota, to both her father and her brother, demonstrate that the Scottish chronicles are apocryphal and not to be relied upon, for no Egyptian princess would have endured such a peculiar married life. On the contrary, although the family relationships are not exactly the same, we know that Ankhesenamun [Scota] had had a number of related husbands. Far from these convoluted consanguinity rules consigning this Scottish chronicle to mythology, they may actually confirm that it is historical fact.

Secondly, there is the detailed description of Gaythelos' departure from Egypt. It is reported that Gaythelos was a part of pharaoh's forces who were pursuing the Israelites out of Egypt – again placing this story at the time of the (second) biblical exodus. But then Bower goes on to relate a quite different account where the people of Egypt, not content with ousting Moses and the Israelites, demanded that the pharaoh and his army left the country too! Now while this may sound peculiar, this is exactly what happened. What the Bible fails to mention is that one of the leaders of the Israelites was a pharaoh too, and his name was Akhenaton [Aaron]. So although Bower was possibly confused by the chronicles before him, they were correct. When the

---

* I suppose this does also make Akhenaton himself a candidate for Gaythelos; as Akhenaton was a prince and a king, he argued with his father, he did marry his own daughter and he had as much opportunity to go to Greece after his abdication as did Aye. However, Akhenaton's name was not Armais, and yet Dannus (Gaythelos) was called Armais by Manetho. More importantly, Manetho places two Amarna pharaohs between Akhenaton and Armais, and so it would seem as certain as anything can be in this research that Armais (Dannus, Gaythelos) was not Akhenaton.

Israelites [the people of Amarna] were exiled from Middle Egypt, a pharaoh was indeed exiled along with them. But then Bower narrates a tale which is quite interesting:

> Gaythelos remained behind after the army [Akhenaton's army] had departed, in the city of Heliopolis, as arranged between himself and the pharaoh; with the purpose of possibly succeeding to his kingdom. But the Egyptian people [Horemheb?] ... gathered their forces together and informed Gaythelos that if he did not speedily hasten his departure ... utter destruction would immediately attend himself and his men. (Author's brackets). SC11

Again, this is probably what happened. Akhenaton departed Middle Egypt as the Amarna experiment began to crumble, and sought to secure a new power-base in Avaris in the Nile Delta, while Aye remained in Amarna and Heliopolis and perhaps Upper Egypt to secure the succession for either himself or Tutankhamen. On this occasion, it was Tutankhamen who became pharaoh, under Aye's guidance and patronage, and it was only upon the death of Tutankhamen that Aye [Gaythelos] was able to take the throne for himself. But the Scottish chronicle may well be correct in saying that the rule of Aye was unpopular, for his reign ended after less than four years. Since there is no record of his death, Aye may well have been deposed and exiled from Egypt, just as the chronicle suggests.

Curriculum vitae

This line of research and reasoning has not only given us a prime candidate for the character called Gaythelos, it has quite possibly begun to change our entire perception of Celtic history. Where there was once a hazy spectre in a mythological tale, there are now images, texts, statues and tombs. We can now put a face to this mythological apparition; we can divine his motives, strategies, hopes and ambitions. We now know, at last, why Gaythelos and his new royal Egyptian bride would have taken to the perilous seas in search of new lands.

So what is the truth behind the claims and counterclaims about the life of Aye [Gaythelos, Dannus]? In fact, both of his documented life-stories, the Celtic and the Greco-Egyptian, may be true and fully compatible with each other. Manetho says that Armais Dannus [Armait Aye] was expelled from Egypt for claiming the throne from his brother, the king. If Aye was the brother of Seti I, as Manetho asserts, then this is entirely possible. Aye's reign was short, and there is no evidence for his death in Egypt, and so he may well have been expelled on an exodus; and it would have been either Horemheb or Seti I who forced Aye out of Egypt. And since Manetho's king-list has misplaced the reign of Horemheb he could not have said this exile was the result of a military coup by Horemheb. Manetho's revised chronology only leaves one possible culprit - it must have been Seti who opposed and deposed Aye.

Thus both of these records mention Aye's exile to Greece, and if Aye had fallen foul of opposition groups within the extended Egyptian royal family, who were opposed to anyone who had been tainted by the Amarna heresy, it is entirely possible that Aye was forced into exile in Argos (Greece, or more specifically the Peloponnese). And Argos was perhaps ripe for picking at the time. At best, Argos was still a land of backward city states during the Amarna era, and perhaps Aye saw the possibility of taking over a fresh new population, and converting them to the Aton religion. Since I have long maintained that Aye must have been of Hyksos-Israelite descent, the new aristocracy of Greece must likewise have become Hyksos-Israelite. This is confirmed in the Torah, which states:

> Arius, king of the Spartans to Onias the chief priest; greetings. It has been found in writing, concerning the Spartans and the Jews, that they are brethren, and that they are of the same stock of Abraham. [B12]

This is interesting for Argos and its people, the Argives, refers more specifically to the Peloponnese than to greater Greece. And yet the Peloponnese is where the Spartans built their empire - they primarily occupied the next valley or inlet just to the west of Argos. Thus, it is entirely possible that Pharaoh Aye-Dannus founded the proto-Spartan nation some 700 years before they rose to their height of power.

Whether Aye aspired to be a king of Argos and Greece or a simple evangelist, it is a fact that the prime city in greater Greece was subsequently called Aten (Athen-s). The name for Athens is said to have been derived from the Greek goddess Athene, however further evidence that the Sun-god Aton was the source of the name for Athens is perhaps demonstrated by the Egyptian name for Greece itself, which was Uainn 𓆑𓃀𓏤𓈖𓂝𓏤. This name was probably derived from *uinu* 𓃀𓏤𓈖𓀭 which means 'light', and the reason for choosing this name is simply that the great god Aton 𓇳 was the bringer of all light and thus all life.* So Uinu became the name for the province of Argos and Aton (Athen) became the name of its primary city.

The parallel Greek myths penned by Apollodorus, Pausanias and

---

* Perhaps it should also be mentioned that the throne name of Pharaoh Akhenaton was Uenu-Aton (or Uenura) 𓈖𓇳 , meaning 'The Only One of Aton'.

Aeschylus closely follow the life of Dannus, as narrated by Manetho, which demonstrates that this was once a widely known and respected mythology or history. In these Greek accounts the father of Dannus (Aye) is said to be King Belus, the king of Chemmis (Egypt). Robert Graves indicates that the *bel* in Belus might be related to the god Bel (Baal). However, since the Hebrew *bel* בעל also means 'lord' or 'master', it is more than likely that this 'name' refers instead this person's status. Thus the father of Dannus (Aye) could have been either a king or a senior courtier, like Yuya.

These Greek accounts confirm the tradition of a dispute between Prince Dannus (Armais or Aye) and his brother King Aegyptus (Ramesses I), which resulted in Dannus' exile to Argos (Greece). They also indicate that on arrival in Argos, Dannus took the kingship from King Gelanor, the king of Argos, and so the people of Greece became known as the Danaoi from that time onwards. The following quotes give a flavour of the Greek traditions that mention the life and times of Dannus, who was obviously a pivotal character in the founding of the Greek nation. The first is from Pausanias of the 2nd century AD.[13]

> After Iasus, Crotopus, the son of Agenor, came to the throne and begat Sthenelas. (These being the original princes of Argos in Greece). But Danaus sailed from Egypt against Gelanor, the son of Sthenelas, and ended the succession to the kingdom of the descendants of Agenor. What followed is known to all alike: the crime the daughters of Danaus committed against their cousins, and how, on the death of Danaus, Lynceus succeeded him. (Pausanias, Description of Greece 2:16) (Author's brackets.)

The crime of Dannus' daughters is a well known element in Greek mythology. It relates that Pharaoh Armais Dannus had 50 daughters, who married the 50 sons of Pharaoh Ramesses Egyptus; but all bar one killed their husbands, and for this terrible crime they were condemned to carry water in a colander for all time. The *Bibliotheca* or *Library* of Apollodorus - an ancient compendium of Greek history and mythology of unknown authorship - says of these daughters:

> But Belus (Yuya?) remained in Egypt, reigned over the country and married Anchinoe, a daughter of the Nile (a princess of Egypt), by whom he had twin sons, Egyptus (Ramesses I) and Danaus (Aye) ... Danaus was settled by Belus in Libya and Egyptus in Arabia. But Egyptus subjugated the country of the Melampodes and named it Egypt (after himself). Both had children by many wives; Egyptus had fifty sons, and Danaus fifty daughters. As they afterwards quarrelled concerning the kingdom (of Egypt), Danaus feared the sons of Egyptus, and by the advice of the goddess Athena (the god Aton?) he built a

ship ... and having put his daughters on board he fled. And touching at Rhodes he ... thence came to Argos and the reigning king Gelanor surrendered the kingdom to him. And having made himself master of the country he named the inhabitants Danaoi after himself. (Apollodorus 2:4) (Author's brackets.)

This paragraph therefore parallels Manetho's account, in suggesting that Seti was in Arabia (Assyria) and later became king of Egypt, at which point Aye was forced to flee to Argos in Greece. There, Aye defeated the local leader and became the king of Argos, with his name being subsequently taken as a title for all the Greeks. The Iliad, for example, calls the Greeks the Danaoi on some 138 occasions. Another account of Aye's exodus comes from a play by Aeschylus of the 5th century BC, who says:

May Zeus ... look graciously upon our company, which boarded a ship and put to sea from the outlets of the fine sand of the Nile. For we have fled Zeus' land (the land of Aton-Ra) whose pastures border Syria, and are fugitives, not because of some public decree pronounced against blood crime, but because of our own act to escape the suit of man, since we abhor as impious all marriage with the sons of Aegyptus. It was Danaus, our father, adviser and leader, who, considering well our course, decided, as the best of all possible evils, that we flee with all speed over the waves of the sea and find a haven on Argos' shore. For from there descends our race... (Aeschylus, Suppliant Women 1-39) (Author's brackets.)

These quotations demonstrate that this mythology or history for the founding of Greece was well established long before Manetho wrote his history of Egypt, and specifically identified Dannus-Armait with Aye and Ramesses-Aegyptus with Ramesses I. And yet these many ancient traditions do represent a plausible life-history for both Aye and Seti, and so all three of the records we have looked at in this chapter might be regarded as being substantially correct.

Thus the account narrated by *Scotichronicon* agrees very well with both the mythological and the known historical life of Pharaoh Aye Dannus. Yes, Aye may well have been forced out of Egypt and flee to Argos. Yes, he may well have subsequently embarked on a much longer odyssey to Spain, as the Scottish chronicles relate. Yes, he did marry a daughter of Akhenaton. Yes, he did become king of Egypt. And finally, yes, he did disappear from the records of Egypt, along with his new wife, leaving no trace of a burial there.

Aye did have a tomb prepared for himself in Egypt: in fact, he had two. His first was carved into the cliffs at Amarna, but with the demise of that regime it was abandoned. Subsequently, he took over WV23 near the Valley of the Kings, a tomb that may have originally belonged to Smenkhkare. But

Aye was not buried in either of these tombs, and both were destroyed by the succeeding pharaoh, Horemheb. No *ushabti* (death figurines) of Aye have ever been found either, and so the evidence suggests that he did not die a normal death in Egypt. So what happened to both Aye and Ankhesenamun? Were they murdered and their bodies disposed of in the Nile? Or were they simply forced out by opposition forces and compelled to go into exile?

Remember that both Aye and Akhenaton were gods, as well as kings. Such people held considerable psychological power over the people, and they were difficult to simply kill off in cold blood. They might well die in battle, of course, but look at the trouble Oliver Cromwell had deciding the fate of Charles I. Having captured the king, he dithered so much that Charles escaped and started a second civil war. Even after Charles' second capture, Cromwell still dithered – simply because of the kings' supposed divine right to rule. Such things weigh heavily on the conscience of a religious man, and so when Cromwell eventually condemned Charles to death he diluted the divine blame (and wrath) with another 58 signatures from all the officials within his regime.

It is entirely possible that exactly the same kind of dithering happened with both Pharaoh Akhenaton and Pharaoh Aye. Both of these kings had tombs prepared for them, but both escaped burial in some manner. A likely scenario in both cases is that they went into exile with a small band of loyal followers. Manetho suggests that Akhenaton was initially exiled to Avaris in the Nile Delta, where they stayed for thirteen years. But then the opposing Egyptian pharaoh, who Manetho calls Amenophis (an unknown Amenhotep) gathered an army in 'Ethiopia' (probably Nubia and Thebes) and chased the 'polluted people' and their 'leprous priests' (monotheist priests of the Aton) to the borders of Syria. However, if we restore Horemheb to his rightful place in the king-list, it is highly likely that it was Pharaoh Horemheb who chased Aye out of Egypt and not an unknown Amenhotep.

Argos

Both Manetho and the Greek myths appear quite certain that Aye-Dannus went to Greece after a short reign. But if Aye went to Greece in 1320 BC, then what about his career during the reign of Tutankhamen? Well, the evidence for Aye's presence in Egypt during this period is equivocal, so we cannot say anything definite on this matter. However, it would appear that Aye was originally a devout Atonist, and so he was unlikely to have willingly stood aside while the Aton cult was dismantled all around him. And although one or two scenes from a later period depict him venerating the traditional gods, this may have been political pragmatism rather than personal choice. Aye's problem was that a senior official called Horemheb had installed himself into nearly every branch of Tutankhamen's administration. He was known as 'Overseer of Overseers', 'Overseer of Every Office', 'King's Deputy in Every Place', and 'Overseer of the Army'. Clearly this was the man who pulled all the strings in Egypt at this time, not Pharaoh Tutankhamen.

More sinisterly, Horemheb also adopted the title 'King's Two Eyes Throughout the Two Lands', an ominous title if ever there was one. So Horemheb was also the chief spy-master, and since he was obviously not an Atonist, there is no way in which Horemheb and Aye could have worked together within the same administration. Thus the evidence, be it only circumstantial, is that Aye may have withdrawn from Egypt during Tutankhamen's reign. Sometimes it is better to go into exile, voluntarily or otherwise, rather than to see all you have worked for and believed in destroyed.

But where might Aye have gone to? In the quote from Apollodorus just mentioned, Aye-Dannus was being linked with Libya rather than Egypt. This is because other traditions, like those mentioned by Diodorus Siculus, say that Dannus built the Temple of Ammon at the Siwa Oasis, which lies on the borders of Libya and Egypt. However, this alternative account is interesting, as it suggests that the temporary exile of Aye during the reign of Tutankhamen may have been in Siwa. And it would only have been a short journey from Siwa back to Egypt proper, to claim the throne of the Two Lands after the death of Tutankhamen. Conversely, commander Horemheb, who was apparently away on a campaign in Hati at the time, was too late to claim the throne on this occasion.

But the renaissance of Atonism under Aye was not to be. The people had tolerated the new cult of the Aton for many years, but perhaps it seemed that this new god just created problems for the people. The taxes grew to pay for the new city at Amarna; the priests in Thebes had been thrown out on the streets; neighbouring kingdoms were in constant rebellion; there were setbacks in the foreign wars; and a plague may have swept through the country. As deities go, clearly this 'Aton' guy was of the bargain-basement variety. Understandably, the people were fed up with the political turmoil and craved stability. Under the circumstances, it is no wonder that the Theban priesthood, assisted by the power and influence of the most senior army commander, Horemheb, were able to steer the boy-king Tutankhamen back towards the worship of the old gods.

As far as many people in the country were concerned, things had been heading back towards the right, traditional direction under Tutankhamen, when Aye suddenly became pharaoh. One suspects that Aye would have attempted to move back towards Atonism, but the priests, the military and the common people refused to follow, and a leader without followers is no longer a leader. Disillusionment was the real reason behind Aye and Ankhesenamun's probable exile from Egypt. Whatever the political imperatives for this exile were, the records of this era - the historical Egyptian, the mythological Greek and the legendary Celtic - all seem to suggest that Pharaoh Aye-Dannus [Gaythelos] and his new bride Ankhesenamun [Scota] were forced into a great exodus to a new life in new lands.

But this was no hurried exile, scrambling away for fear of immediate execution. No, to have assembled a flotilla of ships implies that Aye was asked politely but firmly by the administration to leave, and given sufficient time and resources to organise himself. As Bower says:

> So Gaythelos gathered together all his followers and left Egypt with his wife Scota. Because he was afraid to return to the regions from which he had come (Greece) because of old feuds, he directed his course westwards.

> Gaythelos with his wife and his whole household and the other leaders were taken in skiffs and embarked on the waiting ships, trusting in guidance of their gods. As their prows cut through the waves of the sea, they headed towards the western regions of the world. [SC15]

Here was a well organised expedition, possibly using the navy of another nation hired especially for this purpose. Judging by the sound of the text it would appear that these were very large ships, for the exiles required small dinghies to get out to the main fleet - and this is one of those interesting detailed asides that suggests this story was based upon an eyewitness account of an actual event.

Aye would have known that he needed a large amount of wealth (gold), supplies, livestock and skilled artisans, if he and his supporters were ever going to survive in a new land and he may have needed 500 or more people to set up a viable colony. Such journey would have been a huge undertaking in the Bronze Age, even for a hugely wealthy royal family from the region's richest nation, and would have required a large fleet of sizeable ships, just as the Scottish chronicle reports. But Egypt was a nation with a large fleet of river boats, and may not have had many or any ocean-going ships. The great trading nation at this time, that plied the trade routes of the eastern Mediterranean, was Minoan, as we shall see later, and so Minoan ships may have been hired to take Aye and his large retinue of courtiers, officials and artisans to new lands.

Finally, it is worth noting that the accounts we have looked at all mention an exodus to Greece, while *Scotichronicon* is confident that these exiles also went to new lands in the west. One possibility, is that this mighty armada initially travelled to Greece, and journeyed to the west at a later date. Or perhaps these exiles split into two groups, that travelled in opposite directions. Who knows? With this being such a hoary old semi-mythological history, is unlikely that we will ever know the precise details of Aye-Gaythelos and Ankhesenamun-Scota's exile.

Amity brig

If you desperately need to transport a large number of people, it is surprising what can be managed and what the people can endure. When a sturdy new ship named Amity was built in Canada in 1816 she was thought to be large, but in fact she measured just 23 x 7 meters (18 x 5 meters internal) and grossed just 142 tonnes. Thus her dimensions were about the same as a Viking longboat in length but somewhat wider in the beam. Perhaps, more interestingly, the Amity was only half the length of the boat that was buried beside the Great Pyramid – which was built at least a thousand years before the voyage of Gaythelos and Scota. Clearly, the ancient Egyptians had the technology to build ships the size of this 'modern' two-masted brig named Amity.

Despite the Amity's modest size, this sturdy brig was built to sail the Atlantic, which she did until 1823 when she sailed to Australia instead. But the voyage that is of more interest to this story is the one she took from Sydney on November 9th 1826, arriving in Albany, Western Australia, on Christmas Day the same year.

The brig reached Princess Royal Harbour on Christmas Day 1826, but no-one was put ashore until the next morning. The party comprised of 23 convicts –

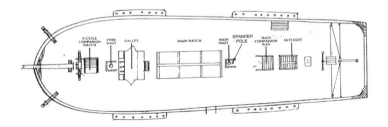

Fig 13. The rotund lines of the Amity brig.

mostly tradesman, 18 rank & file soldiers, a sergeant, a captain, a surgeon, a storekeeper and the commander Major Edmund Lockyer, with stores for six months (including sheep & pigs). [16]

So forty-six people, plus the crew and all their stores and livestock were jammed into a space smaller than the floor area of an average house. But this was not for a cruise around Botany Bay; this was a six-week journey through some of the roughest and most unpredictable seas in the world.

While it is true that the Amity was built of sturdy black birch and American larch, with a high prow and deck to survive the roughest waves, it is also a fact that the Great Pyramid boat was constructed of even tougher Lebanon cedar, and had an equally prominent bow. The only thing that would have detracted from the Great Pyramid boat's design is the shallow draught and low sides; but there again she would only have been dealing with a moderate Mediterranean swell instead of the roaring rollers of the Atlantic or the Southern Ocean. Besides, the Vikings seemed to have coped reasonably well with unpredictable North Sea squalls using a very similar design to the Egyptian one.

So, a small ship the size of the Amity can carry around fifty people and their supplies; but what of the ancient open-deck equivalent? Well, in a very similar fashion the *Lebor Gabala* chronicle, which has occasionally been quoted in *Scotichronicon*, says that each of Gaythelos' boats held sixty people:

> three score (the passengers) of every ship,
> a clear saying,
> and women every third score. [17]

Given this broad agreement in ancient maritime capacity, we now have a pretty good idea of the number and size of Gaythelos' vessels. Further details on the type of ships that would have been available to Aye-Gaythelos will be discussed in a later chapter. But the evidence given thus far demonstrates that even if Aye-Gaythelos' party of exiles had numbered a thousand, only about twenty ships of this size would have been required to transport them across the Mediterranean. A fleet of this magnitude should have been well within the capabilities and technology of the nations concerned, and so is entirely possible that between 500 and 1,000 people set off from Egypt towards the western horizon, in search of a new homeland.

Less than two decades after Moses and Aaron [TuthMoses and Akhenaton] departed on their exodus to Avaris and beyond, a new exodus was being organised in Egypt. This dramatic event evaded the quills of the Hyksos-Israelites, presumably because they were scratching a living in new lands and had their own survival to worry about. The trials and tribulations of Egypt had been left behind them for a few centuries, and the Hyksos-Israelites had little time for the political machinations in their former homeland. So if Aye-Gaythelos was to leave his mark on history, he would have to write his own Day Book or Bible. He appears to have done just that, and the end result, after many translations, editions, revisions and versions, was *Scotichronicon*.

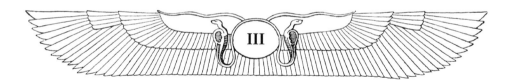

Aye and Gaythelos

If Gaythelos was indeed the Amarna Pharaoh called Aye, perhaps we should take a short detour at this point and look a little closer at the man and his motives.

As we have seen, Aye was probably quite old by the time he came to the throne, and the new wife he then took was actually his granddaughter, Ankhesenamun. It is often said that Aye was a commoner, but since his daughters, Nefertiti and Mutnodjmet, both became queen, this is highly unlikely. Aye was honoured and decorated under Akhenaton, presumably for his role as army commander in keeping law and order in Egypt during Akhenaton's religious reforms. These would have been hugely unpopular amongst the powerful, traditional priesthood, and no doubt Aye's heavy hand kept a lid on any unrest.

The traditional honour given to officials in Egypt was the golden collar or torq, and Aye is portrayed as receiving dozens of these torqs from Pharaoh Akhenaton. Since Scota was a daughter of Akhenaton, it is not so surprising to see this same tradition migrating across to the western reaches of Europe, and so in Ireland and Britain we see Bronze Age torqs turning up in many burials. The later chapter on Ireland will uncover some interesting aspects about this Irish tradition, which will link directly back to the Amarna era and to Aye himself.

The name 'Aye' was probably derived from *a-iy* or *a-yi* 𓇋𓇋 𓏏𓏏 meaning 'I Am'. This is a contraction of his full name, which was Aye Atif-neter (𓇋𓏏𓆣 𓊹𓇋𓏏) meaning 'I Am God's Father', with the 'god' in question probably being a pharaoh. It is generally thought that this title referred to Nefertiti, who was probably Aye's daughter, and so the title actually meant 'I

III   Aye and Gaythelos

Am Pharaoh's Father (In-Law)'. However, it is entirely possible that this title referred to Tutankhamen instead, as we shall see again shortly. This claim was important to Aye, because he needed to overtly demonstrate that he was of the royal bloodline, to be a legitimate claimant to the throne. As we have already seen, since the bloodline in Egypt was maternal, Aye must have been very closely related to the bloodline for the royal bloodline holder – Nefertiti, not Akhenaton – to have been his daughter.

However, within the framework of the new, revisionary Egyptology that has been forged within this series of books, Aye is also known to have been a chronological contemporary of the biblical Moses. So it may or may not be significant that when Moses asked 'god' for his real name, he replied:

> And god said unto Moses: I AM, it is I AM. Say unto the children of Israel that I AM has sent me (Moses) unto you (the people). [B1]

> חה ויאמר אלהים אל-משה אהיה אשר אהיה ויאמר כה תאמר לבני
> ישראל אהיה שלחני אליכם

It would appear that both Aye and the Hebrew god were called 'I Am'. But, just as with the Egyptian term for 'god', the Hebrew equivalent can also be translated as 'leader' (pharaoh, vizier or president). So the 'god' in this verse could easily have been a person. Interestingly enough, the Hebrew word for this individual called 'I Am', is actually *hayah* היה; while at the same time an alternative vocalisation of Aye's name might be Aya. So the names for these two leaders, H-aya and Aya, appear to have very similar meanings and pronunciations. If these characters could, just for the sake of argument, be considered to be the same, then this verse from the Book of Exodus may actually be saying:

> And Moses said unto (the vizier or president), Who am I, that I should go unto Pharaoh [Akhenaton], and that I should bring forth the children of Israel [the people of Amarna] out of Egypt [Amarna]? And Moses said unto the vizier, When I come unto the children of Israel [Amarna] ... they shall say to me: What is his [the vizier's] name? What shall I say unto them? And the vizier said unto Moses: **Aye**, it is **Aye**. Say unto the children of Israel [Amarna] that **Aye** has sent you (Moses) unto them. (Author's brackets.) [B2]

While this is a radical suggestion, the context of this verse would suit this interpretation too. The era in question was just before the second biblical exodus [the Amarna exodus] and Moses, the high priest of Heliopolis, was getting advice from a leader [the vizier, Aye] as to what should be done about the children of Israel [the people of Amarna]. The advice from the leader

[Aye] was that he had seen how bad life was getting in Egypt [Amarna] for these people, and he would tell pharaoh [Akhenaton] to bring the people out into the land of the Canaanites (meaning 'lowlands', the Nile Delta).

Since I have already established that Moses was TuthMoses, the brother of Akhenaton, his acting as an intermediary between Aye and Akhenaton would be entirely understandable. Since we know that Akhenaton's regime became unstable towards the end of the Amarna era, it is highly likely that influential administrators, like the vizier Aye, would have been advising Akhenaton as to his best exit strategy. One option would have been the abandonment of Amarna, and an exodus of the whole population to a safer region – perhaps in Lower Egypt or even elsewhere.

Ayi or Iye (Aye)   *Yiuia or Iyuia (Yuya)*

Fig 14. *Spelling of the names of Aye and Yuya.*

Although some readers might not like the analogy, this is a bit like the last days of the Third Reich. Despite the fact that Hitler's empire had almost entirely collapsed around him, and his command stretched not much further than his bunker in Berlin, all of his courtiers were either so in awe of him or so afraid of him that no one would give him an honest assessment of the situation, let alone any honest advice. The apparent exception to this was Albert Speer, Hitler's chief architect, who seemed to be able to disagree with Hitler without suffering serious harm.

This biblical quote seems to be indicating that the same was true of Akhenaton, and everyone bar Aye was afraid to give him a true assessment of the political situation in Egypt. Again readers may think this assessment of Akhenaton's character unwarranted and unfair, but just think of what he had achieved in about five years (assuming a previous co-regency). Akhenaton had assumed control of the army and taken on the most powerful institution in the land, the priesthood, and closed them down. Likewise, he had taken on the hearts and minds of the people and convinced them, either through persuasion or fear, that their entire belief system was wrong and heretical. A weak, ineffectual leader, as Akhenaton is often portrayed as being, just could not have achieved this.

In the book *Jesus*, a comparison was made with England's Henry VIII and Oliver Cromwell, two leaders who dared take on the might of the Catholic Church. They faced the same problems that Akhenaton faced, in terms of the power and influence of their opposition. They both battled through and succeeded in their campaigns, but neither of these leaders could be portrayed as politically weak, as Akhenaton has often been.

Exodus

We know that the people of Amarna fled somewhere after the fall of this regime, and it is likely that Akhenaton and many in his immediate family fled too; as no trace of their deaths have been discovered, either in Amarna or Thebes. So the context of the biblical account fits the known historical facts, and it is possible that here in the Book of Exodus we have a verbatim record of a conversation between Akhenaton's brother, TuthMoses, and Aye (Aya). Having seen so many convergences and connections between biblical and Egyptian history, this suggestion is entirely probable.

Remember that this is the second exodus from Egypt, as the major mass-migration event of some 500,000 people travelling to Jerusalem was actually the Hyksos exodus that had occurred some 250 years earlier. The biblical account has conflated these two exodus events into one story, with Moses as its leader – although the pitched battle between the armies of the biblical Jacob and Esau (as reported by Josephus Flavius) may well represent another biblical memory of the earlier great exodus.

It is not always wise to build speculation upon speculation, but this argument can be taken one stage further. If Aye was indeed the biblical character who conversed with Moses, and who was sometimes referred to as 'god' (or vizier), then it should be recalled that the next major meeting between these two characters was at (or in) Mt Sinai. Wherever this location may actually be, the purpose of the meeting was for Moses to collect the 'divine' commandments and give them to his people:

> And the lord (vizier) said unto Moses, Come up to me <u>into</u> the mount (Sinai) ... and I will give thee tablets of stone, and a law, and commandments which I have written; that thou mayest teach them (to the people). [B3]

So it is possible that this verse could be translated as Moses [TuthMoses] receiving the laws or commandments from the vizier Aye, and not from the god-figure. As it happens, the throne name of Aye was Kheperu-ra Ir-maat ⟮⊙ 𓏤𓏤 𓎟⟯, which means 'Image of Ra, Creator of Laws'. So once again, the titles of Aye dovetail precisely with the biblical accounts of Moses' meetings with this 'vizier' (or god). Aye was known as the Image of the God and the Creator of Laws, and this 'Image of God' (Aye) was giving those 'Created Laws' to Moses during the exodus [from Amarna].

If both of these verses have been translated in the correct manner, then it would appear that both the high priest of Heliopolis (Moses) and the king of the Two Lands (Akhenaton) were showing deference to Aye, and that in many respects Aye was the senior ranking individual. Actually, this is not so unlikely as it may seem. Aye was not only the elder of these three, but he was also a son of Yuya (Yiuia) 𓏤𓎡𓏤𓅓 , hence the similar names.

The meaning of Yuya's name is not fully known, but bearing in mind the translation for Aye, it is likely that the initial *y (i)* 𓇋 means 'I' once more. The *yu (iu)* 𓇋𓅱 syllable was probably derived from the same root as Aye's double reed suffix 𓇋𓇋 , which means 'am' or 'to be'. The final part of Yuya's name, the *ia* or *ya* 𓇋𓅓 , may mean 'praise' or it may simply be an exclamation. Thus Yuya's full name may well mean 'I Am Praised' or perhaps 'Hail, I Am'. In other words, Aye's name probably echoed his father's (Yuya's) and so Yuya would also have been regarded as a god-figure in the same way that Aye may have been.

To say that Yuya achieved a rank equal to a god (a pharaoh) may seem like an exaggeration; however, he did manage to end up with one of the most prestigious burials ever discovered in Egypt. This was also a burial that was not disturbed during the government-sponsored looting of the Valley of the Kings, during the later twentieth dynasty, and that may not have simply been a fortuitous accident. Whatever the power-base of Yuya and Aye really was, it was very influential and very effective.

Dannus

The biblical assistance we have had in identifying the meaning of these names is very useful, and perhaps it can shed some light onto the other name that was given to Aye – Manetho's alternative name of Dannus. Manetho is often derided as being unreliable, but we can be reasonably certain that the name Dannus was given to Aye because Manetho's Dannus was exiled to Greece and the name subsequently became the primary title for most of the Greek people – the Danaoi Δαναοι. As Strabo recounts:

> Dannus, the father of fifty daughters, on coming to Argos (Greece) took up his abode in the city of Inarchos and throughout Hellas (Greece). He laid down the law that all people hitherto named Pelasgians were to be named Dannans (Danaoi). [S4]

So the name 'Dannus' eventually referred not simply to a person, but to an entire nation. So what did Danaoi mean? Since this was obviously not a Greek name, I have not seen any attempt at a translation from the Greek. In Celtic traditions, the similar title of 'Tuatha de Dannan' was said to refer to the 'People of the Goddess D-Anu'. If the term D-Anu had been derived from the Egyptian, then this may have been from the word D-Anu ⌐ 𝌆⊗ meaning 'The Temple of Heliopolis'.

However, there is an alternative to this translation because the exact Egyptian spelling of Aye's alternative name appears to have been preserved in the ancient records; for the Danaoi Greeks were referred to by the Egyptians as the Djainiua ⌐𝌆. The hieroglyphic spelling of this title would seem to preclude any association with the city of Anu or On (Heliopolis).

The precise meaning of 'Djai-niua' has never been resolved, but the first thing that was evident was that the 'n' glyph seemed to be optional. So, the task was to look for a word that also had an optional 'n'. The result, for the center portion of the name, was *au* 𝌆 or *niu* 𝌆, which both mean 'us' or even the genitive, 'our' (this word also retains the same 'red crown' determinative glyph). The prefixed *a* 𝌆 may refer to an emphatic particle, and so *a-niu* 𝌆 probably means 'Our!' This seemed rather similar to the names for Aye and Yuya, which also referred to 'me' or 'I'. The only difference here being that *a-niu* was now in the plural, because it referred to a whole nation – perhaps it was no longer 'I Am', but 'We Are'. This would leave the initial *da* ⌐𝌆 or ⌐𝌆, which simply means 'the' or, perhaps more likely, 'seed' (offspring). So it is likely that the name for Dannus and the Djainiua (Danaoi) people means either 'Our Seed' or 'The People'. If Dannus was Aye, who was called 'I Am', then the name 'The People' for the nation as a whole would be quite appropriate.

What was this peculiar title of 'I Am' trying to indicate? It tends to sound a little self-important; a mark of these people's special status: 'I Am', but you are not. Actually, while there may be a bit of self-indulgence in this name, the true meaning can only be teased out by looking at the biblical equivalent. As was noted before, the name used for this important person (god) in the Bible was 'I Am', which is the same as Aye's and Yuya's names. However, in the Bible we have a further translation in a closely related language – Hebrew. The Hebrew version of this name is Hayah היה, which was derived from Havah הוה, with both meaning 'exist', 'to be' or 'I Am'. Note once again that if the initial 'h' is dropped from Hayah we can derive Ayah, or the name of Pharaoh Aye.

Much more interestingly, both of these words are very closely related to Khavah חוה meaning 'life'. Obviously to 'exist', one needs to have 'life', and so we can presume that the similar spelling indicates that these were originally the same word. However, the Hebrew ה and ח are too similar for copyists to always transcribe them correctly (yes, they are supposed to be different consonants), and no doubt two variations of the same word have crept into the language through such errors.

Readers who have digested the book *Eden in Egypt* will now see in which direction this argument is going. In this book, I have already argued that the biblical Eve was Akhenaton's second wife, Kiyah ⌣⏐𝕊 𝕴𝕴 ♟ . As it happens, the Hebrew name for Eve is Khavah חוה, which was derived from Khayah (Khiyah) חיה, with both of these words meaning 'life'. But now it would appear that we have a very fortuitous and convenient meeting of terms and people.

a.   Kiyah may have been a daughter of Aye, and Aye was called 'I Am' both in the biblical and the historical record.

b.   Kiyah was possibly the biblical Eve, who was called Khavah חוה or Khiyah חיה in the biblical record. (Note the similarity in spelling to Havah חוה and Hayah היה meaning 'I Am'.) Thus Khiyah's nickname may have been 'I Am', exactly the same as her father's was.

Is it really possible that Kiyah was another daughter of Aye, a sister to Nefertiti? Certainly, the Egyptian royalty liked to keep marriage within the family and this was especially true of Akhenaton, who married three of his daughters. Aye did have another, younger daughter called Mutnodjmet, but she seems to disappear from view at Amarna after the fourth daughter of Akhenaton was born. Or maybe she did not disappear. Could the rather reclusive daughter called Mutnodjmet have had the nickname of Kiyah?

Incidentally, this is not the only confusion in regard to Mutnodjmet's name. Having spent many hours pondering the original spelling of her name, it seemed most likely that she was using the flat-topped seedpod ⏺

Fig 15. A vastly improved version of Queen Kiyah's portrait, by Lena Wennburg.

, rather than the domed and multi-seeded pod ⟨, both of which mean 'sweet smelling'. This may seem like a trivial point, but it would mean that the true pronunciation of her name would be Mutbenrit 🦅⟨◠🦅 instead of Mutnodjmet, and this is a significant difference if one is looking for connections between names in differing languages.

This discrepancy remained a mystery until the *Rock Tombs of El Amarna* was referenced, and there it can be seen that Professor Davies calls Aye's daughter Benretmut. What he has done here is to place the god-name, Mut, at the end of her name, as perhaps it should be anyway; but essentially, Mut-benrit and Benret-mut are the same name. Despite Mutbenrit probably being the true pronunciation of her name, this book will continue with the standard pronunciation of Mutnodjmet to avoid confusion with other reference works.

Fig 16. Spelling of Mutbenrit (or Mutnodjmet).

For Akhenaton to have married two sisters is actually quite likely, and it would explain a great deal about the role and position of Kiyah within the royal family. Certainly Mutnodjmet was the younger sister to Nefertiti, just as Kiyah also appears to be the younger wife of Akhenaton. In short, there is nothing to prevent this association, and it would also go a long way in explaining the rivalry between Nefertiti and Kiyah. The two wives would obviously have been sisterly rivals for Akhenaton's affections, but if Kiyah was Mutnodjmet there may have been a theological split too.

Mutnodjmet was quite pointedly not conforming with Amarna traditions, by keeping an old god-name in her name, and she is also never shown participating in the ceremonies of the Aton. Basically, she was pointedly saying, 'I do not believe in your Atonist rubbish, and I want nothing to do with it.'

Despite this overt rebellion against the Aton, Mutnodjmet was still shown with the royal family as a friend of the elder princesses, and even had her despised and banned name (the goddess Mut) etched into many scenes. For this to have happened, she must have had the protection and sympathetic understanding of the king, Akhenaton, for everyone else in Amarna appears to have changed their names to delete the old god-names and to mention the Aton instead.

Indeed, so contentious was Mutnodjmet's name that someone, at a later date, chiselled out the Mut portion from many of her depictions. Now while there has been a great deal of ancient desecration of the Amarna tombs, with Theban Amun supporters hacking out the name of the Aten and Akhenaton from every location possible, this particular piece of damage would not have been their work. For a start, a stranger from Thebes would have been unlikely to have spotted a minuscule reference to Mut within these large tableaus; and even if they did do so, as supporters of the traditional gods they would have had no problems with this particular god-name. It was the Aton they despised, not Mut.

No, the vandal who chipped the Mut out of Mutnodjmet was obviously an Aton supporter, and so this little piece of desecration must have been performed before Amarna was fully abandoned. That someone would creep into Aye's tomb and cut out just this particular hieroglyph demonstrates how contentious Mutnodjmet's name really was, and how peculiar it is that she was allowed to keep this name. And in a remarkably similar fashion another Aton supporter crept into Kiyah's small temple, after her fall from grace, and excised all her titles and cut the eyes out of her images. Was this the work of the same vandal, because these were one and the same lady?

There is also the question of why Mutnodjmet, being a devotee of Amen and Mut, would want to stay in the Atonist capital of Amarna. While it is true that Mutnodjmet's sister and parents resided there, would she not have felt more comfortable in Karnak with a relative? Her unique, aloof position in Amarna was even being ridiculed by the Amarna artists, who gave her two dwarf companions in some of the scenes:

> These servants (dwarfs), for whom ridiculous titles and names are invented, and their mistress (Mutnodjmet), who stands apart without participating in the worship of the Aten, invite comment. Were it not for the youth of the princess and her Egyptian aspect, I would venture to suggest that (she was foreign)...[5]

In fact, one of the dwarfs was called 'Vizier of the Queen' and the other 'Vizier of his Mother', with the term 'vizier' normally referring to a governor or even prime minister. It is not clear which 'queen' and 'mother' were being referred to by these titles but if the intended subject was Mutnodjmet, as Professor Davies maintains, then this may be important in linking Mutnodjmet with Kiyah – for the latter lady most certainly did become queen. What is actually intended by these comical dwarfs is not entirely clear at this stage, but it can hardly be complimentary for Mutnodjmet to have these two dwarfs constantly in tow. However, since all of this tomfoolery was displayed within the tomb of her father, perhaps the intended ridicule was not too onerous.

Nevertheless, the conventional wisdom is that Mutnodjmet was a nonbeliever, aloof and alone, with constant ridicule and sniggering behind her back; and yet she stayed at Amarna. Why? One possibility is that she was rapidly becoming the king's favourite, the pretty younger sister of Nefertiti with an alluring rebellious streak, and so Akhenaton would not allow her to leave. There might also have been scheming Theban priests, who were taking advantage of Mutnodjmet's favoured status and theological rebellion to undermine Akhenaton's religion. This is exactly what happened with Anne Boleyn, whose anti-Catholic opinions and favoured status in the royal court of England were used by the Lutherans to undermine Henry VIII's nominally Catholic religion.

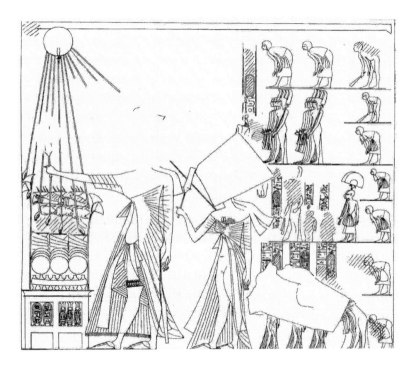

Fig 17. Mutnodjmet is standing, with her two dwarfs, in the register above the three daughters of Akhenaton. Note that Akhenaton may well be wearing a garter in this picture. The book 'Eden in Egypt' has a chapter on the Order of the Garter.

Mutnodjmet was older than Akhenaton's daughters, and would have reached maturity in the middle of Akhenaton's reign, which is exactly when Queen Kiyah rises to power in the royal court. It is also about this time that Mutnodjmet disappears from the scenes and texts, so did she have a name-change and reappear as the king's favourite, Kiyah? Certainly it would have been completely unacceptable for the devout Atonist, Akhenaton, to have married someone with a name like Mutnodjmet, which mentions the banned goddess Mut, so was 'Kiyah' invented as an acceptable nickname? Was the name Kiyah adopted as a compromise, because it did not mention the Aton and simply and playfully echoed her real name? Certainly Kiyah, like Mutnodjmet, seems to have been a reluctant Atonist, as Professor Aldred points out:

> On a separate register Kiyah, followed by an infant, presumably her daughter, also makes an offering (to the Aton). But despite the single ray of the Aton, which brings an ankh to her nostrils, and the fact that this is a major icon from her own chapel, her position seems merely incidental compared with the princesses ... In the writer's opinion, this indicates that the princesses are of superior status to Kiyah. [6]

That may be one possibility, but it does not explain why Kiyah was lovingly described as the King's Favourite Wife. Would such a favoured consort still be portrayed as having low status? Another explanation might be that Kiyah, like Mutnodjmet, was actually a reluctant Atonist, and did not want to be shown making offerings to the Aton, especially within her own chapel. So the possibility exists that Kiyah was actually a daughter of Aye, the younger sister of Nefertiti, and perhaps she was even Mutnodjmet herself.

As was explained previously, the meaning of Kiyah's name is not known, but it is thought to have been derived from *kiy* meaning 'monkey'. While this derivation initially sounded like a professional wild guess, it may not be that far wide of the mark. Readers will recall that Mutnodjmet's real name was actually Mutbenrit, and the suffix to this name, that of *benrit*, means 'sweet smelling'. However, the very similar word *benet* just happens to mean 'baboon'; and so Mutnodjmet and Kiyah may both have been known as 'little monkeys'.

This similarity demonstrates that Kiyah could indeed be a nickname for Mutnodjmet, but it would also pose a serious question about the courtiers' and scribes' intent here. It has been assumed that 'monkey' was an affectionate pet-name for Akhenaton's second and favourite wife, but with all the previous ridicule surrounding Mutnodjmet, could this term actually be yet another carping remark about her traditional beliefs? If so, it would seem strange that Akhenaton would allow such open disrespect of his favourite wife, Kiyah; but then it is equally strange that such an important official as Aye would allow similar disrespect for his daughter, Mutnodjmet.

All in all, this is quite a muddle, but there is a way of making sense of it all. Professor Davies is certain that the title of the dwarf who was called 'Vizier to the Queen' was made in reference to Mutnodjmet. But he then faces a problem, because Mutnodjmet was not a queen at this time, and she would not be so for another ten or so years (depending on when exactly this scene was carved and painted). Davies then toys with the idea that Mutnodjmet was a pseudonym for Tadukhipa, a princess of Mitanni who had entered the harem of Akhenaton's father, Amenhotep III. Tadukhipa was a queen, as is required, but she would have been much older than the images of Mutnodjmet portray. So what is the answer to this conundrum? Why was Mutnodjmet being feted as a queen?

The answer is that Mutnodjmet not only *eventually* became Queen Kiyah, as has already been suggested, but she was actually betrothed to Akhenaton even at this young age. While it is known that the pharaohs took child brides, as did the biblical patriarchs and indeed Muhummad, there was one Israelite sect that did things slightly differently. The Jewish Essene – who resided on the shores of the Dead Sea in the first centuries BC and AD – also took child brides, but unlike their contemporaries they were not allowed to have sexual relations with their betrothed until the girl had had three menstrual periods. Was Akhenaton adhering to this same ancient law? Was Mutnodjmet a child bride who was not yet allowed to consummate her marriage?

This is certainly a possibility, and it may well explain why Mutnodjmet is always depicted as following the royal couple, rather than her parents, Aye and Tiy. Even when Aye was being given honours, Mutnodjmet still stands behind the royal couple rather than her father. It would also explain why hints to her queenly status were being made by the dwarfs, but there was no official recognition of this – because she was not officially a queen as yet. She was betrothed, but not yet married and certainly not yet consummated.

This might also explain the strange appearance of the 'comical' dwarfs. Perhaps they were not court jesters, designed to ridicule Mutnodjmet; instead, they were representative of the courtiers and officials who served a real queen but, because Mutnodjmet was only a child-queen, she only received childlike courtiers. The dwarfs were like a child's toys or dolls – playthings to amuse her until she could handle the responsibility of running a real queenly office with real courtiers. This scenario would also explain the lack of embarrassment over this 'ridicule', for it was not ridicule at all, but simply a child playing with her real-life dolls.

That said, Mutnodjmet still appears to be a theological outsider, always standing on the periphery of the worshipping scenes and never participating, as Akhenaton's daughters do. Is it possible that such a young individual could have made such a fundamental and radical theological choice in life at such a tender age? Well, the author did just that and vigorously rejected any association with Church ritual from the age of seven onwards.

Fig 18. Hieroglyphic spelling of Kiyah.

Downfall

The precise chronology of the end of the Amarna era is not certain; however, the following will not be too far from the truth. Nefertiti appears to disappear from the records in about year 14 of Akhenaton's reign, and is often presumed dead; although an alternative scenario is that she became more powerful and metamorphosed into Smenkhkare, who became a co-regent pharaoh with Akhenaton in year 15. Since the female pharaoh Hatchepsut had done something similar a few generations previously, and since Smenkhkare and Nefertiti held many names in common, this is actually quite likely.

However, as Cyril Aldred points out, the only *shabti* (funerary figurine) of Nefertiti named her as a female Nefertiti, not a 'male' Smenkhkare. If Nefertiti did metamorphose into Pharaoh Smenkhkare in later life, it is very unlikely in the extreme that she would then be buried as 'Nefertiti'. Thus, in Aldred's opinion, Smenkhkare would have to be a young son of an Amarna royal, and not Nefertiti herself. However, if that is true, it is peculiar that Nefertiti could die during the relatively well-documented year 14, and nobody mentions a word about it. The great, influential queen dies and nobody depicts her funeral anywhere? This does seem rather unlikely and the only other possible suggestion is that she went into exile somewhere.

If Nefertiti was not Smenkhkare then this would mean that this ephemeral pharaoh was a young Amarna prince who was aged about 16 to 18 years during Akhenaton's year 15. This makes Smenkhkare's parentage highly uncertain. For Smenkhkare to have become pharaoh before Tutankhamen indicates that he must have had a greater claim to the throne. However, since Smenkhkare not acknowledged as a son of Akhenaton and Nefertiti, and was was too old to have been a son of Akhenaton and Kiyah, this would make it highly unlikely that Tutankhamen was a son of Akhenaton – for any son of Akhenaton would surely have had primacy, even if he was only an infant or a son by a minor wife. So the age and short reign of Pharaoh Smenkhkare strongly suggests that Tutankhamen was not a son of Akhenaton. The alternative and more likely suggestion is that Tutankhamen may have been a son of Aye, and in this scenario it is entirely possible that Smenkhkare and Tutankhamen were brothers.

This argument may actually make more sense of the tombs in the Valley of the Kings, as there has long been a heated discussion as to who the occupant of KV55 was. This unknown pharaoh was buried in an unfinished tomb in a modified sarcophagus that had once belonged to Queen Kiyah. It is likely that Kiyah had 'eloped' with Akhenaton in year 17, leaving her pre-prepared sarcophagus unused. Smenkhkare died just one year later without any funerary furniture having been made by that time, so the mortuary staff borrowed the sarcophagus that had been prepared Kiyah and other furniture taken from the tomb of the late Queen Tiye, who is likely to have been moved (minus her funerary furniture) to a small annex in the tomb of Amenhotep II, for some strange reason.

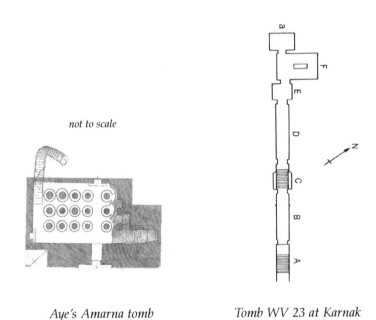

Aye's Amarna tomb   Tomb WV 23 at Karnak

Fig 19. *The two unused tombs of Aye.*

Smenkhkare was probably buried in the West Valley (instead of the King's Valley) in tomb WV23; but this tomb was later commandeered by Aye, and so Smenkhkare was finally laid to rest in the rather bare surroundings of KV55. By the time that Aye emigrated, leaving his tomb empty, the cult of the Aten was already finished and so either during this move or perhaps during a later raid on Smenkhkare's tomb, all the king's cartouches and most of those of the Aten were excised. Hence we are left with an unidentified Amarna pharaoh who is too young to be Akhenaton himself, lying on the floor of a bare, unprepared tomb known as KV55.

Regarding the other Amarna royals, Akhenaton's daughters Meritaten and Ankhesenpaaten (Ankhesenamun) were very much alive in year 14; but Kiyah seems to disappear from the scene at this time, and her small temple at Amarna had been usurped by Meritaten, Akhenaton's daughter-wife, with Kiyah's names and images being altered accordingly to suit the new owner. Since Kiyah was still being sent wine from her estate up to year 16, it is thought unlikely that she was dead, but perhaps she was in disgrace. Of course, had Kiyah been the biblical Eve it is likely that she was indeed in disgrace. The precise events and reasoning regarding Eve's fall from favour in the Book of Genesis are difficult to decipher, but if Kiyah were the rebel princess Mutnodjmet then perhaps we may have a better understanding of this affair.

Mutnodjmet [Kiyah] had always been an unwilling participant in the new Atonist theology of Amarna, and so it would have been very easy for her to fall foul of enemies within the administration. One possible enemy would have been her sister, Nefertiti. There may always have been social tensions between the two of them, resulting from sharing a king and husband, but it is highly likely that there were theological tensions too as Nefertiti was a devout Atonist, whereas Mutnodjmet [Kiyah] was not. Whatever their differences, both Nefertiti and Kiyah disappeared from Amarna at about the same time; although there is little evidence of a link between these two events.

Approximate ages for the key players at Amarna

Event		Akhenaton	Nefertiti	Kiyah	Smenkhkare	Tutankhamen
Akhenaton co-regency	(1)	18	17	5	1	
Akhenaton coronation	(12)	29	28	16	12	2
Nefertiti disappears	(14)	31	30	18	14	4
Akhenaton abdicates	(17)	34	33	21	17	7
Smenkhkare coronation				21	17	7
Tutankhamen coronation						8

Note: a. Regnal year for Akhenaton in brackets.

b. The ages of Akhenaton and Nefertiti when they first came to the throne is unknown, but it is thought that they were still in their teens.

III   Aye and Gaythelos

Iconoclasm

It was at about this time, in years 15 to 17 under the co-regency rule of Smenkhkare and Akhenaton, that the destruction of the cult of Amun intensified, and the image of Amun was erased from every temple in Thebes.[7] But this orgy of destruction was perceived as being the final straw, especially by the unemployed Amun priesthood at Thebes, and so there was a popular revolt against these onerous religious reforms.

Conventional wisdom has it that Akhenaton died in year 17, as his small but influential empire was crumbling around him; but there is no evidence for this death at Amarna, apart from a couple of 'magic bricks' (funerary bricks) in KV55 that may have belonged to him. What is more certain is that Smenkhkare dropped the epithet of 'Beloved of Akhenaton' at this time and became the sole pharaoh ruling Egypt. Smenkhkare then married Meritaten, who then must have unexpectedly died or moved away because Smenkhkare then hurriedly married Ankhesenpaaten (Ankhesenamun).

Whatever the precise circumstances were in Amarna at this time, it is fairly certain that both Akhenaton and Kiyah were now gone, presumably into some kind of exile, while the young Smenkhkare was desperately trying to patch up a rapidly failing regime, and the revolutionary Amarna experiment was rapidly drawing to a close. Manetho mentions that Moses [the brother of Akhenaton] retreated from the 'quarry on the east-bank of the Nile' [Amarna] to Avaris with 80,000 followers and managed to hold the army of the next pharaoh at bay. Presumably this was more of a reference to Horemheb than the boy-king Tutankhamen, as it was the army commander Horemheb who was effectively running much of the administration after the Amarna regime toppled. Significantly, it was Horemheb who became the next pharaoh after Aye, and it was Horemheb who subsequently married Mutnodjmet, Aye's daughter and Nefertiti's sister. Had Mutnodjmet been Kiyah, as has been suggested, she would have been a doubly suitable candidate for a diplomatic marriage with Horemheb. She would have been the wife of a previous king (Akhenaton) and also a known sympathiser of the traditional gods of Egypt.

Significantly, Mutnodjmet was then given the title of Heiress; but heiress to what exactly? Since this title is thought to have legitimised Horemheb's claim to the throne, it is likely that this title was referring to a royal heiress. But how could humble Mutnodjmet, who was just the daughter of Aye and a peripheral figure in the Amarna court, be a royal heiress? As Mutnodjmet this is highly unlikely, but if the same lady was also known as Queen Kiyah, then she could indeed be legitimately titled as a royal heiress.

While the parallel royal family of Yuya and Tuyu were obviously very important people who were of the royal bloodline, they were not royal themselves. So neither Nefertiti nor Mutnodjmet [or Kiyah] could claim the title King's Daughter; and neither could Kiyah [Mutnodjmet] claim to be King's Great Wife, as that title went to her older sister, Nefertiti. However, upon the exile of Akhenaton [to Avaris], Kiyah-Mutnodjmet could indeed claim to be the heiress to the throne – the king's sole surviving bloodline wife.

Kiyah-Mutnodjmet would have been middle aged by the time she married Horemheb. Mutnodjmet was certainly older than Meritaten, Akhenaton's oldest daughter, as she was always portrayed as being taller than the princesses at Amarna. Meritaten was born in year 1 of Akhenaton's reign, so this would make Mutnodjmet at least four or five years old at this time, and therefore about twenty-two years old by the time Akhenaton abdicated in year 17.

However, if Kiyah was one and the same as Mutnodjmet, then the former would also need to be five years older than Meritaten, and this is more or less what the images of Kiyah at Amarna seem to show. Surprisingly enough, it would seem that the probable ages of both Kiyah and Mutnodjmet match very nicely, so Kiyah-Mutnodjmet could indeed have been the wife of both Akhenaton and Horemheb. A suitable chronology for the life of Khiyah-Mutnodjmet might be as follows:

Event	Kiyah-Mutnodjmet's age
Co-coronation of Akhenaton	5
Mutnodjmet goes missing from Amarna	13
Kiyah becomes Akhenaton's second wife	13
Birth of Tutankhamen	14
Coronation of Akhenaton	16
Co-coronation of Smenkhkare	20
Abdication of Akhenaton (reigned 5 full yrs)	21
Coronation of Smenkhkare (reign 1 full yr)	21
Coronation of Tutankhamen at (age 8, reign 9 yrs)	22
Coronation of Horemheb	34
Kiyah-Mutnodjmet's marriage to Horemheb	34

The above assumes that twelve years of Akhenaton's reign was in a co-regency with his father, Amenhotep III, and that one year of Smenkhkare's reign was in a co-regency with Akhenaton.

Nubia

In the last chapter it was noted that Gaythelos [Aye] was supposed to have headed a Greek army that came to the aid of Pharaoh [Akhenaton]. While it was stated there that the use of Greek mercenary forces in this era has not been documented historically, the identification of Gaythelos with Aye sheds a great deal more light on this story. Bower quotes one of his many sources as saying:

> The Ethiopians had overrun the whole of Egypt in those days from the mountains right to the city of <u>Memphis and the Great Sea</u>. So Gaythelos ... was sent with a great army to help his ally Pharaoh [Akhenaton]; and to cement this alliance the king gave him (Gaythelos) his only daughter in marriage. (author's square brackets) SC8

If these events did indeed occur in the time of Akhenaton, as is likely, then this 'overrunning of Egypt' has to be taken with a pinch of salt, as no historical evidence for a Nubian incursion on this scale exists; although this could be an exaggerated account of some of the periodic Nubian advances into Egypt. However, Professor Watt, the translator of *Scotichronicon*, goes a stage further and indicates that this account has no basis whatsoever, and is simply a literary device invented to explain why Moses should have had an Ethiopian (Nubian) wife:

> And Miriam and Aaron spake against Moses because of the Ethiopian woman whom he had married: for he had married an Ethiopian woman. B9

Watt goes on to say that there is also 'no biblical basis' for this myth of a battle between Moses and the Ethiopians, and for Moses marrying a Nubian. However, this merely exposes the deficiencies in Watt's theological education, for there *is* a biblical-type record of a dispute between Egypt and Ethiopia (Nubia); and this story is to be found in the parallel accounts of Josephus Flavius, the historian who compiled his own version of the Torah. As has been explained in my previous works, Josephus had access to the original Torah from the ruined Temple of Jerusalem, and so his version of biblical history is far older and much more authoritative than the Aleppo Codex Tanakh that has been used by orthodox Judaism and Christianity. By using this more authoritative source, Josephus says of this incident:

> The Ethiopians (Nubians), who are the next neighbours to the Egyptians, made an inroad into their country ... (the Egyptians were) overcome in battle, some of them were slain, some ran away in a shameful manner ... the Ethiopians proceeded as far as <u>Memphis and the sea itself</u>.

> The Egyptians under this sad oppression ... (decided) to make use of Moses the Hebrew, and take his assistance ... the king commanded his daughter (Thermuthis)* to produce him, that he might be general of their army.

(Moses) came upon the Ethiopians (Nubians) before they had expected him and joining battle with them. He beat them and deprived them of hopes they had against the Egyptians ... and (Moses) gave (the Nubian princess Tharbis) an oath to take her to his wife; and that once he had taken possession of the (Nubian) city he would not break his oath to her. No sooner was the agreement made ... when Moses had cut off the Ethiopians (Nubians), he gave thanks to god, consummated his marriage and led the Egyptians back to their own land.[J10]

This series of quotes is interesting in many ways. Firstly, the obvious similarity between Bower's source and the works of Josephus demonstrates that the Scottish chronicler was very familiar with the works of Josephus, as well as those of Manetho. Both accounts indicate that Egypt had been overrun from Memphis to the Mediterranean and both indicate that a foreign prince became an Egyptian army commander who led the battle for freedom. Josephus says that this foreign prince was Moses, while Bower says that it was Gaythelos.

Another striking similarity between these two accounts can be seen in the role of the pharaoh's daughter, Thermuthis.* The Moses story, as we all know, has Moses being discovered as a baby in an ark (basket) on the Nile by pharaoh's daughter. Pharaoh then orders his daughter to bring Moses to him. In reality, the biblical symbolism of an 'ark on the Nile' is a retelling of the Osirian myth, and so Thermuthis was probably Moses' biological mother. This is why Moses was regarded as a prince of Egypt, because that is exactly what he was [thus Moses was TuthMoses, Akhenaton's brother, and Thermuthis was Tiye, Akhenaton's mother]. However, in both accounts, we now have a pharaoh's daughter who is closely associated with the Moses-Gaythelos hero figure. In the biblical account she is possibly his mother; in the Scottish chronicle she is said to be his wife. However, the general thrust of the two stories displays a very common theme and, when taking Josephus' version into account, both texts indicate that the hero figure (Moses-Gaythelos) married a royal princess.

This demonstrates the wide variety of sources available to Walter Bower *et al*, and that these documents have been distilled and transcribed reasonably faithfully into his chronicle of the Scots. This gives us some confidence that the other sources he used, which are no longer available to us, were also transcribed reasonably faithfully into his account.

The second and more important reason for the interest in these

---

* Thermuthis is an alternative Greek name for the goddess Isis. See the book *Cleopatra* for further details.

two accounts is the curious fact that Josephus says it was Moses who pacified the Nubians and married the princess, whereas Bower indicates that it was Gaythelos who did this. The close similarity between these two sources would seem to indicate that Gaythelos was actually another name for the biblical Moses, rather than the historical Pharaoh Aye. However, in my previous works I have already argued that Moses was TuthMoses, the elusive elder brother of Akhenaton, and so at the very least this alternative link between Gaythelos and Moses would place the Scota story within the Amarna era once more, which would confirm many of the arguments already made.

Is it possible that Gaythelos could have been Moses, the brother of Akhenaton? TuthMoses [Moses] was the elder brother of Akhenaton, but by how many years we do not know. Aye was the father-in-law of Akhenaton, through his daughter Nefertiti, but if we presume that Nefertiti was a child bride of around fourteen years of age, then Aye need not be that much older than Akhenaton. Thus TuthMoses [the biblical Moses] and Aye could well have been of the same generation in the extended Amarna family.

This gives us an intriguing possibility. Aye seems to be the most likely candidate for the character known as Gaythelos, and yet Moses is also now a candidate who shows similar attributes. Could, therefore, TuthMoses [Moses] and Aye [Gaythelos] have been one and the same character? Both Gaythelos and Moses are being intimately linked to an exodus event, and Aye also seems to be connected in some manner, so were all these names originally connected to the same individual? Was Aye also called Moses?

Whilst this proposal is intriguing, on balance it does not stand up to scrutiny. Gaythelos became a king, and yet Moses never claimed the throne. Perhaps the most important reason why this comparison fails, however, is the fact that Gaythelos is not named in the Scottish chronicle as being Moses. Had there been any hint of the biblical Moses being the founder of the Scottish people, this triumph would have been trumpeted from every rooftop; but it was not. Also, *Scotichronicon* makes a clear distinction between Gaythelos and Moses; and in many places the chronicle indicates that Gaythelos was a part of the Egyptian regime who was chasing Aaron, Moses and the Israelites [Akhenaton, TuthMoses and their followers] out of Egypt. Although it might seem historically unlikely, the latter assertion may actually suit the role of Aye.

Although Aye was a follower of Aton and vizier to Akhenaton, it would appear that towards the end of the Amarna regime Aye made a break with much of Amarna theology. In the reliefs in the tomb of Tutankhamen and in the remaining reliefs in his own Theban tomb, WV23, Aye is shown in the company of the traditional gods, not the Aton. Whether this was due to a religious conversion or because of political pragmatism, Aye had effectively turned his back on the Aton and the Amarna theology. It is possible that Aye was trying to save the remains of the Amarna dynasty in the only way he knew how, but to any pious Atonist he would have been seen as a traitor. In their eyes, Aye would have been an integral part of the oppressive Theban regime who had thrown Akhenaton and TuthMoses [Aaron and Moses] out of Amarna – just as *Scotichronicon* indicates Gaythelos did.

On balance, therefore, the link between Moses and Aye does not work, and Gaythelos was most probably Aye. The confusion between Aye and Moses in these two accounts has probably occurred because they both held similar positions. If a skirmish with Nubia had developed during the Amarna era, it is possible that TuthMoses (the brother of Akhenaton) would have been called upon to command the military, as he is known to have held the title 'Commander of the Horse'. However, this is also a title that was held by Aye, and since Aye is likely to have been the senior of the two commanders, it would have been Aye who was ultimately in charge.

This may be the reason for the differing accounts as to who married whom. Josephus says that the hero married the defeated Nubian princess, while Bower indicates that the hero married the princess of the victorious Egyptian pharaoh [Akhenaton]. With two commanders on the field of battle, both accounts may have been correct. It was the younger Moses [TuthMoses] who married the Nubian princess, Tharbis, while the more senior Aye eventually married the daughter of Akhenaton (although by the time this latter marriage occurred, Akhenaton would have been in exile for many years).

Following the fall of Amarna and the exile of Akhenaton, relations between Aye and the two brothers, Akhenaton and TuthMoses [Aaron and Moses], are likely to have deteriorated significantly. But despite all of Aye's desperate diplomatic, marital and theological manoeuvreings, it is likely that he, like Akhenaton before him, was also pushed out of Egypt in another exodus event. This is where the valuable extra material within *Scotichronicon* fills in a few of the missing historical details, for the Scottish chronicle explains that:

> Gaythelos remained behind after the army (of pharaoh) had departed the city of Heliopolis, with the purpose of (Gaythelos) possibly succeeding to his kingdom. But the Egyptian people ... gathered their forces together and informed Gaythelos that if he did not speedily hasten his departure from their kingdom, utter destruction would immediately attend himself and his men. [SC11]

The chronicle is quite clear in saying that there were two exoduses at this time. Firstly, the [Amarna] Israelites were being chased out of Egypt [out of Amarna towards Avaris] by a pharaoh. The pharaoh indicated here would have been a reluctant Tutankhamen, who was being manipulated by General Horemheb. But Gaythelos stayed behind with the intent of becoming pharaoh, which is exactly what Aye did in the historical record. Then, at a later date, Gaythelos [Aye] was also advised by the people to leave Egypt, and this may well be historically true too. Thus Gaythelos and Aye seem to have had similar intentions and appear to have led similar lives, which again suggests that Gaythelos was Aye.

This history rather makes Aye-Gaythelos appear to be an antihero figure, a 'traitor' who turned upon his own (Amarna) people when the odds were stacked against them. This uncomfortable fact was probably noted by Walter Bower, and so later chapters of *Scotichronicon* begin Aye-Gaythelos' transition from an unstable adventurer-prince into a wise king and leader. Subtle parallels are then drawn between the wanderings of Gaythelos and Scota and the wanderings of the Israelites. Then, again like Moses, Gaythelos dies after seeing his people's initial promised land (which lay just off the coast of Spain) from a hilltop. These parallels are not being built into the story to indicate that Gaythelos was Moses, but to renovate the former's tarnished image and to portray him as having equal standing with the legendary lawgiver. Anything Moses could do, Aye-Gaythelos could do better.

The final thing to note in this section is that since Aye-Gaythelos left Egypt on an exodus, it is imperative for this explanation's integrity that this character was not buried either in Amarna or Thebes. Accordingly, Aye's Amarna tomb was completely unfinished, and while his Theban tomb (WV23) was finished, there is no evidence that it had ever been used. Upon initial examination by Belzoni in 1816, it was noted that many of the wall paintings in WV23 had been deliberately hacked out in antiquity, as had the images of all the Amarna pharaohs and queens apart from Tutankhamen; and likewise, Aye's sarcophagus had been pulverised. It wasn't until 1972 that Otto Schaden made a thorough inventory of all the remnants in the tomb, and during this investigation he noted a few fragments of artifacts and some plaster blocking from the entrance to one of the rooms. The latter was taken as being evidence that the room had been sealed after a burial, but the sparse remains of plaster blocking did not have any royal seal impressions, which would have been stamped on the blocking of any completed royal burial. So, as is the case for Akhenaton, Kiyah and Nefertiti, there is no evidence for Aye's burial either at Amarna or Thebes.

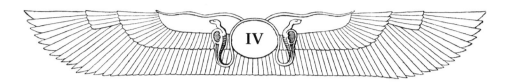

Ebro River

The small ship ploughed through the crashing waves on a stiff easterly breeze, the small square-rigged sail tugging and heaving on the yards. Every now and then a puff of spray swept across the open deck and soaked all of those huddling within. In a small, hastily-erected cabin, Aye-Gaythelos and Ankhesenamun-Scota sat shivering on a small, ornate couch, feeling decidedly queasy.

What a turn of events for a once proud royal family and all of their senior courtiers and officials. Here were the pampered elite of the most powerful nation in the world, and they were reduced to owning just a couple of square meters on the deck of a heaving ship. Here were officials, whose idea of a long 'sea voyage' was crossing the Nile from Karnak to the Valley of the Kings, and now they were crashing through a rough swell and could not see the land on any horizon. Half of them may have been convinced that Aton would look after them in their hour of need, and perhaps the other half thought Aton had deserted them, and so they cowered in the bowels of the small ship hoping that their deaths would be swift and painless.

But perhaps the Aton was still smiling on these refugees, if weakly, for the Scottish chronicle states that the royal flotilla did not flounder in the open seas. Instead, they landed in several coves along the North African coastline. But these were not the ultimate destination of these refugees, just short stops to rest, recuperate and to gather provisions and water. It is likely that their destination was uncertain, and the flotilla was blindly searching for a likely place in which the people could settle, but they found nothing but desert scrubland along the North African coastline and so they soon pushed on once more. It is also thought that Minoan ships of this era never deliberately sailed at night, and so many stops would have been made each evening along the coast.

Eventually, after seeing the Spanish coastline across the straits of Gibraltar, they altered course and travelled eastwards and northwards, heading up along the eastern coast of Spain. Once more they dropped of at several spots *enroute*, but found nothing to match their former homelands along the Nile valley and the fertile Delta region.

Bower makes a comparison here with the fate of the Hyksos-Israelites, who were supposed to be wandering around the Sinai peninsular in a similar fashion at this very same time. The Aye-Gaythelos exodus would have taken place just twelve or thirteen years after Akhenaton and TuthMoses left Egypt, in about 1320 BC, and so the Aye-Gaythelos exodus can rightfully be equated by Walter Bower with the biblical exodus. Time after time, the Hyksos-Israelites seem to have been pushed out of Lower Egypt, and on each of these occasions they took their culture, hopes and ideals all across the Mediterranean. More importantly, they also took their technology and leadership skills and imposed or instilled those attributes onto more primitive populations in many diverse locations. One of those locations was now going to be Spain.

> In this way the wandered for a long time over unknown seas in various directions, passing through many places, enduring many perils and various vicissitudes according as they were driven about by the violence of opposing winds, until forced at last by lack of food they landed safely on the shores of Spain beyond all their expectation. [SC1]

But Spain was not an uninhabited land, and their arrival caused a bit of a stir amongst the local population:

> The local inhabitants rushed together on all sides in resentment of their arrival. Their aim was to oppose them in armed warfare; soon a fiercely contested battle was joined and the inhabitants were defeated and turned to flight. Then, after he had won the victory, Gaythelos pursued the inhabitants and plundered a considerable part of their territory. He returned to the shore and pitched his tents on a small mound on higher ground. [SC2]

It should be borne in mind that the Egyptians had a professional standing army that was quite well equipped. They had chariots, horse, bows, spears, swords, daggers, armour, shields and decades of experience fighting the Hittites and other nations. The Spanish tribes, on the other hand, were probably farmers and hunters with a mixed bag of agricultural and hunting weapons and no experience of fighting a disciplined army. For the Egyptian soldiery who accompanied Aye-Gaythelos, this was probably a turkey-shoot.

The battle was quickly won and the chronicle then goes on to relate how Aye-Gaythelos and his followers established themselves and built a strong town called Brigantia, in the middle of which they constructed a large tower. Now this tower could have been a defensive keep, but a following chapter will discuss the possibility that this was actually a religious shrine of some nature.

Fig 21.   Map of Spain, with the Ebro river flowing through Zaragoza. (Courtesy Tourizm Maps.)

Balearics

The chronicle states that the new town of Brigantia was situated on the river Ebro. Now this is the modern name of the river in the north east of Spain, which runs from just south of Bilbao to an exit a hundred miles or so south of Barcelona. Since this is the modern name for the river, it has largely been discounted as a true account of Aye-Gaythelos' landing in Spain, but it will be shown shortly that this was indeed the location at which they landed. Further confusion has arisen because the chronicle then goes on, confusingly, to assert that Ireland could be 'seen' from a hill near the town of Brigantia:

> On a certain clear day as he was looking out from Brigantia he saw land far
> out at sea. So he armed some energetic and warlike young men and sent them
> off to explore in three small ships. ᔆᶜ³

Note that the chronicle does not mention Ireland at all, just that land could
be seen. It would seem that Orosius, a Spanish historian and theologian of
the fifth century AD, has taken this account rather literally, and since the
ultimate destination of Aye-Gaythelos' followers was Ireland, he indicated
that Brigantia was the 'lookout' for Britain (Ireland). It is probably this
suggestion that has led some modern historians, including Professor Watt, to
speculate that Brigantia was actually located on the northwest tip of Spain
at La Corunna, a point in Spain where there is no landmass between the
Spanish and Irish coastlines. But this argument defies logic. I suppose that it
could be argued that the chronicle was using a literary allusion, but the fact
of the matter is that it is impossible to see Ireland from Spain no matter how
clear the day was, as it lies well below the horizon.

What, then, was the text meaning when it stated that an island could
be seen from Brigantia? From where on the Spanish coast can you see an
island? The solution to this is given in every nautical manual where it is
stated that the distance to the horizon (in nautical miles) is 1.17 times the
square-root of the height of the observer (in feet). The hills just to the west of
the mouth of the Ebro river rise to some 4,000 feet (1,200 m), and so from the
top of these peaks you would be able to see 74 nautical miles (nm) or about
150 km. But the distance to the nearest island, Mallorca, is about 120 nm, so at
first glance it would appear that Aye-Gaythelos would have been able to see
nothing but water from his salient near the Ebro river. But, the mountains on
Mallorca also rise to some 4,500 feet, which alters the calculation considerably.
In fact, the top 3,000 feet (900 m) of the Mallorcan mountains may have been
visible to Aye-Gaythelos on a fine clear day, although to the naked eye these
rocky pinnacles would have been very small indeed.

The view from the top of the El Port mountains above the river
Ebro is as impressive today as it was in the era of Aye-Gaythelos, the only
difference being that one can now drive to the top in about half an hour. The
only problem on the day that I visited the area was the usual Mediterranean
haze, so it was not simply a few isolated island peaks that were lost from
view, but the entire horizon. As the chronicle says, it would have to have
been an exceptionally clear day to see the minuscule tops of the Mallorcan
ranges.

But perhaps Aye-Gaythelos never saw the mountains at all. All
one would need to see was a range of cumulus clouds springing up in the
morning in the same location, day after day. Any sailor worth his salt would

know that one of the prime initiators of cumulus clouds is land, especially a mountainous land adjacent to the sea. Regular cumulus clouds building up in the morning would strongly indicate that there was an island out there in the Mediterranean, even if the island itself was well over the horizon. The reason that these nearby islands had not already been discovered by these exiles' roving ships is that sailors in this era only ever hugged the coastline. Thus a trip from Egypt down the North African coast would have revealed the peninsular of Spain, across the Gibraltar strait, but these nervous navigators would never have seen the islands of Mallorca and Ibiza.

The chronicle then goes on to relate that the young bloods in the exiled community did make this hazardous journey to the nearby islands (knowing that something was there) and started another settlement in the Balearics; and that the people made the crossing so often that this stretch of water became known as the Sea of Hibernia, after the son of Aye-Gaythelos. It is now called the Gulf of Valencia:

> They put into a nearby harbour on this island and after beaching their ships went all around exploring the island. After seeing as much of the island as they could they sailed back to Brigantia, reporting to their king Gaythelos on the very beautiful tract of land that they had found in the Ocean. [SC4]

> So because Hiber (the son of Gaythelos) sailed so frequently to that island and so often returned ... he bequeathed his own name for all time to that sea and island. Just as the sea was called Hiberic, so also the island was called Hibernia. [SC5]

There are several confusing and contradictory statements about this newly discovered island. It is said to be in the boundless ocean, which is thought to refer to the Atlantic; but the people of Brigantia sail regularly to and from this island, which makes it sound like a nearby island (for Ireland is a very long way from the Ebro). Likewise, the island could also be seen from the mainland, which reinforces the view that the island was not that far away. This really does not sound like a commentary on the discovery of Ireland at all, and the simple answer to this dichotomy is that two groups of islands were eventually discovered by the Brigantians. The later accounts in *Scotichronicon* do indeed relate to Ireland, so this island was discovered at some point in time, but it would appear that the first island that they discovered – the island that was seen by Aye-Gaythelos from Brigantia – was Mallorca.

If this is so, then the chronicle supports the idea that Aye-Gaythelos first landed on the mouth of the river Ebro, as the chronicle states, and not along the remote and wild Atlantic coast of Spain at La Corunna. This argument is supported by the very name that this river has been given. It has been assumed by some historians that Ebro is a relatively modern name for this river, and so it cannot be related to the original story of Aye-Gaythelos in any manner. But this is not so. In a similar fashion, Professor Watt argues that this river was included in the chronicle because its name sounded similar to Hibernia, the original name for Ireland (the name for the river Ebro having the same epigraphic root as the name H-<u>iber</u>nia):

> The name (of the river) in its Latin form 'Hiberius' resembles 'Hibernia', or Ireland; hence its inclusion (in the chronicle). [SC6]

In other words, like the name for Queen Scota, the name of the river is a 'reverse inclusion' that was fabricated by Walter Bower to entwine mainland Spain into the story-line. However, neither of these assertions is true.

Firstly, the name Ebro is a very ancient name for this river indeed, and its original Roman name was Hiberius (Iberius). Likewise, the Catalonian museum in Barcelona states that the Phoenician and Greek explorers who plied these waters in the seventh century BC called the local people Hibers, because that was the local name of the river that flowed through the region. In other words, the name for the Ebro is at least 2,700 years old.

Secondly, the name of the river was not inserted as a 'reverse inclusion', to link the Scottish chronicle to Spain, as the origins of this name are not native Iberian at all, but native Egyptian instead. *Scotichronicon* looks way beyond the environs of northeastern Spain, towards Egypt, and so the word for a river in the ancient Egyptian language is Eebre (Eebro)   .

This word has also found its way into the Hebrew, where it became Yebel יבל, which can also be pronounced as Eebel. Remember, however, the standard 'r' to 'l' transliteration that often takes place between the Egyptian and the Hebrew – due to the fact that the Egyptians did not have an 'l' consonant in their language. In other words, the Egyptian original of Eebere (Ebro) has become the Hebrew Eebele. So Professor Watt is most likely to have been wrong in his assertion. The Scottish chronicle clearly states that these names were brought from Egypt to Spain and thence to Ireland and Scotland, and having researched the situation that is exactly what we find. That this intricate and ancient Scottish chronicle could somehow link Egypt, Spain and Ireland through mere chance and coincidence is unlikely in the extreme. That this story could have been fabricated in a Scottish monastery, long before the Egyptian language had been deciphered by Francois Champollion, is simply not credible; and so the only remaining option is that the chronicle is probably true, and a people did migrate from Egypt to Spain, Ireland and Scotland, and they took the Egyptian name for a river with them.

There is always the possibility that the alternative name for the Israelites – the Hebrews or Ebriy עברי – also came from the same epigraphic root. The biblical Concordance maintains that the name 'Hebrew' was derived from Eber עבר, the son of Salah. However, the Nile was a sacred river of Egypt, the lifeblood of the nation, and for the nation (of Hyksos-Israelites) to be named after the sacred Eebere river would be quite logical. The leading 'h' may be due to this being the Hebrew equivalent of 'the', and so the H-Eberews (Hebrews) may well have been called 'The Nile People'. But, as we have seen, Spain was called (H)iberia and Ireland was once called (H)ibernia; and so many brothers from the Orange Lodges in Northern Ireland claim that both Spain and Ireland were originally known as the 'Land of the Hebrews'. This is said to be the reason for the Star of David appearing on the flag of Ulster, as we shall see in a later chapter.

But if some of these Egypto-Hebrews had been exiled to Catalonia, what would be more natural than to take this name, which may well have been used for the Nile itself, and to bestow it upon the river they had just discovered in this new land. This was the New Nile, just as the most influential American city became New York. Thus the name of the river Ebro itself strongly indicates that a people who were using the Egypto-Hebrew language landed and settled in this very location, and what better candidate for this do we have than the royal couple – Aye-Gaythelos and Ankhesenamun-Scota?

In addition, the location they found in Spain was absolutely ideal for a party of renegade Egyptians. I have long maintained that the Amarna regime was allied to the Hyksos, and so their main power-base outside Middle Egypt was situated in the Nile Delta, at Avaris. Thus the emigrants, in their flotilla of small boats, would have drawn heavily upon Delta farmers and Delta livestock to sustain themselves in their new lands.

What they found, when they arrived at the river Ebro, was a delta region that was very much like the one they had left behind in Egypt only a few months previously. Although it is much smaller, the Ebro Delta would have had much the same topography, plant life, sunshine and annual floods as the Nile Delta in Egypt. The only difference was that the floods came in the spring, rather than the summer/autumn inundation in Egypt, as the snows of the Pyrenees melted.

One can imagine these refugees calling in at each and every major river system that they found along the North African and eastern Spanish coastline, just as the chronicle suggests. Each time, the farmers would have leaped out of the boats, run their fingers through the parched soils and shaken their heads in despair. Most of the rivers, even in eastern Spain, are seasonal, and dry up during the long hot summer. Few, if any, of these sites would have been suitable for farming without major irrigation projects, which these refugees did not have the time nor the equipment to build. Then, at long last, the migrant farmers laid their eyes upon the Ebro Delta, fell to their knees and blessed Aton for his deliverance.

The Ebro gets its waters from the Pyrenees, and the snow on these high peaks slowly melts all through the long, hot Iberian summers. This supplies the Ebro with a spring flood, just in time for the spring planting, and a steady flow of water throughout the summer. In the autumn and winter the rains return and replenish the supply of water and snow, so that the Ebro stores up its stocks of water once more for the coming growing season. The Ebro was manna from heaven; it was deliverance for Aye-Gaythelos and Scota.

Ebro river

As the surging Ebro river pours into the Mediterranean it takes with it tons of silt, that have built up over the years into a sandy promontory or delta, that juts out from the Spanish coastline. The land itself is reasonably fertile, but perhaps the modern irrigation of the region masks a more hostile environment. Away from the river channels and freshwater lagoons, the land can be dusty, arid and barren. Perhaps deep-rooted trees once covered this region, but today the fallow areas of the delta well away from the river are reduced to sandy scrublands.

However, any Delta farmer from Egypt worth a bushel of grain would have seen the opportunities of this delta region. Areas of the Nile Delta can be similarly barren, without man's intervention, but the perfectly flat fields and the adjacent river – which is actually slightly higher than some of the surrounding land – makes for an ideal irrigation system. All that needs to be done is to create small clay-lined field walls across the flat landscape, perhaps add a *shaduf* at one end to lift the water from the river, and the irrigation system is complete. For very little expenditure in labour, an Egyptian farmer could have had several fields up and running within a few weeks, each capable of producing two crops a year. Most of the current Ebro Delta is given over to paddy-fields for rice, but there were other crops of many varieties growing in the same field systems, which demonstrates the fertility and versatility of a delta region.

Had Aye-Gaythelos and Ankhesenamun-Scota landed on the Ebro Delta, they would certainly not have gone hungry. Apart from the rapidly expanding field system, the river itself teems with fish, even in the modern era; while the lagoons are similarly populated with wildfowl of every description. In fact, the Ebro river is a major destination for modern European fishermen, looking for a river untouched by pollution and rich in aquatic life. In 2006, the largest fish ever caught in Spain was reeled in on the banks of the Ebro – a 2 m long, 100 kg catfish. In short, there would have been plenty of protein available for the tired refugees from Egypt, to tide them over until the first crops were harvested. And there would have been good scope for population growth too. There are over 300 square kilometers of Ebro Delta that can be irrigated and farmed, with each field producing two crops a year – enough to feed a vast population.

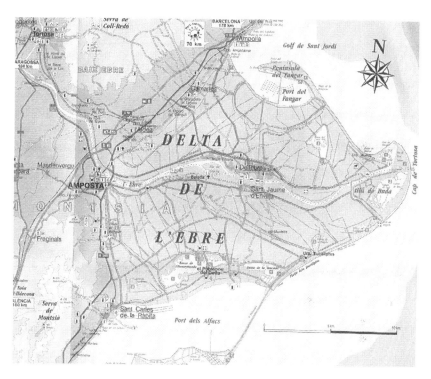

Fig 22.   Map of the Ebro Delta.

The area would have been ideal for transport too. The Ebro is plenty wide and deep enough for Minoan-style boats to navigate upstream for miles, should they have needed to. At the very least, the armada of boats from Egypt could have been taken deep into the delta to protect them from storms at sea; rendering them safe for future generations to use in their travels across the Mediterranean. The river may also have given a degree of protection to the community, as there may well have been small eyots, or river islands, upon which a small settlement could be built. There is just such an eyot in the river now, but since these features can shift and change over the years there is no certainty that this particular eyot is an ancient feature.

Brigantia

There is only one spot on the east coast of Spain that an Egyptian Delta farmer would declare as 'home' and that is the Ebro Delta – and to highlight this truism the Ebro river betrays its true origins by bearing an Egyptian name. Here, Aye-Gaythelos and his followers built Brigantia, a small fortified town that was dangerously exposed in a faraway land.

There are two possibilities within the Egyptian language as to how the name of this new town was derived. The first is somewhat tentative, but it is possible that Aye-Gaythelos was influenced by the wetlands that surrounded his new town, and so the name that was chosen was Baregta 𓅱𓎛𓈖𓈖 meaning 'pool', a word which evolved into Bregata (Brigantia). Pools were not only necessary for life in otherwise hot and arid lands, they were also a central component of every Egyptian temple complex. The priesthood underwent a ritual cleansing in these pools before any ceremony commenced, and it is probably from this ancient tradition that the immersion rituals of John the Baptist evolved. Thus every Christian baptism is a vestigial re-enactment of this ritual priestly cleansing in a large sacred pool. We shall be exploring the settlement of Ireland in a later chapter and, of course, one of the largest cities in that land became known as Dub-linn, or the 'black-pool'.

However, perhaps the second option for the name of this town is the more compelling of the two. Brigantia was set up as a fortified town, in order to repel attacks that were being carried out on a daily basis by the local population. From the evidence at Avaris, Yehudiyeh and Tanis – the fortified Hyksos cities discovered in the Nile Delta – the favoured way of fortifying a city was to build a slope all the way up to the top of the city wall, which is called a glacis. This may seem like a counterproductive thing to do – to build a nice wheelchair-friendly slope all the way up and over your fortifications – but the logic behind this feature is actually quite sensible. The slope was made as smooth and as slippery as is possible, which is why it became known as a glacis, as in glacier: from the French *glacier* meaning 'ice' or 'slip'. So, the enemy is disadvantaged by trying to climb up a steep, slippery incline, while the defenders at the top of the ramp have a clear field of vision for loosing off their arrows. Conversely, a wall offers an attacker the opportunity of hiding at the bottom of the wall under a wooden shield, and undermining the wall (which was invariably made of mud-brick in Egypt, and easily undermined). A glacis slope presents no such opportunities for the attacker.

Bearing all of this in mind, another possible translation from the Egyptian is *b-rigata-t* 𓏲𓂝𓏏𓎛𓈖𓈖 meaning 'glacis', the inclined ramp around a fort. This sort of name for a city also has a precedent within Egypt, for Tanis was once called Thar 𓄿𓂋𓏤𓊖 , meaning 'fortress', as well as

*Fig 23. Osiris sitting on a sacred pool,
denoted by the zigzag lines.*

Tchan (Greek, Tchanis) which referred to the surrounding dyke or moat. It is uncertain if the city of Tanis was in existence at this early era, as it was probably constructed in the eleventh and twelfth centuries BC by the descendants of Hyksos-Israelite refugees. So too was Yehudiyeh, which was also a Hyksos-Israelite city in the Nile Delta, as the Judaic name might suggest. Interestingly, the defences at Yehudiyeh included a glacis.

Since the people of Brigantia eventually migrated once more to the greater British Isles, it is probably from the name of this city that the name for the Celtic Brigantes people was derived. The Classical Gazetteer of 1851 says of these people:

> **Brigantes** *(Celtic* 'plunderers'), a people of Britain, occupying the whole of Maxima Cesariensis, with the exception of the portion occupied south of Alaunus. l. by the Otadeni. *Durham, Cumberland Westmoreland, Lancashire, and Yorkshire.* II. of Hibernia, s. *Waterford and part of Tipperary.* [7]

Interestingly enough, the capital city of the Celtic Brigantes tribe is given as being Eboracum, a Roman name for modern York which is strangely reminiscent of the river Ebro. Note that this venerable reference book uses the classical names for cities and countries, and so Ireland is called here Hibernia. Interestingly, the Brigantes people of Britain were also settled in southern Ireland, which was the eventual destination of the Brigantians living on the River Ebro. The derivation given for the name 'Brigante' is also interesting, as we still use the term 'brigand' today to refer to a 'bandit'. The Gazetteer then goes on to describe Hibernia (Ireland) as:

Hibernia. an island in the Atlantic, west of Britain. Its principal people, the Hiberni, would appear to have come from Iberia (Spain), and it was their name which Caesar extended to the whole island. The Scoti, who formed a portion of its later population, were Scandinavian immigrants, and were called by the natives Daoine Gaul or Gaulte, meaning 'foreign or barbarous men' whence Donegal. [8]

Note the general acceptance that the people of H<u>ibernia</u> (Ireland) came from <u>Iberia</u> (Spain) – and brought the name of their former country with them. The Scandinavian origins for the Scoti is less convincing as they are also being called the Daoine, and any classical scholar would know that the Danaoi came from Greece, from whence Aye-Gaythelos is also supposed to have originated.

Stratigraphy

With a secure settlement on a river island and food being produced in quantity, Aye-Gaythelos may well have felt quite at home in Brigantia. However, farmers have to go out into the fields, fishermen need to sail the river, carpenters need to find forests, and hunters have to travel to the lagoons; and no doubt the resentful aboriginal population along the River Ebro were harassing each and every movement these new immigrants made. Had Aye-Gaythelos a sizeable army with him, it would have been relatively easy to stamp his authority on the region and pacify the locals. However, with perhaps less than a thousand citizens, including women and children, the community was dangerously exposed, and it is no wonder that a voyage was contemplated to the less well-inhabited Balearic Islands, and a new colony started there.

But Brigantia, by all accounts, was still active over many generations, and so a sizeable town with many deposition layers may well have been left somewhere in the Ebro Delta. Another obvious location for Brigantia, apart from an eyot or river island, would be Deltebro, a small rise in the land to the north of the river that lies just 4m higher than the rest of the delta lands. Had this location been defensible, with a mud-brick glacis fortification, it would have stood above the flood-level of the river and been a favourable location for a town. However, it is *still* a favourable position for a town and so the whole area is currently occupied. Unfortunately, the chances of doing any archaeology in this region are pretty remote, and so the true location of Brigantia may well remain hidden under this town for centuries to come.

In fact, Bronze Age archaeology for this entire region is surprisingly minimal. Besides a few flint shavings and a deposit of bronze axe heads, the museum for the Catalan region, located in Barcelona, has no artifacts whatsoever prior to the seventh century BC. Likewise, the charming small museum of the delta, situated in Amposta, has nothing from the Bronze Age for the delta region. However, the historical scenario being described in this chapter may well have resulted in this archaeological situation. The native tribes were described as being primitive, and so are unlikely to have joined the Egyptian Bronze Age. Aye-Gaythelos and his community were certainly well within the Bronze Age, technologically, but their community was so small that it probably left few clues to its existence. Only on the Balearic Islands did a Bronze Age culture really start to flourish, and on these islands there are many clues that point towards the Minoan Empire, if not the Egyptian Empire, as we shall see.

Some Bronze/Iron Age burials have also been located in the south of Spain, at Granada, but no great settlements. Nevertheless these burials are interesting, for they are pot burials and one of these alabaster pots is engraved with the cartouche of Pharaoh Takelot II (Meriamun Hedj-kheperre) of the twenty-second dynasty (c. 850 BC). The inscription on the pot says that its owner was from a foreign land and travelled through many countries, which is undoubtedly true. But what this man was doing in Granada is not entirely clear. Even the size and duration of stay for this band of hardy Egyptian exiles is a matter of conjecture, although I would presume that they were actually of Egypto-Phoenician origins.

Back towards the Ebro, in Catalonia, the only early archaeological remains date from the Iron Age, about 600 BC, when small, fortified villages were being constructed all around this region. Typically, they were located on hill tops, built in an oval fashion, with the rear walls of each house being used to form a contiguous defence wall. This is the same design as is to be found in Israel, another location in which the Hyksos-Israelite exiles

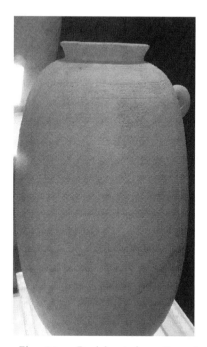

Fig 24.   Burial pot from Granada inscribed with the cartouche of Takelot II.

from Egypt found themselves. Although it has to be said that the similarity between these two designs could be due to coincidence rather than common ancestry, it is interesting enough. The appendix has a short dissertation on the similarities between these Israelite settlements and Hyksos Egyptian settlements.

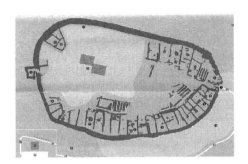 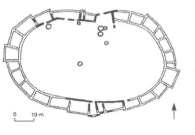

Fig 25.   *La Moleta del Remi*   *Isbet Sartah fort,*
                 fort, Catalonia   *Israel*

Mallorca

As was discussed earlier, although the natural environment along the Ebro Delta was very productive and benign, Aye-Gaythelos grew concerned that his fledgling empire was being attacked so often in Brigantia that it may never grow and prosper as he had hoped. He needed to find an alternative, more suitable location:

> Gaythelos suffered many kinds of calamity in that place (Brigantia). His whole mind was intent of the protection of his people, as befits a practical and careful leader ... Although he had been successful in inflicting heavy losses on the enemy on many occasions, he never gained a single victory without some loss to his tiny nation, which he saw would grow smaller as a result of daily and unending decrease instead of increase in numbers. [SC9]

Thinking that he had offended the gods by taking over land that had been given (by the gods) to other nations, Aye-Gaythelos determined that they must search again for uninhabited lands. So he sent out his boats and scanned the horizon from a large hill, as already discussed. There, on a particularly clear day, he saw cumulus clouds over Mallorca, and realised that there must be an island out there in the deep ocean. But it would appear that Aye-Gaythelos died not long after this discovery, which would not be so surprising given that he was already quite old when he left Egypt. However, this account may have been a literary allusion to link Aye-Gaythelos with Moses, as this was the same fate that befell the Hyksos-Israelite lawgiver – to be able to see the promised land from Mount Nebo, but never reach it. So, like Moses, it was to be Aye-Gaythelos' sons who went in search of new lands in and around Brigantia.

> So after he heard his father's words Hiber sailed to the aforesaid island with his brother Hymec and took possession of it, not by force but finding it empty and completely uninhabited, as certain authorities claim. After taking possession of the island he entrusted it to his brother and his family and returned to Spain. [SC12]

The mention of an island at this stage in the chronicle must again refer to Mallorca and not to Ireland. One cannot, of course, see Ireland from Spain, and the mention of regular travel between this island and Brigantia again favours the Mallorca identification.

River and Sea

The importance of the names being used in *Scotichronicon* is once again highlighted by the names of Aye-Gaythelos' sons. One of these sons was called Hiber and the other was called Hymec, and both of these names are quite interesting as they too appear to have been Egyptian titles. The name Hiber is obviously a derivation from *ebro (yibro)* 𓏭𓂋𓈖 meaning 'river'. Conversely, the name Hymec (Heemec) is most probably derived from the Egyptian *eema (yima)* 𓇋𓈖 meaning 'sea'. Both of these names are prefixed with an 'h' meaning 'the', as in 'H-ebrew'. Like *eeber*, the name *eema* has also filtered down into the Hebrew, where it became *yam (eam)* ‏ים‎ meaning 'sea'. Interestingly enough, the word Yam more specifically refers to the Mediterranean, and also refers to the west. Since Aye-Gaythelos was heading westwards across the Mediterranean, such a name for his son would have been doubly fitting.

Incidentally, having identified so many Hebrew words that have been derived from the ancient Egyptian, I have already proposed that Hebrew is simply a later dialect of the Egyptian language. This should not be so surprising, since the Hebrews were in fact the Lower Egyptian Hyksos and so they and their leaders (pharaohs) would have spoken fluent Egyptian. Some of these words have also found their way into the English, and in this particular case we still use the term 'immerse', which was derived from the Egyptian *eema* or *yima*. See the book *Eden* for further details.

So the two sons of Aye-Gaythelos were called River and Sea in the Egyptian language, which is quite fitting considering that Aye-Gaythelos and Scota were delivered from Egypt by river and sea. In fact, if one were to add to the speculation here, it should be noted that Ankhesenamun-Scota was Aye-Gaythelos' new wife, who he married when he was crowned pharaoh of Egypt, just three or four years before they both made their exodus to Spain. Thus these sons of Aye-Gaythelos may well have been born during this great exodus from Egypt, and if one had been born while at sea and the other delivered as they reached the great river in Spain, it would only be natural that their names would have become Sea and River (Eema and Eebro).

That these may well have been Egyptian-influenced names is also supported by the conveniently similar but contrasting nature of the names. One of the central planks of Egyptian theology, which was later inherited by Hebrew theology, was dualism. To the Egyptian priesthood the universe, the world and all life was created in a dualist fashion. Thus the gods in their great wisdom formed the male and the female, king and queen, day and night, light and dark, desert and marsh, chaos and order, and Sun and Moon (which are identical in apparent size), amongst many other dualist features. Even the gods themselves came in symmetric pairs, who complemented or opposed each other. While the complete answer to life, the universe and everything was unknowable, you can be sure that it would be dualist. While it is true that the new theology of Akhenaton dampened many theological concepts in Egypt, this dualism remained intact, and so the fact that a king like Aye-Gaythelos chose the names River and Sea for his sons is completely in line with standard Egyptian theology and culture.

Ireland

The tale thus far appears to be marooned upon the Balearic islands, so where does Ireland come into this story? What probably happened is that Hiber went to Mallorca first, as that was the closest island and could be seen (by his father Aye-Gaythelos) from the mainland. It would have taken a number of years to settle and build up the population, but after a generation or three there may well have been a vibrant enough population to expand out to other locations. The texts mention that there were constant battles with the indigenous Spanish tribes, as we have already seen, so spreading out across Spain was not the easiest option. Instead, they went island-hopping to Mallorca, Minorca and Sardinia, as will be discussed in the next chapter, and only then did they undertake the long and hazardous journey around the

Iberian peninsular to Ireland. In fact, the chronicle says:

> Supreme power at last fell to ... King Micelius Espayn. One of his predecessors (Gaythelos) had acquired for himself and his peoples a place to live in freedom that was independent but too small for such a numerous population ... Micelius had three sons called Hermonius, Partholomus and Hibertus. He prepared a fleet and sent them across to Ireland with a sizable army, knowing that they would find there extensive but practically uninhabited land to cultivate. [SC13]

Micelius was the great grandson of Aye-Gaythelos, through Hiber. So this account indicates that it had taken the people of Brigantia just four generations to become powerful enough to build and crew a fleet capable of sailing to Ireland. If they had started with just 1,000 people in Brigantia and trebled the population each generation, they would have become 80,000 strong in four generations. This is assuming that each couple had six surviving children, which is just about possible given the high birth rate of the time. This population of 80,000 would have been at least doubled by a large number of captured slaves and newly converted citizens from the native lands. Assuming there were no major catastrophes, the potential total population after four generations of 160,000 would just about be large enough and vibrant enough to construct a fleet of ships to go looking for and colonising new lands.

These simple demographic calculations indicate that Aye-Gaythelos could not really have started in Brigantia with much less than 1,000 followers, otherwise the colony would not have been large enough to achieve the kind of expansion that has been recorded. The *Lebor Gabala* indicates that there were about 60 people on each ship, which would equate to a fleet of about 16 ships. The Irish chronicle goes on to indicate that there were just three or four ships on this exodus, all tied together to prevent them from getting dispersed; but this figure seems to be unreasonably low, given the subsequent battles and history that the various chronicles relate. The chronology and geography of the *Lebor Gabala* is seriously distorted, in comparison with the equivalent passages in *Scotichronicon*, so perhaps this figure relates to the later exodus to Ireland.

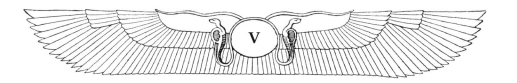

Minoans and Phoenicians

An important question that has not, as yet, been addressed is how a king and queen of Egypt assembled this large flotilla in the Nile Delta and how they navigated the largely uncharted waters of the western Mediterranean. Although the Egyptians possessed boat-building skills for their extensive Nile fleet, they were not exactly renowned in this era for their seafaring skills. Although Aye-Gaythelos and Ankhesenamun-Scota were fleeing an unstable political situation, and necessity is the mother of invention, a long voyage without the necessary knowledge and skills might be foolhardy in the extreme.

The alternative option is that the Egyptian royalty were able to employ the skills from other nations that bordered the Mediterranean, and an obvious candidate for this might be the Phoenicians, the Mediterranean's most celebrated seafaring nation. But this suggestion is not as straightforward as it may at first seem. The reign of Pharaoh Aye has been classically dated as 1325 - 1321 BC – the late fourteenth century – while the rise of the Phoenicians as a seafaring nation has been traced only to the eleventh century BC onwards. However, there must have been the nucleus of a seafaring empire extant in the Mediterranean at an earlier date than this, because the vast armada of the Sea People invasion of Egypt took place in the mid twelfth century BC.

This gives us the tantalizing possibility, already explored in my books *Solomon* and *Eden*, that the earlier voyages of Aye-Gaythelos and Scotia were related to, and laid the foundations of, the Phoenician empire. The researches thus far have unearthed evidence that points towards the Sea People invasion of Egypt in the twelfth century BC being masterminded by Hyksos-Egyptian diaspora royalty, who were trying to utilise mercenary armies from all over the Mediterranean to regain control of Egypt. These military exploits, and the need for subsequent reinforcements and materials, may well have laid the foundations for a maritime trading empire which, I believe, may have evolved into the separate empire of the Phoenicians. To investigate this suggestion further, perhaps a review of the Phoenician empire is required.

Unfortunately, the origins of the Phoenicians are shrouded in mystery, and classical mythology merely suggests a homeland in Scythia, modern Ukraine. However, in complete contrast to this, it is a fact that the majority of Phoenician art and architecture displays distinctly Egyptian influences and styles, and so a close cultural link to the exiled Hyksos-Israelites is entirely possible.

Whatever their origins, the Phoenicians eventually took residence along the Levantine coast, with their main port cities of Tyre, Byblos and Sidon. Utilising their maritime skills to the full, new colonies were established from the eleventh century BC onwards, at diverse locations across the Mediterranean. Eventually, the Phoenicians were to establish cities in nearly every Mediterranean coastal nation bar modern Italy and Greece. But where did this maritime tradition come from? What were the imperatives that drove the Phoenicians onto the capricious seas?

The most probable answer, to which classical history subscribes, is that military and political pressures forced these people out into the Mediterranean. But the new twist to this history is that this was not pressure from the Hittites upon the peoples of the Levantine coasts; instead, this was a few centuries earlier, the pressure came from Upper Egypt and it was applied to the Hyksos pharaohs of Lower Egypt. The first wave of migrants would have set out from Egypt circa 1580 BC, as Ahmose I swept to power in Lower Egypt, as Ahmose I swept to power in Lower Egypt and forced the Hyksos peoples out of the country and into new coastal settlements all across the eastern Mediterranean. This, however, was not the only civil war in Egypt, and the religious reforms of Akhenaton in the fourteenth century BC destabilised Egypt in a strikingly similar fashion. Once more, sections of the Lower Egyptian Hyksos people and monarchy were being pushed out across the Mediterranean in a flotilla of small craft.

But none of this explains where the maritime expertise, utilised by both the Hyksos-Israelites and by Aye-Gaythelos, came from. Undoubtedly the fourteenth century BC Egyptians had the boat-building skills necessary, and this is amply demonstrated by the impressive cedar boat that was buried next to the Great Pyramid at Giza. Any nation capable of constructing such a leviathan would be amply equipped to build boats capable of circumnavigating the Mediterranean. But what of the navigational skills for open-water sailing?

V Minoans and Phoenicians

Santorini

The source of this maritime expertise in this pre-Phoenician era may come from a surprising location – Thera (Santorini). Between 1625 and 1600 BC, the great volcano on the island of Thera erupted with devastating violence. The force and fallout from this eruption were sufficient to create the biblical plagues in Egypt, which resulted in the Hyksos-Israelite exodus, and yet it may also have provided some of these exiles with their means of deliverance.

Luckily for the inhabitants of Thera, the volcano must have given them a reasonable amount of warning about its intentions, for no buried population was ever found in the ruined city of Akrotiri, and it would appear that the people had all fled the island. This exodus and the subsequent destruction of the island of Thera actually formed the basis for Plato's story of Atlantis and a fresco of the city of Atlantis is actually on display in modern Santorini, as is related in the second edition of the book *Tempest*. But the destination of these exiles from Thera is unknown, and it is presumed that they fled to the Minoan empire in Crete, whose society and nautical technology were virtually identical to the Theran's. However, around this same time a number of Minoans began arriving in the city of Avaris, in Lower Egypt, and their distinctive artwork has been discovered in the remains of this city.

The excavations of Avaris by Manfred Bietak uncovered some exceptional frescos that were undoubtedly Minoan, both in their design and execution. The fresco or secco painting technique was unknown in Egypt and the Levant at this time, but many fine examples of this type of artwork have been discovered at Knossos in Crete. In addition, the characters in the Avaris frescos wear distinctive Minoan costumes, and the subject matter in these frescos – that of bull-leaping – is uniquely Minoan. Indeed, the styles employed are more typically Theran than Minoan, indicating that the artists came from Thera (Santorini).

The colours used in these paintings are also interesting, as the bull-leapers' skins are invariably depicted in lighter tones, which range from yellow though to white. Archaeologists have speculated that the lighter-toned athletes may be female, but that is contradicted by a similar image of a yellow skinned young boy and a white skinned prince (with feathers) at Knossos. It is not entirely clear if these skin-tones represent a fashion or genuinely fair-skinned people, but there is a similarity here with Egyptian depictions from around this era.

In the tomb of Userhat, a royal scribe who worked under Amenhotep II and was buried at Thebes, many of the people in the wall scenes are depicted as having blonde hair. This is not simply artistic licence, as some of the people in these scenes have black hair. So was this a new fashion for light coloured wigs or were there pockets of other nationalities living and working among the general population?[1]

While the prospect of a tribe of blonde-haired people living in the Near East in this era may seem unlikely, it would appear that the later Greeks also had a number of blondes in their midst – despite the predominant Greek phenotype having wavy, raven-black hair. I have already identified Helen of Sparta as being related to the Hyksos-Egyptian royal line in some manner, in the book *Eden*; however, surprising as it may seem, Helen is also said to have been blonde. The poems of the Spartan poet Alcman were inspired by the legends of Helen, and yet despite the typical Greek beauty being raven-haired, these poems acclaim the beauty of blondes. Thus, Helen has traditionally been viewed as being a blonde or perhaps a blonde-ginger-haired beauty, which is how she was portrayed in the recent film *Troy*.

This portrayal caused howls of protest from the politically correct brigade, who declared this to be yet another Hollywood distortion of the truth. However, while I could not find a direct reference to Helen's hair colour in the *Iliad*, Homer does mention many a golden-haired Greek in his epic, including Achilles, Meleager and Agamede. In addition, Helen was married to the 'yellow-haired' King Menelaus; and while Homer gives Helen a gloriously erotic and supernatural parentage, she was probably closely related to Menelaus, and thus also blonde. The historian Bettany Hughes says of Helen:

> We hear of a female poet (rare in Greece) called Megalostrata who, like Helen, was 'golden-haired'.[2]

In a similar fashion, the biblical Mary Magdalene was also envisioned as being blonde or blonde-ginger, although descriptive evidence for this within the Bible is lacking. Nevertheless, many a Renaissance painting portrays her as being blonde-ginger, just like Helen; and the crypt of Mary Magdalene under the church at Saint-Maxim has her (supposed) relics crowned by a distinctive blonde wig.

If there were blondes in Egypt, it is entirely possible that some of those people could have been related

Fig 26. Blonde Egyptians, from the tomb of Userhat.

to the (possibly) lighter-skinned Minoans. However, having done all this meticulous work on the possibility of Minoans living in Egypt, the conclusion of Manfred Bietak was:

> I have proposed very cautiously, as a working hypothesis, the possibility of an inter-dynastic marriage between the Hyksos [Israelites] and a Minoan princess.[3]

While Bietak suggests the possibility of a dynastic alliance, the obvious link to the destruction of Thera cannot be ignored. This is made perfectly clear in the following quote:

> Excavations conducted by the Australian Institute ... at Avaris, have now revealed thousands of fragments of wall-painting apparently stripped from the walls of the Hyksos palace when it was overthrown by (Ahmose I) who founded the eighteenth dynasty. There on Egyptian soil were wall paintings which were unmistakably Minoan in character. What were they doing there? Who painted them and why?[4]

The answer to both of these conundrums is more than obvious. Modern dating of the Thera eruption places the exile of the population of Akrotiri and the other cities on Thera to about 1620 BC, while the classical date for the destruction of the Hyksos capital city of Avaris by Ahmose I is around 1580 BC. Thus any exiles from Thera could have been resident in Avaris for some forty or so years before the city was overrun by the forces of Ahmose I. Forty years would have been quite sufficient for the exiled royalty of Thera to have created their own palace in Avaris, and decorated it with scenes that reminded them of their abandoned and destroyed homeland. So these were not 'anomalous' Minoan frescos in Avaris, but Theran-Minoan artwork which had been created by the refugees from the island itself.

Despite this obvious chronological connection, academics still seem confused on the precise origins of this artwork, and one researcher says of the Avaris frescos:

> Whether we are seeing Knossians (Minoans), as suggested by the sport, or Therans, as suggested by the blue hair ... the people from (one of these islands) came to Egypt and brought with them images of their religious practices ... The mystery of what they were doing there and why the paintings were commissioned remains unsolved.[5]

Why is there any mystery? The previous quote gives us two options for the origins of this artwork: Thera or Knossos. We also know that the era for these paintings being commissioned in Avaris was just before the attack by Ahmose I or, in other words, just after the Thera eruption. We also know that one of these islands was destroyed, but the entire community was evacuated just before the Thera eruption, as no decimated population has ever been discovered in the well-preserved ruins of Thera.

It would seem to be perfectly obvious, therefore, that a substantial number of the Theran population must have been evacuated to Lower Egypt, where they reconstructed a palace full of classical Theran artwork. But this evacuation was not simply from Thera, because Tacitus says of this evacuation:

> It is a tradition that the Jews, as fugitives from the island of Crete at the time when Saturn was expulsed by the violence of Jupiter and forsook his kingdom, settled themselves upon the extremities of Libya (Egypt).' [6]

The 'violence of Jupiter' has to be a reference to the Thera eruption, while the confusion with the Jews comes from the fact that the Hyksos-Israelite and Akhenaton-Moses exoduses from Egypt were the basis for the conflated account of the biblical exodus. The Israelites were, as I have demonstrated in previous works, the Hyksos Egyptians from Lower Egypt, and it would appear that they had a long-standing alliance with the Minoans, many of whom were now living in Avaris. Likewise, the Israelites were related to the Spartans, as we saw previously. The reference to Crete is interesting too, as this implies that Crete was also badly hit by the Thera eruption and many refugees were also fleeing from the Minoan empire on Crete, which would certainly explain the slow demise of the Minoans from this time onwards.

Following the civil war and the exodus from Egypt, during the reign of Ahmose I, the Hyksos and Minoans drifted back to the Delta lands of Lower Egypt, taking their distinctive culture and artwork with them. But this flowing naturalistic style of artwork was so different to the formal religious artwork of Egypt that it was probably considered to be highly revolutionary. In fact, this naturalistic artwork was so progressive that it was to greatly influence a later pharaoh from Lower Egypt and thereby cause a complete religious reformation within Egypt. That later pharaoh also happens to be central to this story, for he was the revolutionary iconoclast, Akhenaton – the father of Ankhesenamun-Scota.

As an aside, the bull-leaping imagery that is so familiar to us from Thera and Crete may not simply have been a circus trick for the entertainment of the aristocracy. Instead, it may have had stellar and thus religious connotations. The era for these depictions was just after the constellation of Taurus had given way to Aries, in the precessional cycle of the Cosmos. Thus the standard image of the leaper on the back of the bull's neck can be directly

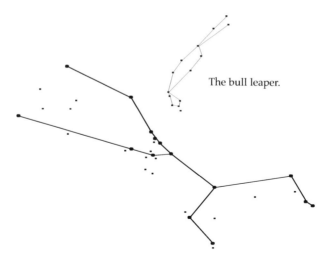

The bull leaper.

Fig 27. Taurus, with Minoan bull-leaper.

compared to the stars that stream off from the 'neck' of the constellation of Taurus. In which case, the acrobat's display in the arena would have had subtle and mystical undertones for the assembled priesthood and royalty. In the stellar diagram in fig 27, only the neck and horns of the bull can be seen in the constellation of Taurus, but the outline of a 'bull-leaper' jumping over the horns of Taurus can be clearly seen in the layout of the minor stars of this constellation. The image this projects is strikingly similar to the artwork of the Minoans, and this may have been the inspiration for this athletic display (see plates 15 & 16, for images of a Minoan bull-leaper).

And while some historians will claim that stellar imagery is not at all common in Minoan art, the seal-stone from Gournes does exhibit circular 'buttons' on the limbs of the bull, that can readily be interpreted as representations of stars, as can be seen in fig 28.

Fig 28. Seal-stone of Gournes.

V Minoans and Phoenicians

Minoan Amarna

The reason for some of the Theran exiles establishing their new colony in Egypt, rather than Crete, is uncertain. It is known that the Hyksos retained close links with the Minoans, as many artifacts from Egypt have been discovered in Crete and *vice versa*. Examples are the Egyptian sistrum discovered in Arkhanes Phouri in Crete, and the decoration of the tomb of Hepzefa in Egypt, which follows Minoan principles.[7]

Both of these similarities date from the twentieth century BC, which demonstrates that there were close contacts between these two cultures long before the Thera eruption in the seventeenth century BC. It is possible that this close connection was based upon a common heritage, as has been suggested, although direct evidence for this is somewhat lacking. It is thought by many historians, including the venerable Manetho, that the Hyksos people were a Semitic people who migrated into Egypt from the lands to the east; in other words, from the lands that had also been occupied by the proto-Minoans. So it is not beyond the realms of possibility that the Hyksos and Minoans shared a common heritage, if not a common ancestry.

Oblique evidence in favour of this suggestion is to be found in the previous quotes. All of these Egyptologists are indicating that the Hyksos people of Lower Egypt had allowed the Theran-Minoans into their country, and that they may have even adopted some of the Minoan's revolutionary artistic styles. However, when Ahmose I captured Avaris in about 1580 BC, both the quasi-religious naturalistic scenes of bull-worship and the naturalistic scenes of the Nile Delta wildlife were hacked off the walls and destroyed. Clearly, the Theran-Minoans were far more closely allied to the Hyksos-Israelites in Lower Egypt than they were to the Upper Egyptian regime of Ahmose I.

This similarity between the Therans and the Hyksos-Israelites is likely to have been intensified after this exodus, as they now had the significant bond of a common tragedy and thus a common heritage and history. Certainly, this bond must have endured through the following generations, because some two hundred years later another pharaoh of Egypt was again adopting and promoting the naturalistic art forms of the Theran-Minoans. As we have already seen, this pharaoh was Akhenaton, who I have long argued was related in some way to the previous Hyksos-Israelite regime in Avaris. Akhenaton's artistic reforms have often been said to have been unique and revolutionary, but this is not at all correct. While Akhenaton's artistic preference was unique to Middle and Upper Egypt, it has exact parallels and similarities with the Theran-Minoan artwork of Avaris:

V Minoans and Phoenicians

> Much comment has been made on the Minoan character of the nature scenes at Amarna, which along with the large quantities of Mycenaean pottery found at the site has suggested to some (that there was) an Aegean influence in the art. However, nature scenes are not typical of Mycenaean art but of Minoan art; and Minoan painting was a thing of the past by the time of Amarna. [8]

In this quotation, Vivian Davies is pointing out that although the artwork at Amarna looks distinctly Minoan, the Minoan empire had all but collapsed by this time. So how did Minoan artwork suddenly appear at Amarna?

The answer to this is a simple continuation of the arguments that have already been put forward in this chapter. There were probably strong cultural links between the Theran-Minoans and the Hyksos-Israelites, who may have both lived along the northern Nile Delta and the eastern Mediterranean coastline. Eventually, the two strands of these people forged diverging empires in different lands, in Egypt and Crete/Thera. Although this scenario may seem contrary to my previous assertions – that the Hyksos-Israelites were native Lower Egyptians – this alternative Laventine homeland for the Hyksos may have been the result of a previous exile from Lower Egypt during the turbulent period at the end of the Old Kingdom (c. 2200 BC), when Egypt suffered divisions and conflict that were strikingly similar to the Hyksos era.

When the island of Thera exploded in about 1620 BC, many thousands of Therans chose to emigrate back to their related cousins in Avaris, in Lower Egypt. Although these lands and the city at Avaris were overrun in about 1580 BC, during the civil war with Upper Egypt, the common bond of these privations ensured that these two peoples stuck together in whatever lands they were exiled to. When the Hyksos-related Amenhotep pharaohs again rose to power in Egypt a century or more later, these Theran-Minoan influences were still strong within this community. Hence the style of Theran-Minoan artwork survived the slow demise of the Minoan empire on Crete, and hence Akhenaton (Amenhotep IV) had a strong appreciation for this 'unusual' naturalistic artwork.

It should perhaps also be pointed out that some aspects of Minoan culture were definitely *not* supported by Akhenaton, and that included bull-worship. Akhenaton was the brother of the biblical Moses (TuthMoses), and so he was closely linked to the (second) exodus from Egypt. Yet the biblical accounts make a great play on the difficulties that Moses was having with bull worshippers.

I had long been puzzled as to why Apis-bull worshippers would have been allied with the Hyksos-Israelites on the exodus out of Amarna. That the Upper Egyptians still worshipped the Apis is well known, but why any of these people should wish to follow Moses and Akhenaton's Atonist regime on the exodus remained a complete mystery. However, if these renegade bull worshippers were not Egyptian Apis worshippers but the remnants and descendants of the Theran-Minoans, who had long venerated the bull in their own idiosyncratic way, then the mystery may well be solved. But if this is so then the alliance between the Therans and Akhenaton must have fallen apart during this (second) exodus, because the Bible reports that Moses killed 3,000 of his followers at Mt Sinai, when he discovered them worshipping a golden calf.

Script

Perhaps at this point it might be useful to look at the unique script of the Minoans. There are three stages in the development of the Minoan script and language, and although the dates of these stages are far from certain, they appear to mimic the major periods of civic unrest in Egypt. The first stage is notable for the usage of pictorial symbols, which represents the simplest form of writing possible. It is presumed that these glyphs and symbols have pictographic meaning, but none has yet been deciphered.

Then, in about 1650 BC – which is more or less at the same time as the Thera eruption and the resulting Hyksos-Israelite exodus from Egypt – the first usage of symbolic letters of a rudimentary alphabet were used, which is called Linear A. Unfortunately, although some of these alphabetic characters are similar to the later Linear B characters, the precise pronunciation for this alphabet and the nature of the language it represents are both unknown.

Finally, in an era variously described as being between 1400 BC and 1325 BC – which is more or less the era of the Akhenaton and Aye exoduses from Egypt – Linear A was superseded by the more sophisticated Linear B script.

The exact language represented by the Linear B script was unknown for a long time, but then a nonspecialist in the field of etymology, Michael Ventris, demonstrated that the Linear B was a syllabic alphabet and that the tablets that had been discovered were written in an archaic form of Greek. At first this discovery did not go down too well with the establishment, especially those from Greece who were effectively being told by a non-academic Englishman that the artifacts in their museums were actually written in their own language. However, despite all the protests, it became abundantly clear that Ventris was correct, and that the Linear B tablets in both Mycenae in Greece and Knossos in Crete were all written in an early form of Greek. Fired on by this discovery, many have subsequently tried to show that the earlier Linear A script tablets were also written in Greek, but that attempt has so far failed, and the Linear A texts remain undeciphered.

Thus far, the evidence seems to show that Linear A was used by the Minoans for their own language, of which we have no knowledge. However, the fact that the Minoans started using this new hieroglyphic script around the time of the Hyksos-Israelite exodus from Egypt may imply that they were influenced by the Egyptian hieroglyphic script. Similarly, while the language that the Minoans were recording with this Linear A script is unknown, further Egyptian influences are not impossible. At some later date it is thought that the Mycenaean Greeks adopted the Linear A alphabet and adapted it for their own language, and this became the Linear B script and language. Both the new script and the new Mycenaean-Greek language subsequently supplanted the original Minoan script and language back in Knossos. At a much later date, the Greeks then adopted the simpler Phoenician script but maintained the same language; and it is this Phoenician alphabet that we recognise as the foundation for all modern Greek and Latin scripts. [9]

The general thrust of this chronology and argument is that there may well have been Egyptian influences upon the Minoan and Greek languages, which were provided by the many exiles fleeing from Egypt; including Aye-Dannus. It is not the intention of this book to look into this concept in any great detail, but the idea occurred because some similarities had already been noted in the second edition of the book *Eden*. The primary similarity was the name for the Trojan horse, which was called an *h-ippos* ιππος in Classical Greek. However, due to a rather dramatic historical mistranslation, the Trojan *ippos* (a horse) was actually based upon a Greco-Egyptian *appis* (a bull), which was a Greek rendering of the Egyptian *hep* 𓏲𓂝𓆑 (the sacred Apis-bull of Egypt).

I had initially thought that this Greek adoption and alteration of the term for the Egyptian Apis-bull had been a comparatively recent event, perhaps dating from the classical Greek era. However, the Mycenaean word for a horse (in Linear B) was *iqo*, which Michael Ventris has identified with the Greek *h-ippos*. Since the Egyptian word is the more ancient of the two, it must have been from the Egyptian *hep* 𓏲𓂝𓆑 that the Greek *iqos* or *h-ippos* was derived. It might seem unlikely that the Mycenaeans would confuse a bull with a horse, but such linguistic changes are far from uncommon; as can be seen with the similarly named but physically unique hippopotamus ιππο ποταμος, or 'river horse'.

Another interesting word in Mycenaean Greek is *eqeta*, which became the Classical Greek *heqetai* ηεψεται. This denoted a special leader who was closely allied to the royal court and performed a prestigious but largely honorary role in the Mycenaean army. This position has proved to be a bit of a mystery, especially as the *eqeta* used the prestigious and expensive chariot for transport, and so John Chadwick says of these leaders:

V Minoans and Phoenicians

> The 'Followers' *(eqeta)* are important men, presumably followers of the king and members of his household ... Why does each unit have a royal officer *(eqeta)*, not apparently in charge, but attached? My guess is that he is the communications section. [10]

While that may be entirely possible, a more tenable scenario is that the royalty of the Mycenaeans were not of the same culture or nationality as the common people. Indeed, they may have been of exiled Hyksos-Egyptian stock, and had taken over the Mycenaean people by force and become their *de facto* leaders. In this case, each army unit would require a member of the new Hyksos-Israelite royalty to oversee it and ensure its loyalty. While this may seem to be a tenuous suggestion, the name for the Mycenaean *(h)eqeta* may well have been based upon the Egyptian *heqa* 𓉐𓏤𓁐 meaning 'ruler' or 'royalty'. Indeed, the related Egyptian title of Heqetai 𓉐𓏤 means the 'Ruler of the Two Lands' or the 'Ruler of Egypt'.

Further similarities are to be found in the two classes of Mycenaean royal landholdings, which are given as the *te-menos* and the *te-ret*. Since these two terms are paired in this fashion, they are very likely to have been taken from the equivalent Egyptian words *ta-meh* 𓇾𓏤 and *ta-resi* 𓇾𓈖 , which mean 'land of the north' and 'land of the south' respectively. Actually, these were rather important Egyptian titles, and should really be read as 'Lower Egypt' and 'Upper Egypt' respectively. For the exiled leaders of Egypt to adopt these familiar titles in a foreign land would be quite logical. Likewise, if the Mycenaeans had been influenced to this degree by the exiled Hyksos-Israelites (c. 1580 BC) then this would indeed have been a logical destination for the exodus of Aye-Dannus some three centuries later (c. 1330 BC).

Of course, this is not to say that the language of the Mycenaean Greeks is going to prove to be a complete derivation of the Egyptian language, as Hebrew appears to be. As was mentioned previously, more often than not a ruling elite in a new land has to adopt the language of the native people and not *vice versa*. However, it is also common that some phrases and customs of the new ruling class become established within the native language, and no doubt these words would include mention of the ruling elite itself, their right to occupy the land and the names of their gods.

The navy

The primary point to be made in these discussions of the Minoan empire is that the Theran-Minoans, many of whom were resident in the Hyksos-Israelite capital of Avaris in 1580 BC, appear to have had a close relationship with the Lower Egyptian monarchy. More importantly, perhaps, they would also have had the maritime experience that the Hyksos-Israelites would have needed during their first (great) exodus from Egypt. So, during this first exodus out of Lower Egypt, some of the refugees may have taken to their boats and established colonies elsewhere in the Mediterranean. Some may even have gone to Crete and Greece, and spread their culture and language there; perhaps even aspiring to positions of power and influence.

The legends of Greece herself indicate that this transfer of culture from Egypt to Greece was effected in several eras. We have already seen the legends of King Dannus [Aye] fleeing to Argos (Greece) and taking over the region. Likewise, in a much later era we find the *Pseudo Callisthenes* relating a similar story about Pharaoh Nectanebo II (Nakhthoreb) of the thirtieth dynasty fleeing to Macedonia (Greece), where he 'established himself as a magician'. It was from an illicit union between Nakhthoreb and Queen Olympias that Alexander the Great was supposed to have been born. [KN11]

Now this fabulous account of the paternity of Alexander is the stuff of pure legend, but it does indicate a strong desire for Alexander to have been of Egyptian royal blood, which is probably correct, as one of the primary goals of his great military expedition was to conquer Egypt and become pharaoh. But although it is entirely possible that Nakhthoreb fled to Greece there was probably a great deal of Egyptian royal blood already in that region, which had been taken there during the first great exodus from Egypt. Moving on two centuries from the first exodus, we arrive at the exodus of Akhenaton and his followers. As we have seen, the evidence from the archaeology and from the naturalistic artwork of Akhenaton's regime, suggests that the Theran-Minoan influence among the Hyksos-Israelites was still strong, even within the city of Amarna. And so Akhenaton may have been able to call upon the Minoans to provide a seaworthy fleet and navigate a long voyage, following his exile - skills that Aye-Gaythelos was also going to rely upon some 13 years after Akhenaton's exodus.

It is also worth noting that the demise of the Minoan empire in mainland Crete (as opposed to Thera) was suspiciously concurrent with the demise of the Amarna regime, and again one may suppose that there was a link between the two. The Minoans had retained close contacts with the (exiled) Hyksos regime, and may have depended to a great extent upon them for trade, as the latter regained their power base within Egypt. But as the Amarna regime rapidly collapsed, and the influence of Mycenaean Greece in the Mediterranean grew in equal measure, so the traditional economy of the Minoans had to rapidly evolve and adapt. Instead of looking south to their colleagues and cousins in Egypt, they now had to look towards a new and possibly threatening empire in the north. But this transition had obviously been painful, for the Minoan empire appears to have finally collapsed at this time.

V   Minoans and Phoenicians

However, it is entirely possible that the link between these two failing empires, in Egypt and Crete, was even closer than this. Although this is merely speculation, Aye-Gaythelos and Ankhesenamun-Scota required dozens of ships to evacuate their proto-nation out of Egypt, and the Minoans were still a reasonably powerful maritime nation at this time. Were dozens of Minoan ships either commandeered or purchased by Aye-Gaythelos and Scota, leaving the Minoan mainland susceptible to Greek raiding and maritime dominance?

Phoenicia

We have looked at the Minoan empire in some detail and witnessed its eventual demise. However, nothing in human history is static and where one empire fails a new nation normally rises to fill the strategic and commercial vacuum. The seafaring economy of the Mediterranean was to be no different, and so as the last of the Minoans ebbed away, the mainland Greeks rose in maritime power and influence. But such was the scale of the available commerce that there was room for another player in this market, and so a small nation from the Levant began to make inroads into this Greek dominance of the seas. This new nation was, of course, the Phoenicians. However, one researcher in the field reports that the rise of the Phoenicians may have been closely and causally linked with the demise of the Minoans:

> The Phoenicians and the Celts may have originated in the Indus Valley, and also from the Knossos Civilization of Crete. [12]

As mentioned previously, a cultural link between the Minoans and Phoenicians would make a degree of sense, as both were major maritime empires and the latter simply seem to have taken over when the former declined. That the Phoenicians may have been linked to the Minoan's allies, the Hyksos-Israelites, is implicit in their original name, as they appear to have called themselves the Kenaani or Canaanites כנעני. This term is traditionally said to mean 'merchant', while the land of Canaan כנען referred to 'lowlands'. The book *Cleopatra* translates the term 'merchant' as more accurately meaning 'banker'.

The Book of Leviticus relates that the land of Canaan was given to the Israelites after Joshua conquered it, and since Joshua was of the next generation after Moses, this event would have been just after the exodus of Aye-Gaythelos and just before the rise of the Phoenician empire. This account, and the previous arguments that have been discussed, therefore demonstrate possible links between the Hyksos-Israelites, the Minoans and the Phoenicians.

These may have been simple trading links, although it is much more likely in this kind of era that any such links were also cemented with a royal alliance, with Minoan princesses being packed off to Avaris and Amarna. The offspring of these diplomatic unions would then be free to travel back to Crete and take with them the intermingled Egyptian-Minoan culture.

Further evidence that the Phoenicians and Minoans were closely related can be seen in the name given to a Phoenician boat, which was *kefti* . But the Egyptian name for the Minoans was the Kefti , and the Bible calls them Kaphtor כפתר. Thus the Phoenician boat and perhaps the Phoenician people themselves were easily confused with the Minoans.

The biblical accounts say that the Kaphtorites (the Minoans) were none other than the Philistines, which it actually calls the Pelesheth פלשת. The Pelesheth (Philistines-Minoans) are obviously the historical Peleset, who were one of the many tribes of the Sea People alliance who attacked Egypt during the reign of Ramesses III. Since I have always maintained that this Sea People alliance was organised by the exiled Hyksos-Israelites (and thus also the exiled Amarna regime), and used as a mercenary force to destabilise the Upper Egyptian Theban regime, the Hyksos-Israelites and the Peleset (Peleseth-Philistines-Minoans) should have been close allies. Why their presence on the Levantine coast sometimes led to friction and skirmishes, according to the biblical accounts, is not entirely clear. However, the biblical Concordance, in its usual circuitous manner, does confirm that all these tribes were much the same or at least very closely related:

> **Kaphtor:** the original home of the Philistines, perhaps on the southwest coast of Asia Minor, maybe in Egypt or close by, or more probably on the island of Crete.

> **Philistine:** an inhabitant of Philistia; descendants of Mizraim who immigrated from Kaphtor (Crete) to the western seacoast of Canaan.

> **Canaan:** the fourth son of Ham and the progenitor of the Phoenicians and of the various nations who peopled the seacoast of Palestine. [13]

The result of these observations is that Kaphtor was Crete, the Egyptian Keftiu; the Philistines came from Crete; the Minoans came from Crete; the Canaanites were the Phoenicians; the Phoenicians came from Canaan; Canaan and Philistia were neighbouring countries; both the Canaanites and the Philistines were immediate descendants of Ham; and the Philistines were the descendants of Mizraim. However, in the Bible, Mizraim means Egypt, and so the Philistines were descendants of Egypt!

Thus it would appear that the Minoans, Phoenicians, Canaanites and

Philistines were pretty much one and the same people. The Concordance also implies that the Philistines (Minoans) were of Egyptian origins. Although it is not clear if this refers to Upper Egyptians or the Hyksos-Israelite Lower Egyptians, the strong links between the Minoans and the Lower Egyptian monarchy in Avaris would strongly suggest the latter.

It has already been demonstrated that the Canaanites were substantially an Egypto-Israelite nation, as has been discussed in the book *Solomon*. That their descendants, the Phoenicians, may well have been similarly descended from Egyptian exiles (the Hyksos-Israelites) is confirmed by the overtly Egyptian nature of their artwork. Time and time again, the artwork and motifs of the Phoenicians are demonstrably based upon Egyptian antecedents. The excavations at Phoenician Carthage, for example, unearthed the following trinkets:

> This material is of undoubted Egyptian inspiration ... The most common figurative themes are the *wadjet eye, ujat, uraeus,* and the Ptah-Patechus. We also have the hawk, Horus, Bes and Thoth. Less frequent are certain divine beings like Isis, Min, Khonsu, Shu, Khnum or Amon-Ra, Sekhmet, Anubis...[14]

In other words, nearly every Egyptian deity can be found within the sparse remains of the city of Carthage. Even Phoenician architecture is overtly based upon Egyptian styles, with the typical Egyptian cornice at the top of a building being a favourite theme. These cornices were even adorned with multiple *uraei* and the winged solar disk, rendering them almost indistinguishable from their Egyptian equivalents, except perhaps in the quality of their workmanship. But if Phoenician art was based upon Egyptian styles, then their language also shows great affinity to Hebrew:

> The affinity (of Phoenician) with other languages of the first millennium is considerable, and seems to show a strictly parallel development, particularly as far as Hebrew is concerned ... The comparison between Phoenician and Hebrew does indeed show autonomy, but above all it shows coexistence and parallel development.[15]

The evidence suggests that these two languages were closely related, and their development was closely related and in step with each other. However, in the book *Eden* it has already been demonstrated that Hebrew was a direct descendant of the Egyptian language, and so the equivalence and parallel development of the Phoenician language suggests that it too was a dialect of ancient Egyptian. For a nation like the Phoenicians, who had adopted (or maintained) the majority of Egyptian customs, architecture and theology, this would not be too surprising.

However, while the Hebrew and Phoenician languages may have been based upon ancient Egyptian, their script was not – although some historians do maintain that the Phoenician script could have been based upon the cursive Egyptian demotic script. What is far more certain is that this new Phoenician script became the basis for the later Hebrew, Greek and Latin scripts, and so this aspect of Phoenician culture has become a central component of all Western cultures. This topic is discussed in more detail in Chapter VII.

Purple palms

As we have seen, the historical Greek name for the Canaanite people was the Phoenicians, and the traditional reasoning for this new name for the Canaanites is that the word was derived from the Phoenician word *phoinikhon* meaning 'purple', which was derived from the Mycenaean or ancient Greek word *poniki*. This name was supposed to be a reference to the purple dyes that were made from the *murex* snail in Phoenicia. This may be partly true, but the Phoenician reference to purple may also be an oblique reference to the Lower Egyptian royalty, who were distinguished by the Red Crown. In addition, the *murex* purple dye was so expensive that it was the preserve of the royal family, a tradition that survived into the Roman era and the emperor's cloak of purple.

This meaning for their name also links the Phoenicians directly with the Minoans once more, for the origins of the *murex* dye trade actually lie in Keftiu (Crete). In her recent excavations, Maria C. Shaw discovered evidence for *murex* purple extraction at Kommos, a port in southern Crete. She says:

> I have excavated part of what seems to be an installation for extracting purple in a MMIIB context at Kommos ... In the area involved I found crushed *murex* and some channels carved in the ground filled with *murex* shells. [16]

The Knossos tablets refer to the purple dye being called *po-pu-ro*, [17] and this term is more or less identical to the Greek *porphyry* πορπηιρι, which is in turn the origin of the English term 'purple'. One would presume that the Minoan term, *po-pu-ro*, was the original here and it is the Greeks who have adopted this word. But it is unlikely that the Phoenician equivalent of *phoinikhon* has been derived from *porphyry*, which leaves the true origin of the former name rather uncertain. In other words, the Phoenician word for purple may simply have been derived from the Phoenician's eventual monopoly of the purple dye market, and not the other way around. In which case, the Phoenician's well-known title may have predated their entry into the lucrative purple trade, and so we may have to look for another origin for their name.

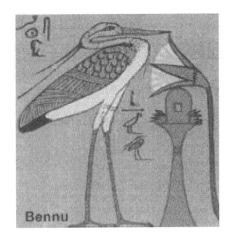

Fig 29. *The Egyptian Phoenix.*

One possibility is that the name for the Phoenicians was derived from the Phoenix, the fabulous bird from Egyptian mythology that was capable of regenerating itself. This attribute, of dying and being reborn anew, may have been considered to be quite fitting for this nation's name, especially if the Phoenicians were the reborn descendants of the Minoans. But there is a flaw in this argument, because the traditional Egyptian name for the Phoenix was the Bennu . So how did the Egyptian Bennu become the Phoenician Phoenix? The answer to this probably lies in the tree with which the Phoenix is associated.

The traditional observation is that the Bennu (Phoenix) is associated with the persea or avocado tree, as that is where it is supposed to have perched. However, the Bennu-Phoenix is more closely related to the *benra-t* tree, which is actually the date-palm. The reason that this strange association has come about is due to the graphic symbology of the palm frond. The Bennu (Phoenix) bird was, in essence, a representation of the Sun, and its regeneration after a long time-span denoted the movement of the Sun through the heavens. The most likely event that this story was trying to explain was the rising of the Sun in a different astrological constellation every 2,000 years or so, due to the precession of the equinox (the slow wobble of the Earth around its central axis). This was the 'regeneration' event in the cyclic life of the Bennu-Phoenix: when the Sun faded from one astrological house and was born again into the next.

In Egypt, the Sun-god Ra was invariably depicted as a flying sun-disk, as can be seen at the beginning of each chapter in this book. These flying Sun symbols were normally placed over doorways, no doubt so that Ra could see all who entered the building. However, in a changing religious environment the flying Sun-disk may have become an unacceptable motif, hence the later Judaeo-Israelite invention of the 'flying scroll'.

Zechariah is said to have had a vision of a huge flying scroll that was the width of the porch of the temple, which is probably an exact description because this was actually the winged Sun-disk of Ra that was displayed above every entrance-way in Egypt, and probably over the doorway to the Temple of Jerusalem too. The symbolism of this new flying scroll imagery is identical to the winged Sun-disk, but the theology can now omit any references to the Sun-god Ra, if that is expedient to the new Judaic priesthood.

> Then I turned, and lifted up mine eyes, and looked, and behold a flying roll. And he said unto me, What seest thou? And I answered, I see a flying roll; the length thereof is twenty cubits, and the breadth thereof ten cubits. [B18]

In ancient Israelite iconography, the scroll is normally portrayed as being rolled up and seen edge on; in other words we see just a circle with two wings attached, or the symbol of Aton-Ra. However, the rectangular dimensions given in this verse convinced some ancient scholars that the scroll had been unwound and opened, thus presenting a rectangular image. It was from this ingeniously revised symbology that the mythology of the Persian flying carpet was derived.

But this is not the only way of covering up the Hyksos-Israelite veneration of Aton-Ra, and an alternative to the flying scroll might well be two golden palm fronds. These innocent-sounding palm fronds happen to

Fig 30. The palm-frond symbol of Ra in the Peitavas synagogue, Riga.

look rather similar to a pair of bird's wings, so the image of Aton-Ra can be overtly displayed once more, but again the true symbology is hidden. A good example of this is to be seen in the Peitavas synagogue in Riga, Latvia. This synagogue happens to be one of the few synagogues in the world that are decorated in the Egyptian style, and above the pylon-styled doorway there are two golden palm fronds in just the same position and layout as the Egyptian flying Sun-disk. Again, the symbology remains hidden, and none of the congregation need know that Adhon, the Judaic god, is actually a reference to Adon (Aton-Ra), the solar deity of Akhenaton. See the book *Eden* for a colour picture of this synagogue and the golden palm fronds above the doorway.

It seems highly likely that the Phoenicians have gone through exactly the same process of obfuscation as the Israelites, and the evidence for this lies in the terminology that is used. While most classical interpretations will still maintain that the Phoenicians were named after the word *phoinikhon* πηοινικηον, referring to the colour purple, the biblical Concordance does not agree with this analysis at all and uses the Minoan/Greek term *porphura* πορφυρα for 'purple' instead.

So if the term *phoinkhon* was not readily used for a colour, from where did the Phoenicians derive their common Greek title? In fact, the Concordance refers to Phoenicia as Phoinike φοινικη, or the 'Land of Date-Palms'. So the Phoenicians were actually named after the Greek term for a date-palm, which was called a *phoinix* φοινιξ. So it would seem that the fabulous Phoenix-bird was closely related to the date-palm in both the Egyptian and the Greek languages. But this was probably not any old date-palm symbolism. As has already been explained, this is likely to have been a reference to the two 'palm fronds' (or wings) that were placed over the entrance-way to all the temples in Egypt, in an image of the flying Sun-disk of Ra. So, it would seem that the Phoenicians were named after the Sun-god Ra, but they used the covert symbology of the palm frond to display this, just as the Riga synagogue does to this day.

This same symbolism is also probably the origin of the Christian Palm Sunday; a festival which is supposed to celebrate Jesus entering Jerusalem on a donkey and palm fronds being strewn in front of him by the faithful. So, Jesus was just about to be crucified and 'resurrected' (reborn) and the people of Jerusalem are said to be spreading *phoenix* fronds (palm fronds) in front of him, and yet nobody within the establishment bothers to mention the obvious symbolism. Theologians will not mention the fact that Jesus was being overtly identified with the self-regenerating Phoenix in these verses, but presumably this is because the authorities do not wish to admit to the more 'pagan' elements that lie behind classical Christianity. Instead, it is sometimes said that palm fronds were used in this manner because the palm was a symbol of victory; but why would a humble palm frond be a symbol of victory? The simplest answer is that the palm frond was also a symbol of the almighty Ra, who led armies to victory in battle. Accordingly, the Christian palm frond festival is celebrated on Palm Sunday, the day of the Sun.

However, the humble palm frond has another epigraphic twist that connects the Phoenicians with the Hyksos-Israelites, and thus with the collapsing Amarna empire. The Phoenicians rose to power in the eleventh century BC, when the Hyksos-Israelites were re-establishing their dominance in Egypt under the leadership of the twenty-first dynasty pharaohs, which included Pharaoh Psusennes II. The wife of Psusennes II was a lady called Maakare MuTamhat, who has already been equated with the biblical Queen Maakhah Tamar in the book *Solomon*. This queen was deified after her death and became a tremendously influential figure of respect and worship, much as the Virgin Mary has achieved within the Catholic world today. However, an alternative Hebrew name for the date-palm is *tamar* תמר, and so through their title the Phoenicians may also have been paying their respects to the great mother-goddess of the Hyksos-Israelites.

At the end of the book *Solomon*, it was argued that Tanis in the Nile Delta, the newly established capital city of Psusennes II, may have been called the 'City of Palms'. This may be true for several reasons. Firstly, since Queen Maakhah Tamar resided in this city, its name would have been (in the Hebrew) the City of Tamar עיר תמר, which actually means the City of Palms. Secondly, the entire temple complex at Tanis is comprised solely of the most beautifully carved, pink-granite date-palm columns imaginable. Thirdly, it is mentioned in the Bible that the Israelites were driven out of the City of Palms for a period of eighteen years, an event that appears to coincide with the aggressive campaigns of Ramesses II (Ramesses the Great), who did indeed take control of Avaris and the Nile Delta lands for a while.

But that is not the whole story, for the city of Tanis may have had an alternative name in another language. The Hyksos-Israelites had been unceremoniously kicked out of Avaris in the Nile Delta several centuries before the reign of Psusennes II (on the first exodus, *circa* 1580 BC). However, Pharaoh Psusennes was now in the process of building a new capital city further north than Avaris, a city which we know today as Tanis. This city was rising, Phoenix-like, out of the sands of the Delta, and Psusennes II was physically using building materials from the abandoned city of Avaris to construct his new capital city. The comparison between the Phoenix myth and the founding of the new city of Tanis upon the ashes of the old city, could not be more fitting.

This comparison is greatly reinforced when it is recalled that the temples in the new city of Tanis were made from hundreds of finely carved, pink-granite date-palm columns taken from Avaris, and in the Phoenicio-

Greek languages the date-palm is known as a *phoinix* φοινιξ. Thus the city became known as Phoenix (Phoinike Φοινικη), or the City of the Date-Palms, as has been suggested. This convenient synergy – between the Phoenix-like rising of a new city that was made from the ashes of its old self, and those ashes comprising *phoenix*-shaped (palm-shaped) granite columns – is striking to say the least.

What this may imply is that the Greek name for the Phoenician people may have been derived from this very city. When the reborn City of Palms (Tanis) rose majestically from the sands, the Phoenicio-Canaanite observers in the Levant may have made the obvious link between the palms and the mythology of the fabulous Phoenix bird rising from its own ashes. Thus the Egyptian *bennu* became known as the Phoenicio-Greek Phoenix. There is only one problem with this scenario, and that is the troubling fact that this would make the Phoenician people more closely linked (or originally linked) to Tanis and the Nile Delta than to the cities of Palestine and the Levantine coast.

Now this might have been a huge and immovable stumbling block, were it not for the fact that a very strong argument has already been put forward in the book *Solomon*, that the original city of Jerusalem was actually located at Tanis. While that theory was put forward quite tentatively in the first instance, more and more evidence keeps turning up to support that original idea. Here again there is further independent evidence, from the history of the Phoenicians, to suggest that the Nile Delta was the most important biblical location from the time of the Judges all the way through to the era of Nebuchadnezzar.

Ashtoreth

That the Phoenicians may have had links to the Hyksos-Israelites is hardly surprising. They sprang from the same geographical location as many of the Hyksos-Israelites, and they worshipped the same gods. Although there were strong movements against polytheism within Judaic culture, Baal was still worshipped throughout the Levant and by the Phoenicians. The scale of the undercurrent of polytheism within Judaism can be glimpsed in this biblical quote from Kings:

> And the high places that were before Jerusalem, which were on the right hand
> of the mount of corruption, which Solomon the king of Israel had builded for
> <u>Ashtoreth</u> the abomination of the <u>Zidonians (Phoenicians)</u>, and for Chemosh
> the abomination of the Moabites, and for Milcom the abomination of the
> children of Ammon, did the king defile.[19]

Here are three 'pagan' gods and goddesses whom King Solomon had built temples for; a list that includes Ashtoreth, which is the biblical spelling for the Phoenician mother-goddess Astarte. This is being made clear in the quote above because the temple of Astarte was made for the Zidonians, the inhabitants of the Levantine city of Sidon, who were also called the Phoenicians. But the gods of the Phoenicians were not only the same as the gods of the Hyksos-Israelites, they were, of course, also the same as the traditional Egyptian gods. Astarte is only a Phoenician version of the Egyptian Ast (Est) or Isis: the mother-goddess of fertility and the wife of Asar (Esar or Osiris).

It is also likely that the cult of Isis was present within the Minoan empire. During the excavations of Knossos, a deliberately broken and carefully interred figurine of a goddess was discovered in the produce-storage areas. These finely crafted goddess figures are distinctively bare-breasted and cloaked with the winding coils of a serpent. Because of her attire, this goddess quickly became known as the snake-goddess, and there was much speculation as to whether the prominent snake signified duplicity as in the biblical Eve or perhaps the wrath of a Seth-like deity.

However, if the direct links between Keftu (Crete) and Egypt were more readily accepted, it would seem much more likely that the snake-goddess is actually a depiction of Renenutet, or the goddess Isis in the form of a snake. Since I have already demonstrated, in the book *Solomon*, the close links between Isis and the bare-breasted symbology of the God's Wife, these figurines depict

Fig 31. The Minoan snake goddess and the Phoenician Tanit.

Isis in every detail.

In her serpent guise, Isis is said to represent youth, fecundity and, more importantly, the fertility of the harvest. It is thought that these two Minoan figurines were deliberately buried during civil disturbances in Knossos following the Thera eruption and the associated failure of Minoan agriculture. With Renenutet-Isis being the goddess of the harvest, who had probably failed to do her duty for several seasons, it is not surprising that they were broken and buried in the now empty Knossan food magazines.

Although Renenutet-Isis had failed the people of Keftu (Crete), there were many nations around the Mediterranean who still revered her. Not surprisingly, one of those nations was the Phoenicians, who are likely to have been the descendents of the Minoans, as we have already seen. However, perhaps due to her abject failure to ensure the harvest in Knossos, the Phoenician Isis had now become a stylised figurine known as Tanit. But despite the priestly obfuscation, it is abundantly clear that the Phoenicians were still venerating the Minoan snake goddess, who was a manifestation of Renenutet-Isis.

Such was the enduring status and influence of the cult of Isis, that at the start of the first millennium AD even the Christian religion could not suppress her; and so Isis was adopted and represented in the Christian world by the ubiquitous imagery of the Madonna and Child. Moreover, she is also represented by the celebration of Christian Easter [Ast-er]. The primary fertility symbol of Ast (Isis) was the egg, as can be seen from the spelling of her name, and so the primary symbol of Easter has always been the Easter-egg. Christianity has long dodged tricky questions by upstart youngsters about where in the Bible the Easter-egg symbolism came from, and since eggs are not mentioned anywhere within the New Testament (apart from a comparison with a scorpion) the priesthood have sought solace in fairy-tales about not being able to eat eggs during Lent and other such nonsense. The truth is infinitely more believable: Easter is the festival of Ast or Est (Isis-Astarte) and it celebrates the spring equinox and the springtime generation of new life – which is symbolised in Pharaoh Akhenaton's Hymn to the Aton by the hatching of an egg.

This egg symbology was also important in Minoan theology. One of the enduring mysteries of Minoan culture is the beds of smooth beach-pebbles that adorn their ritual centers. When discussing the Theran-Minoan artwork in Avaris, it is said that:

> Other fragments (of the frescoes) depict the ground in terms of pebbles or gravel, a characteristic of Minoan art ... and the so-called 'Easter-egg' pebbles, which are very much a Minoan iconographic form. [20]

The Easter-egg pebble is not only classically Minoan, its precise symbolism is unknown. However, in the light of Phoenician worship of Astarte (Ast or Isis), and the latter's close association with the Easter-egg, the symbolism of these beds of 'eggs' becomes more obvious; especially since Christians still give decorated eggs each Easter, presumably as a gift to or from the gods. Finally, it would seem that some of the Phoenicians also worshipped Aton (Adon), the one and only god of Akhenaton:

> The name 'Adon' appears in a number of Phoenician inscriptions in Cyprus, including one from Idalion.[22]

The quote is actually referring to Adhon, the Judaic god. However, Adhon is not just the name of the Judaic god it is also the title of Akhenaton's new god of Egypt, the Aton 〔⌒☉〕. This deity and his name was not only taken and adapted by the Hyksos-Israelites into their all-powerful god, it was also taken by the Greeks and turned into the god Adonis; where only the Aton's regenerative properties were retained.

Here we might also glimpse the reason for the Phoenicians adopting the palm imagery for the Sun-god Ra. The reforms of Akhenaton had expunged all the other gods and idols from Egypt, and his people were expected to worship only the one hidden god (Aton) through Akhenaton himself. This meant that all the images of the gods were erased, and that included the flying Sun-disk too. If a core of early Phoenicians had been influenced by Akhenaton's religious reforms, it would have been expedient to replace the flying Sun-disk with the flying scroll or even with two palm fronds – the *phoinikhon* or *phoenix*. In the book *King Jesus*, we shall also look at the Egypto-Parthian people of Palmyra, Syria, who similarly replaced the traditional Egyptian flying Sun-disk symbol; but in this case the alternative imagery was an eagle with outstretched wings.

Bronze Age boats

Aye-Gaythelos and Scota would have required a large fleet for their great exodus out of Lower Egypt and may have been forced to employ the services of a third party. Both the Minoans and the later Phoenicians were great maritime nations in this region, but what type of vessels would they have had at their disposal during this early era? It is known that the Minoans had seaworthy boats in this era as they are mentioned in several texts. However, their precise method of construction was not known until quite recently, since no plans or records of their construction technique have ever been discovered.

Because of this lack of data, early reconstructions were based on guesswork and a few frescos from the ancient city of Akrotiri, located on Thera. A replica boat has been assembled in Heraklion, but it has been assumed here that the design was lightweight, with the majority of the hull being cloth stretched over a wooden frame. While this might be fine for inshore sailing, I am not convinced that this design would be strong enough to withstand the long journeys that we know were made to Greece and Egypt. [23]

A more likely alternative is that the Minoans were using the traditional sewn-plank boat, of which the Giza pyramid boat is the finest surviving example. In this type of construction, massive planks of wood are closely fitted together to form the shape of the hull, and then they are sewn together using withies or ropes. Once the hull is formed, some internal ribbing can be added for additional strength. But, unlike in a modern clinker-built boat, the main strength in the Giza boat – which was built at least 4,500 years ago – is formed by the hull itself rather than the framing. The gaps between the planks would then require a lot of caulking to keep the hull watertight.

Although this is a primitive construction technique, the sheer size of the Giza boat, which is some 43 m long and 6 m wide, demonstrates that a large vessel can be made using these early techniques. All that would be required to make the Giza boat perfectly seaworthy is the addition of some gunwales or elevated sides, to keep out the larger swells of the Mediterranean. Since the next quote seems to indicate that these gunwales were a later addition to a boat, presumably a river boat could be transformed into a seagoing vessel with very little extra work.

At some point between the early dynasties of Egypt and the middle of the Minoan era, maritime construction techniques changed and improved. Although little written evidence is available, it is known that mortise and tenon joints replaced the earlier sewn-plank technique at some unknown time during this period. Perhaps the best description of this from antiquity is from Homer's *Odyssey*. This account says:

> (Odysseus) shaped the planks to fit one another and bored mortises in them all. Then he hammered the ship together with tenons and dowels ... he worked on, laying the decking planks and fastening them to the close set frames, then finished the ship with long gunwales. [24]

The *Odyssey* epic dates from about the twelfth century BC, which means that this 'hull first', mortise and tenon technique had probably evolved during the Egyptian eighteenth dynasty (c. 1580 - 1290 BC) , and lasted through to the Roman era. The technique seems to have been adopted by many nations and used all across the eastern Mediterranean, until it was eventually supplanted by the 'frame first' technique.

In Odysseus' 'hull first' technique, the planks that formed the hull were placed adjacent to each other, and joined together by a line of mortise holes along the edges of the planks and short tenon rods that completed the joint. The hull of the boat was built up in this fashion, and only when it was complete were some internal frames added for extra rigidity. The mortise and tenon joints, together with the frames or ribs, were all held in place with dowels (wooden nails).

Not to scale

Confirmation that Homer was correct in his description was found in the Kyrenia ship, which was discovered off the coast of Cyprus in 1967. This ship dates from the much later fourth century BC, but still used the techniques described in the *Odyssey*. However, in following this ancient construction technique, the boat ended up with a total of about 8,000 mortise and tenon joints throughout its hull, which demonstrates how labour-intensive this design was. Nevertheless, a reconstruction of the Kyrenia boat, made in 1985, showed that the design made an eminently seaworthy craft which required very little in the way of caulking and achieved a remarkable speed of 9 kts with a favourable breeze. A $^1/_5$ scale model of the Kyrenia boat was also made by Coventry Boat-builders in Britain, and is now located in the Manchester Museum. [25]

Although Odysseus was a Greek hero, it is known that

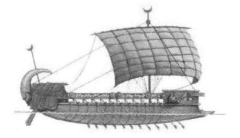

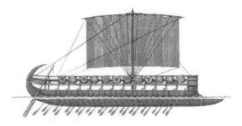

Fig 35. The evolution of the trireme.
a. Early Egyptian 2500 BC
b. Minoan 1500 BC
c. Phoenician 600 BC
d. Roman 100 BC

he travelled to the prime Minoan base of Crete. Had this technology been available to the Greeks, it would certainly have been available to the Minoans (or *vice versa*), who would immediately have noted any new methodologies and techniques being used. However, the original date for the *Iliad* and *Odyssey* is said to be around the twelfth or eleventh century BC, so a question-mark still hangs over the type of vessels used on the voyages of Aye-Gaythelos and Scota, which would have been in about 1320 BC. Had these vessels used the sewn-plank technique or a mortise and tenon construction?

The answer to this question was finally discovered in 1984, with the uncovering of the Uluburun wreck just off the southern coast of Turkey. There, over a period of ten years, a remarkable Bronze Age ship was slowly uncovered that still contained its complete cargo. The sheer wealth of this cargo was astounding, and it led the archaeologists on site to declare that this was a royal cargo. The most notable artifacts were the raw materials, which were cast into ingots, with some ten tons of copper, a tonne of tin and a ton of coloured glass being discovered. Since copper and tin were required for the manufacture of bronze, and the latter was a very useful and very expensive material in this era, this cargo must have represented a king's ransom. In fact, this is just the sort of cargo that Aye-Gaythelos would have needed for his first trip (or exile) to Greece – raw materials for establishing a new colony in Argos.

So, was this wreck anything to do with Aye-Gaythelos and his many exiles and travels? Well, we are never going to find a letter penned by Aye on board, as written confirmation, but the other evidence that was uncovered was interesting nonetheless. Firstly, this ship was dated by dendrochronology to 1306 BC (+/- 25 yrs), a date that fits Aye-Gaythelos' exoduses to Greece and Spain (c. 1320-1330 BC) rather well. This date has been disputed recently, but it is a fact that the only definitively datable artifact found on the wreck was a gold scarab beetle that was inscribed with the cartouche of Queen Nefertiti. While this artifact could have been a family heirloom, still being carried around in later generations, the chances are that this final cargo was being transported during, or shortly after, Nefertiti's reign. Thus the presence of this scarab links the cargo with the Amarna dynasty and also with the Amarna era.

Secondly, there is the sheer variety of the cargo on this vessel. In addition to the raw materials, there were oils, incense, musical instruments, ostrich eggs, bowls, cups, ceramics, lamps, thousands of beads, trinkets, cosmetics, jewelery, ivory, fishing nets and fishing equipment, hooks, harpoons, axes, saws, chisels, adzes, spears, arrows, and swords etc. Either the intention of this voyage was to trade anything and everything possible, or this was instead a cargo that contained everything that a new colony in a foreign land would need for the next decade or so. So the date, the cargo, the link with Amarna and the location of the wreck all favour an association with

Aye-Gaythelos.

Finally, the method of this boat's construction should also be mentioned. Although the Uluburun ship had largely rotted away, it was established that she was of the 'hull first' construction technique with mortise and tenon joints – just as Odysseus' and the much later Kyrenia ships were. The only thing that was not determinable was the ship's origins – from the cargo discovered she could have been Mycenaean, Minoan, Canaanite (proto-Phoenician) or Egyptian.

The boat illustrations in fig 35 show the progression in technology from the Giza boat through to the Roman trireme. Note that the early Minoan boat has much higher gunwales than the Giza boat, to allow for the larger swells of the Mediterranean. The next vessel is perhaps more accurately termed as a bireme, rather than a trireme, as it has two banks of oars. The third illustration is of the better known trireme with three banks of oars. However, since descriptions of these vessels go up to five banks (a quinquereme), it has been suggested that this number may be related more to the number of men per oar rather than the number of banks of oars. Since no remains of a trireme have been discovered, and the available images on pottery and in inscriptions are confusing, argument still rages as to how the oars were arranged.

Note also the high prows on all of these boats, which demonstrates that no sensible designer would send a boat to sea with a low prow that would easily ship water. The bireme and trireme prows were subsequently modified in later eras to permit the offensive ramming of enemy ships, but they still maintain a seaworthy high prow.

Ferriby

The options for the boats that formed Aye-Gaythelos' fleet are the Egyptian sewn-boats or the later Mycenaean mortise and tenon boats. But if Aye-Gaythelos had used such vessels to sail to Spain, and his descendants then further migrated to Ireland, some of this technology would surely have been spread throughout the greater British Islands. Unfortunately, the museum exhibits at Newgrange in Ireland do not support this suggestion, for the boat technology displayed there consists of a coracle – a simple animal-skinned stick-and-string tub.

However, the same museum exhibit then goes on to say that thousands of tonnes of quartz were brought from the Wicklow Mountains, which lie to the south of Dublin, up to Newgrange; a distance of about 90 km or so. It is highly unlikely that a coracle could have been taken out onto the Irish Sea loaded with quartz without being swamped; so it is highly likely that a more seaworthy vessel was available when this henge was constructed, or when any additions to this henge were made. So there must be a gap in the maritime archaeological record of Ireland. Since wood is highly perishable, this is not so surprising, and so most of the evidence for better transport vessels has long since deteriorated and faded away.

But not all of the evidence has disappeared; it is just a matter of striking a lucky find in the anaerobic muds of the major river estuaries around the greater British Isles. In recent years there have been two major chance discoveries of Bronze Age boats in Britain, and these are the Ferriby boats at Hull and the larger Dover boat from Kent.

The first of the Ferriby boats was discovered by Ted Wright in 1931, on the north shore of the river Humber, England. The course of this river had altered slightly in the early part of the last century, and had begun to scour silts and muds that had been laid down thousands of years ago. Encouraged by a local archaeologist, two teenagers began a 'shore watch' to see what successive tides uncovered. They were suitably rewarded for their diligence, as the boats that they eventually found were one of the major archaeological discoveries of the twentieth century.

The first of the boats uncovered was formed from three planks of oak. There was a long center-plank and two side-planks, which were bound together with yew withies to form the bottom section of the boat. When the full structure was exposed, it was found to be 13 m long and nearly 2 m wide, giving it a reasonable load capacity. The sides of the boat were missing, as they may have been deliberately removed for recycling onto a new vessel, which is disappointing as the original layout of the boat now becomes a matter of conjecture. Unfortunately, the excavation of the site was a bit of a shambles and the boats were largely destroyed. The few remains that have been salvaged from the site are not on show at present, which is again quite disappointing.

The presumed archaeological era for these three craft was deduced to be in the Bronze Age, because of a bronze adze blade discovered in the same strata; a blade that closely matched the cutting marks on the boats themselves. However, it was deemed that this type of construction was far too advanced for the Early Bronze Age, and so they were consigned to the Middle Bronze Age, or about 1300 BC. Eager to get a scientific date for the boats, the new technique of carbon-dating was employed in 1951, and this gave a much later date than expected, with a range of 750 - 150 BC being determined. Further testing in 1958 pushed this date back to around 1300 BC, which seemed more archaeologically acceptable.

These tests were both conducted while carbon-dating was in its infancy, and so more testing was carried out in the 1980s, and these tests rendered dates of 1890-1700 BC and 1930-1750 BC for the two main boats. These dates were much earlier than expected and present distinct archaeological problems, for the construction technology of these boats appears to be far too advanced for this date.

However, one does have to wonder about the accuracy achievable for carbon-14 testing in such circumstances. The wood of these boats had been soaked in the Humber muds for over 3,000 years, and when they were discovered the wood had the consistency of soft butter, which is why their excavation was so difficult. In other words, the wood was nearly 80% contaminant and only 20% original material; so in trying to establish a date for these boats, are we dating original wood or the absorbed contaminant? Dating such a find must be a bit like weighing a large, wet bathroom sponge, and agreeing that the sponge itself weighs one kilo. Similarly, dendrochronology was not possible on these remains; not simply because the wood was in such a poor condition, but also because the planks that made up the hull were so thin. If there are not enough growth-rings visible, then dating by dendrochronology becomes impossible.

Dover

The same was true of the Dover boat, which was discovered during the construction of a pedestrian underpass in 1992. This time, the boat was successfully removed and conserved by the more radical technique of cutting it up into sections, and it is now on show in the Dover Museum. The construction technique of the Dover boat was almost exactly the same as the Ferriby boats, except that on this occasion two keel-planks were used instead of one, making the boat much wider. The Dover boat was a fortuitous and important discovery, because it demonstrates that this exact same design was in use across much of Britain during the Bronze Age. Of course, it is always possible that the two vessels were manufactured in the same location and exported around the country, but at the very least this remarkable and advanced sewn-plank design must have been a familiar feature in many British coastal Bronze Age communities.

Not all of the Dover boat was recovered from the site, as some of the boat continued under neighbouring shops, and so a debate still rages as to exactly how long this vessel really was. The favoured solution is that it was not much longer than the 9 m that was recovered, and had a truncated back-end, with what is known as a transom-plank across the back. This, it is said, would make the boat more rigid and more seaworthy. An alternative design is for a symmetric, tapered shape to form the back-end immediately after the recovered sections, which would result in a vessel some 13 m long. This is also said to be a practical design, but less seaworthy than the first option.

The outside contender in this list of options is that only half of the boat was recovered, and so its full length would have been an impressive 18 m.

The problem that the archaeologists have in deciding and reconstructing the probable design of the boat is that the longer the boat gets, the less structurally sound it becomes. The design of the boat, as it is presented to archaeologists, looks more like an estuary cruiser than a seagoing vessel; and if this type of low-sided vessel were too long, it would flex in rough seas and fall apart. However, there are a few points that may favour the longer option.

Firstly, if the 2.5 m wide Dover boat had been constructed to the full 18 m length, it would have had almost exactly the same length to breadth ratio as the larger of the Ferriby boats; which had a 13 m length and a 1.7 m beam. This would make it appear as if the two boats came out of the same boat-yard. If the Dover boat was designed to be rowed, as is highly likely, the designer would want to make it as long as possible; both to cram in as many oarsmen as possible per tonne of boat, and also because a long, thin craft – like all modern racing rowing boats – goes much faster through the water. In other words, there would be evolutionary pressures that would push the design to its absolute limits in length.

In addition, the longitudinal strength of the boat lies not simply in its length, but also in the strength of the planks' joints and the depth of the boat's sides. The current perception, that the boat is a weak design, is based upon the notion that these boats looked like low-sided river punts; but if they had taller sides, like a Viking longboat, they would be much more rigid, longitudinally. Although their construction technique was more advanced than the Dover boat, it is known that the Vikings were able to make equally long and narrow boats, which were more than capable of withstanding the punishing and unpredictable North Sea. The Imme Gram, for instance, is a reconstruction of a longboat that was excavated at Ladby, Denmark, and she measures 21 m by 3m. Likewise, the Athenians also made their trireme war vessels as long and as slim as possible, to make them fast and deadly. The reconstructed trireme called Olympias had a total length of 37 m and a breadth of 5m, giving exactly the same length to breadth ratio as the longest option for the Dover boat. The various length to breadth ratios for these different boats are as follows, and the evidence would seem to indicate that the Dover boat could easily have been constructed to the full 18 meters.

Boat	Length (m)	Width (m)	Ratio
Imme Gram	21	3	7.0 : 1
Olympias	37	5	7.4 : 1
Ferriby	13	1.7	7.6 : 1
Dover	18	2.5	7.2 : 1

Was the Dover boat originally 18 m in length? The keel-planks so far recovered on the Dover boat were created from single lengths of hewn logs, and so the question remains as to whether there were any new sections added and jointed down the length of the hull to increase the length. One of the Ferriby boats did have a keel-plank formed from two jointed sections, so this was a possible solution to increasing the Dover boat's length. However, it would be inadvisable to have the keel- and side-planks all jointed in the same place amidships, as this would weaken the vessel considerably; if there were joints in these planks, they would need have been staggered, and all presumably towards the aft end of the boat. However, these Bronze Age shipwrights would have had a much better selection of trees to choose from than we have nowadays, and so it is just about possible that a straight plank could have been taken from an oak log that was 18 m in length. So, the keel-planks may have just about been created in one piece, and the length of the boat thus determined by the maximum height of the oak tree.

The other question, in terms of the vessel's rigidity and strength, is exactly how high did the sides of the Dover boat go? Again, we are working in the dark here because the sides of the boat have been removed in antiquity. Since this is the same fate as that of the Ferriby boats, one presumes that this was a common procedure – perhaps the bottom of the boat rotted before the sides, and so the sides were removed and reused on a new vessel. Had there been two or more side-planks, which are now missing, this would have made the entire structure more rigid and more seaworthy. The current reconstructions of the boat have a single side-plank added, resulting in low sides that look fine for river use, but are hardly suitable for cross-channel services.

However, it is a fact that the Athenian trireme, Olympias, also had a high length to depth ratio for its hull, as it appears to show a design using a 16:1 ratio. Since Lloyd's of London's nineteenth century limit for this ratio was 10:1, the shipyard building Olympias was skeptical that she would be strong enough not to break in half during a large swell (which is known as hogging – the boat bending in the middle like a hog's back). However, it was pointed out that with the hull-planks of the Minoan and Greek designs being pinned together, as well as some internal ribbing being in place, the ancient hull may actually be stronger than the later frame-only vessels. Accordingly, Olympias was built with the original 16:1 length to depth ratio, and the structure has proved to be seaworthy in all the conditions she has met thus far. If this same ratio were adopted for the Dover boat, the hull would only need to be 1.1 m in depth (from the top of the gunwale to the bottom of the keel). In which case, only two side-planks would need to be added to the hull section that has been found in order to turn this into a seagoing vessel.

For really heavy weather, the Minoans added curtains of cloth or reeds to the gunwales to increase their height, and so deflect the spray without adding to the weight of the vessel. [26]

Another technique, which was used to strengthen these boats longitudinally, was the *hypozomata*, a tensioned rope that ran from bow to stern over a pillar in the center of the boat. This acted like the cables in a stayed suspension bridge, and prevented the ends of the boat from sagging (hogging) in a large swell. This technique was certainly in use during the Greek era, but the design is much older than this as it is known that even the Egyptian reed boats utilised a similar type of device. This became all-too evident to Thor Heyerdahl during his pioneering voyage on a traditional reed boat named Ra I, from Egypt to America in 1969. Drawings of these ancient Egyptian reed boats clearly showed a rope that led from the high stern of the vessel to the center section, and so this rope was installed as per the original design. However, having tripped over this rope countless times during the voyage, it was decided that it should be done away with – even though the rope was obviously under tension. Having cut the rope, the stern of the vessel promptly, but gracefully, slid below the waterline. There is no evidence that the Dover boat had such a tension cable, but there are plenty of possible attachment points at the front of the boat had they been in use in British vessels.

The other crucial aspect of the sewn-boats at Ferriby and Dover, which may have a bearing on their original design, is their origin. Were these indigenous designs, which had evolved and been improved in total isolation within the British Isles over centuries or millennia, or was this construction technique an import from the Mediterranean? The earliest sewn-boat designs are from ancient Egypt, as has been explained, and although similarities between the British and Egyptian sewn-boats are sometimes acknowledged in passing, the current thinking is that:

> Boats of Ferriby type have no known ancestors or descendants but are obviously of a long lineage. [27]

In other words, these Egyptian and British boat designs evolved completely independently of each other. But here are two very similar construction techniques, both involving sewn-planks and internal ribbing, and the only real thing that separates them is geography. Although there are differences between the massive sewn-boat that was discovered beside the Great Pyramid (at Giza) and the Bronze Age British boats, there are a number of similarities too. Both boats were made from rough-hewn planks that were sewn together with rope; both used flat keel-planks, rather than a true keel; both used a variety of grooved edges to the planks to aid their jointing and sealing; both used internal ribs; both used thwarts, or cross-benches; and both were constructed in the Bronze Age. Is it so improbable that the Egyptian technology could have reached Bronze Age Britain, that this option should be dismissed so lightly?

The one major difference between these vessels is the cleats and bracing-struts (dowels) that run across the keel-planks of the British boats, but this additional cross-bracing may simply be an adaptation to rougher northern seas. Both the Ferriby and the Dover boats used short struts that were placed through cleats on the bottom of the boat. Although this might look like a primitive technique, in comparison with the sleeker Egyptian hull, since each cleat is an integral part of the keel-planks, this method is actually much stronger than using additional sewn ribs. This strengthening of the keel would be especially useful when coming ashore onto rocky ground, which could split an unbraced plank. Conversely, it is unlikely that the bottom of the Giza boat had to deal with anything other than soft silts and sands.

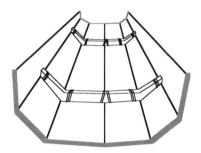
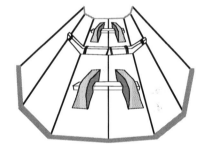

Fig 36.   Ribs in the Giza boat   *Cross-bracing in the Dover boat.*

The cleats along the bottom of these boats also give us a direct link with Irish construction technology. Although no Irish sewn-boats have been discovered thus far, one of the major discoveries of Irish Bronze Age technology was an ancient wagon-wheel. Rather than using spokes, the wheel was formed from large planks of wood; and to link these together in a strong enough fashion, the wheelwright has used cleats and dowels in exactly the same fashion as the Ferriby and Dover boats. Thus it is certain that the technology and techniques required to make a sewn-boat were available in Ireland.

It has to be said that the British sewn-boats were more roughly made than the Giza boat, but this should not be so surprising. The economy of Egypt was far stronger than that of Bronze Age Britain, and so the latter could not afford the luxury of finishing off every detail to perfection. Besides, the

Dover boat is likely to have been a commercial boat, whereas the Giza boat was probably ceremonial – a no-expense-spared government enterprise.

It is worth noting again that sewn-boat technology in Britain has no known ancestry, and the technique was not used by all the communities in Britain. This fact was dramatically illustrated by a more recent find in the Humber river. It would seem that around 450 BC, nearly 1,000 years after the Ferriby boats were abandoned on the north shore of the Humber estuary, another type of craft was plying these same estuary waters. But this new vessel did not represent an improvement on the Ferriby design, nor an adaptation of it. This was no clinker-built, fully ribbed wonder-vessel with iron rivets and billowing sails – instead this was a dugout 'canoe'. Perhaps canoe is the wrong term here, for this single, hollowed-out tree-trunk was nearly 13 m long and weighed in at over six tonnes. This was the Hasholm boat, which was recovered from the Humber in 1984 and is still undergoing preservation in the Hull Museum. So why did the technology in this region regress so dramatically, from the stable, seaworthy, high-technology sewn-boats of Ferriby and Dover, to the rough-hewn hollowed-out log of Hasholm?

Fig 37. Bronze Age wagon-wheel, Dublin Museum.

One possibility might be that the sewn design was not indigenous to the people of this area, and when the designers moved on or died out, the technology went with them. It is known that any high technology in these early eras was tightly controlled by families or clans, and so the continuation of that technology was highly dependent on their survival or continued occupation. Even in the thirteenth century AD, the same kind of cartel was flourishing within the cutting-edge Venetian glass industry. Exclusive access to a new technology was a valuable commodity, and so everything was done to protect the industry and its lucrative income:

> However, it has been plausibly suggested that the move (to Murano in Venice) was made in order to isolate the master glassblowers and prevent their sharing their valuable glass-making know-how with foreigners. In fact, the glassblowers became virtual prisoners on Murano, insulated from any contacts who might divulge their production secrets to potential competitors abroad. [28]

The possibility exists that the sewn-boats in Hull and Dover were an imported design, suitably adapted to the rougher waters of the English Channel and North Sea, but their manufacture was based upon a few skilled artisans working in a limited number of locations. Other communities, either not blessed with living next to a sewn-boat yard or not being able to afford the enormous barter-cost to purchase one, had to make do with low-tech solutions for river navigation.

However, if this sewn-boat building technique did indeed come from Egypt, then we might just be able to make some alternative suggestions as to how these boats originally looked, and thus how they performed in the open sea. Take a look at the Ferriby boat design in the following plan-view diagram, where it will be seen that the keel-planks protrude a long way beyond the side-planks. It is thought that this protrusion represented a ramp at the front of the boat, a design that is again similar to a river punt. The additional side-planking would have met this extended and upturned keel-plank, and so only two more side-planks would be necessary to finish off the vessel.

This low-sided, flat-prowed design would be fine for river work, as the cargo could easily be dragged over the front of the boat, and there would be no problem with waves crashing over the bows and swamping the vessel. However, the discovery of the very similar Dover boat changes this perception completely. It is unlikely that the Dover boat was an estuary cruiser, as there are no large-sized estuaries in this region, and so it must have been a seagoing vessel; even if this was only a matter of hugging the coastline down towards Dorset. Indeed, shale from the Dorset region was found inside the Dover boat, and so it is likely that she had been at least this far down the coast.

But a wide, flat, punt-like prow is not very good in even the slightest of swells. The sea would batter the boat's wide, flat prow, slowing her progress, and the spray would pour over the prow and rapidly swamp the vessel. All in all, this kind of blunt-prowed, low-sided design would not be that sensible on the open waters of the English Channel. Even the dumbest of Bronze Age designers would have spotted the fact that his perfectly acceptable river-boat design was being rapidly swamped as the wave height grew. It would not take a great leap in imagination for this same designer to realise that a seagoing vessel required a higher bow and sides. In the aftermath of a single mishap in the open sea, the design could and would have been quickly changed.

The evidence from Minoan archaeology is that the boats being used in the Mediterranean in this era did have seaworthy high prows, and the Greek myths of Dannus [Aye-Gaythelos] confirm this view. In fact, it is said of the vessel that took Dannus to Argos (Greece) that:

> With Athene's help (Dannus) built a ship for himself and his daughters – the first two-prowed vessel that ever took to sea – and they sailed to Greece together... [29]

It is not entirely certain what is meant by a two-prowed vessel; perhaps Dannus had lashed two ships together to increase the load-carrying capacity for his voyage. But it would seem clear that one of the most prominent parts of a ship's construction was the prow, and this should have been evident to designers of every nation.

Hence, if one looks at the design of the Giza boat, it will be seen that the bow has been made to curve up substantially. A colour picture of this boat can be seen in the book *Tempest*. But the manner in which this has been achieved is interesting, as the following plan-view of the boat demonstrates. Here, it can be seen that the keel-planks on the Giza boat extend well beyond the initial few side-planks, just as they do on the Ferriby boat. But this extension was not so that a flat, stumpy prow could be made, it was so that a high, curving prow could be added to this extension. Note that the prow and stern sections of the Giza design are almost completely separate units, which were not a part of the primary structure, and they were simply attached to the keel-plank extensions. This would make the upturned bow quite weak and one wonders if they could stand a battering from reasonable-sized waves, but perhaps this was not a top priority for a vessel that cruised the Nile and rarely went to sea.

Now take this Giza design and apply it to the Ferriby boat's hull, and it will be seen that exactly the same can be achieved. Instead of the upturned end of the keel-plank representing the bow of the boat, it could instead have been the extended attachment point for a raised prow. In turn, the number of side-planks would then have to have been increased to mate with this new bow section, increasing the depth of the sides of the vessel as well. All in all, these two changes to the design would have made the boat far more seaworthy, and turned an estuary cruiser into a coastal trader.

The same may also be true of the Dover boat. Instead of the

protruding extension on the Ferriby boat, the keel-planks of the Dover boat form a recessed 'U' shape. Into this recess, it is thought there may have been a flat wooden board, making a flat, inclined bow that is again reminiscent of a modern river-punt. As before, this is not exactly a seaworthy design. However, given the large amount of reinforcing that is present around this recessed area, perhaps this was instead the attachment point for a tall bow section. Once again, this new design would have required further side-planking to meet up with this raised bow, and this would again greatly increase the seagoing capabilities of the vessel.

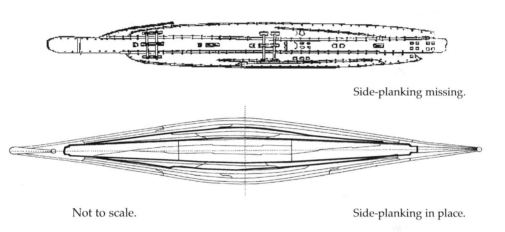

Side-planking missing.

Not to scale.   Side-planking in place.

Fig 38.   The Ferriby boat design (top) and the Giza boat (bottom). [30]

The rather flat bottom of the Dover boat, which is good for an estuary vessel that spends a lot of time sitting on the mud when the tide goes out, would now sport a more streamlined and pointed bow section. The boat would now be suitable for loading in the shallows of the estuary and also pushing through the moderate swell of the English Channel. The traditional view of the Dover boat never did make much sense, but with this small alteration, perhaps the designer was actually a Bronze Age genius. That this was the intended design can perhaps be deduced from the later experiences of Julius Caesar, when he fought his way through Gaul towards Britain in the 50s BC. Caesar, or his biographer, was a great observer of local customs and technologies during his many campaigns, and one of his descriptions was of the standard Breton seagoing vessel:

Their hulls were somewhat more flat-bottomed than those of our ships so that they may more easily approach shoal water and tidal flats. Their prows, however, were quite high, and their sterns too; well suited to the magnitude of the waves and storms. The ships were made completely from oak, very resilient to any forceful blow or rough treatment ... In an encounter with these ships the only advantage ours had was speed and the use of oars; in all other respects their ships were better suited to the character of the region and the force of its storms. To this was added, that whenever a storm began to rage and they ran before the wind, they both could weather the storm more easily and heave to securely in the shallows, and when left by the tide feared nothing from rocks and shelves: the risk of all which things was much to be dreaded by our ships. [32]

This is not a description of a British vessel as such, but one of the Veneti from Brittany, in northwest France. But, of course, the Bretons were substantially a Celtic nation who had very close cultural and trading links with greater Britain, as their name might suggest. However, in addition to Caesar's description, we have a similar description of a British seagoing vessel from the accounts of Strabo. His Geography was written just after Caesar's campaigns in Britain and some of the text may have been drawn from his accounts, but Strabo nevertheless includes some interesting additional observations:

Because of the great tidal variation, they make their ships flat-bottomed and beamy (wide), with high sterns and prows, and they use oak, of which they have an abundance. For this reason, they do not match up (mortise and tenon) joints in the planks but leave open seams which they caulk with tree-moss. [s33]

These two description match the design of the Ferriby and Dover boats rather well. The flat bottoms, the oak fabrication, the open seams and the moss caulking are all features of the Ferriby and Dover boats. Indeed, the similarity is so great, it is almost as if Strabo were standing in the Dover Museum and describing what he saw.

Of even more importance, perhaps, is the fact that both Caesar and Strabo describe the rationale that lay behind the designs of these boats. The flat bottoms were not designed so these boats could cruise up rivers, but rather so that they could beach as far up the tidal flats as possible. In the Mediterranean, which does not have high tidal variations, the tides do not present a great problem. But, as Julius Caesar mentions, the boats of Brittany could sail through estuary shallows without fear of being beached or toppling sideways on rocky outcrops. Caesar also discovered another problem with tides during his invasion of Britain in 55 BC, when his ships were caught out by a high tide and a storm, and were 'dashed to pieces and cast upon the shore'. Tides can be highly destructive and so coastal boats need to be dragged as far up the beach as is possible, which is what a flat bottom achieves.

Strabo also comments on the jointing technique used in the planking. His argument is not that the sewn-boat is more primitive than the mortise and tenon design, but that the oak planks precluded the use of mortise and tenon joints. The only reason I can suppose for this is that the oak planks may have been too hard to easily drill out the mortise holes. While this might be so, it may also be true that the plain butt-joint was a much quicker method of construction, and as long as the boat held together why bother with the more complex mortise and tenon joints? Certainly, the reconstructed section of the Dover boat seems to be adequately strong for its purpose.

While the sewn-boat may seem to be a rough and ready method of construction, it was not just the British shipbuilders who opted for this simpler technique. In 1497, the Portuguese explorer Vasco da Gama was sent out to discover a sea route through to India. After a long and eventful voyage he landed at Calicut in India, where he was coolly greeted by Arab merchants who were fearful of Portuguese competition in the valuable spice trade. However, the point of interest in this present discussion is that the Arab vessels all had sewn-plank hulls. Either the Arabs had not updated their shipbuilding techniques, or perhaps they too found the sewn design simpler and cheaper.

The last and most important point, which is made by both Julius Caesar and Strabo, is the shape of the Breton/British boat's prows. Each and every aspect of the Ferriby and Dover boats matches their descriptions of British boats except, of course, the orthodox interpretation of how the prow was formed. This is why I think that both of these British Bronze Age boats had separate, high prows, which were added onto the keel-planks rather than being an integral part of the keel. Why these ancient shipwrights should make the prow and stern separately I do not know, but the example of the Giza boat suggests that is exactly what they did. This separate prefabrication would also explain why these prows and sterns were missing from the Ferriby and Dover boats as, like the missing gunwales, they could be easily removed and reused on a new vessel.

Here, then, is the evidence that advanced Egyptian or Minoan shipbuilding techniques were available in greater Britain during the Middle Bronze Age period. While I suppose it is possible that there were parallel and independent advances in technology, which produced similar or identical boat-building techniques in Britain and the Eastern Mediterranean, I personally think that this is unlikely. The Hasholm dugout demonstrates that some tribes in Britain were still in the Stone Age, as far as shipbuilding was concerned, and yet others had progressed onto elaborate seagoing vessels. Indeed, the British tribes that had the superior technology preceded the Hasholm dugout by almost 1,000 years.

The simplest way of explaining this dichotomy is through technology transfer from one nation to another. But in this early era, and with such a complex industry as shipbuilding, it is more than likely that this transfer of technology also involved the transfer of significant numbers of artisans. The Dover boat would have required significant improvements in metallurgy, tool making, rope-making, caulking, transport and organisation, in addition to the overall design of the new vessel. If there was a significant transfer of artisans and technology from Egypt or Crete to Britain, during the fourteenth century BC, the chronicle of *Scotichronicon* would provide all the necessary explanations and reasons for this transfer.

Navetas, Talayots and Nuraghi

We now come back full circle to the Minoans, for there is evidence that links the Minoans directly to the adventures of Scota. Shortly after Aye-Gaythelos and his people landed in Spain and founded Brigantia, they supposedly went on an expedition to Mallorca, where it would seem that they founded another colony. But again we have to ask ourselves if this is historical fact or romantic mythology.

In the historical reality of the region, a new people did arrive in the Balearic Islands around the thirteenth or fourteenth centuries BC. We are pretty sure that they were immigrants from overseas because they built boat-shaped stone monuments called *navetas*. Whoever these new people were, they were quite industrious because, on Minorca and all of the other Balearic Islands, a number of ancient monuments were suddenly constructed.

The first of these structures that need to be researched are the halls of pillars. To the south of Mallorca, near the town of Santanyi, there is a large complex of Bronze Age monuments. Within this complex there are several large rooms that are not functional rooms, because the available floor-space is ruined by a large pillar. From the surviving (but smaller) Minorcan versions, it is clear that this pillar once held up a stone roof, but since the rooms themselves were not large enough to be practical, it was the pillar itself that must have been the most important element in this design. Similar pillar-rooms can be seen in the eastern Mediterranean, where they are said to be religious shrines of some kind. The other location to the east is, of course, the island of Crete and more specifically the Minoan empire that was based there. In my travels to Knossos, Phaestos, Tripodo, and in many other Minoan cities, I was able to confirm that special rooms were built which contained a single pillar (see plates 20 & 21 for an image of these pillars).

I have speculated in the book *Tempest* that these pillars were not simply phallic, but they may also have had metrological significance. It is known that the Egyptians and the subsequent Hyksos-Israelites were fascinated by metrology, the study of measurements, and that certain measurement systems were regarded as sacred. The god of modern Freemasons, a society that inherited many of these ancient Egyptian traditions, is known as the Great Architect and measurements and measurement systems are bound be sacred to an all-powerful architect. The pillars in Keftu (Crete) seem to have been constructed using the Egyptian Thoth cubit (Royal cubit) measurement system, and so their function may have been to venerate and preserve a standard of measure. They could also be phallic symbols, and when looked at in that light they do have similarities to the eastern (Indian) lingam.

Whatever their function, these halls of pillars at each end of the Mediterranean are quite obviously the same in every detail, bar one. It is clear that the technology being used in Crete was far in advance of that used in the Balearic Islands, but that is perhaps understandable. When Aye-Gaythelos landed in Iberia with his small proto-nation, they would have had to struggle for their very existence, without spending precious time and energy on religious monuments. They would also have lacked a toolmaking industry for many years, and may not have been able to carve the blocks as neatly as we see at Knossos. Nevertheless, the evidence seems clear – there is a physical and religious link between the Minoan empire and the budding empire in the Balearic Islands, and yet this is where the descendants of Scota and Aye-Gaythelos are reputed to have lived.

The second structures of interest in the Balearics are the truncated round towers, which are called *talayots* in the Balearic Islands and *nuraghi* on Sardinia. An entire chapter has already been written on these strange structures in the book *Jesus*, and this conclusively demonstrated that these towers were not intended as defensive structures, as archaeologists maintain. They are simply too numerous, too small and too vulnerable to defend a population. Their siting is not defensive either, for instead of being at the center of a conurbation, as a castle's keep would be, they are often situated at the more vulnerable extremes. This 'defensive structure' would be the first part of the citadel to fall, not the last. No, these towers are not defensive structures in any way, shape or form. Instead they are religious monuments once more – churches, temples or shrines, call them what you will.

Undoubtedly there is a phallic symbology involved here, and comparisons have already been made with the Egyptian Benben tower which once stood at Heliopolis. A local historian from Sardinia has suggested that the *nuraghi* towers there were originally taller and finished off with a conical roof structure, and an ancient model of a tower seems to confirm this. However, having reviewed the available evidence, I no longer think that this is possible for the similar *talayots* on Mallorca and Minorca. Although the majority of the *talayots* are now ruined, there are many of these towers that retain most of their structure. Looking at the remaining ruins, it is apparent that there is not enough fallen material to account for a taller structure or for a stone roof. If it is claimed that stone-robbers have been at work, then they must have been very careful to strip the tower down symmetrically, and not just attack one side. In addition, the upper surface on some of the virtually complete towers have suffered upper-surface erosion, whereas the underlying layers have obviously not; so it is certain that these *talayots (nuraghi)* have stood in this truncated form for a very long time. In fact, all the evidence points towards the round-towers on Mallorca being designed in this fashion from the very start.* So what, in this case, was their function?

One possibility was graphically suggested by the form of the Erismanzanu *nuraghi* on Sardinia. In modern times this round-tower has acquired an olive tree within the body of the tower, and this tree erupts out of the top of the tower in a rather pleasing fashion, as can be seen in the colour section of the book *Jesus*. Could the towers have been constructed to contain sacred trees? Certainly the towers could easily have had a small layer of earth at the bottom, and some in Mallorca have small conduits running through them that could have been used for watering the tree. The size of the tower looks right for this suggestion; the function appears logical; and we know that the cult of the sacred tree was widespread both in early Egypt and the subsequent culture of the Hyksos-Israelites. But although the idea had its merits there was no evidence for this proposal whatsoever, as any sacred tree in these towers would have long since died and decayed. Besides, any modern archaeologist is likely to have removed any remains of a tree and discarded it as a sign of the site's later abandonment.

Then, just as it seemed that the true function of these towers could never be discovered, a breakthrough was made in the city of Iraklion, Crete. There, in the museum, was a new display of the Minos Ring, which had recently been rediscovered. The ring has led a charmed life, for it was buried some 3,500 years ago, rediscovered in 1928, but then lost again. It spent the next seventy-odd years in the bottom of someone's drawer until it came to light again in 2002, when it went on display in the city's museum.

The Ring of Minos is a remarkable piece of workmanship. Crafted in gold, it is a finger-ring with an oval face upon which is engraved, in the

---

* Many of the *talayots* on Minorca are actually solid, rather than being empty cones. I rather think this is due to the Minorcan versions being made of rough boulders, rather than the cut blocks that were used on Mallorca. Without their infill of material, the Minorcan *talayots* would have quickly collapsed, as the one or two examples that were empty – like the smaller of the two *talayots* at Torello near the airport – clearly demonstrate.

most intricate detail, a scene that portrays the travels of a typical Minoan goddess – through air, land and sea. What this scene actually signifies is not fully understood; however, the main element that caught my eye was the truncated round-towers that were depicted on the ring. For out of the top of two of these towers there sprang trees, and these trees were clearly being attended to by special attendants. Indeed, one of these attendants is picking a fruit from one of the trees, which is clearly a significant event for a fertility mother-goddess and bears an obvious similarity with the story of the biblical Eve picking fruits from the sacred Tree of Knowledge.

Here, then, is the likely function of these round-towers. Within their protective shield there grew a sacred tree, and the implication from the Ring of Minos is that the tower was indeed a protective shield rather than an overgrown 'pot'. The tree on the left of the ring can be seen to be leaning against the side of the tower. This could be artistic licence, but it is also the exact form we would expect if the roots of the tree resided much lower down at the bottom of the tower.

The type of tree involved is open to speculation. The image on the Ring of Minos portrays a broad-leafed tree, which may be the persea or avocado. This tree was particularly sacred to Heliopolis, as it was upon this tree that the Phoenix sometimes perched. However, if the detail of the image

Fig 39.   Expanded view of the Ring of Minos.

can be regarded as accurate then this may not be the persea, as the leaf portrayed on the ring is too blunted and the fruit is in the wrong orientation (the stalk should be on the other end).

However, whatever the species of tree involved, the symbolic value of the tree is rather better understood. The sacred persea tree in Egypt was used to record the names of the pharaohs, and there is a marvellous representation of this to be found in the Temple of Karnak at Luxor, where Thoth is shown inscribing the cartouche of Seti I on the fruits of this tree. A colour picture of this can be found in the book *Eden*.

It would appear that the tree was recording the names of the royal family, so it was not just a sacred tree, it was a family tree; a record of the royal family's history. In addition, when a person dies their body normally decays and their soul can be taken up by the roots of a tree, so the tree absorbs the person's *ba* or soul. It was for this reason that the soul of a person was often regarded as residing within a tree. Clearly, if the fruits of a tree could contain a soul and simultaneously record the names of successive generations of the royal family, they would be very sacred indeed. Again, one can deduce elements of the Adam and Eve mythology within this symbolism.

Whatever the symbolic value of these trees and their fruit, it is a fact that here again we have a direct and unmistakable similarity between the Minoan empire and the new civilisations that were growing on the Balearic Islands, and also on Sardinia. Classical chronology places the beginnings of the Minoan empire some 500 - 700 years before the culture that suddenly blossomed on the Balearic Islands, and the Balearic Islands also have boat tombs that point towards an inward migration following a long voyage. So it would seem highly likely that it was the Minoan culture that travelled westwards, and not *visa versa*. If this is so, then we are looking for a history of a people who travelled westwards, from the eastern Mediterranean towards the Spanish coast, and in the history of Aye-Gaythelos and Scota we have just such a history.

Why look for any other explanation? We have the written history, handed down from generation to generation, and we have the equivalent physical evidence that confirms the story. Moreover, this semi-legendary history can be shown to be historically accurate, in regard to its terminology, numerology, chronology and nominology (ie: onomastics), and so it must have been based upon some kind of historical reality. Once more, the simplest solution to the cultural and archaeological evidence that we see around us, is that the chronicle of *Scotichronicon* is based upon true history. Aye-Gaythelos and his wife Ankhesenamun-Scota did travel to Spain to escape the political turmoil of late eighteenth dynasty Egypt.

Plate 1.
View from the
El Maestrat
mountains in
Catalonia, looking
across the Ebro
Delta.

Plate 2.
Satellite image of the
Ebro Delta. Courtesy
of the Earth Data
Analysis Center.
The ghostly
apparition is the land
of the Ebro Delta -
presumably the wet
paddy fields look
like the sea to the
satellite's camera.

Plate 3. Top.   A reconstruction of the Dover boat.
                 Dover Museum.

Plate 4 Center. The Dover boat. Dover Museum.

Plate 5. Lower.   Model of the Ferriby boat. Hull Museum.

Plate 6. Right. Bronze Age cartwheel employing the same
                  construction techniques. Dublin Museum.

Plate 7. Solid gold cape, discovered at Mold, Flintshire, UK. Thought to be Early Bronze Age and dating from 1600 BC. British Museum.

Plate 8. The Ring of Minos, from Minoan Crete. Dating is estimated to be about 1500 BC. Iraklion Museum.

Plates 9 & 10. Left. Two golden torqs from the Gorteenreagh hoard, Co Clare, Ireland. Possibly dating from 800 BC. Dublin Museum.

Plate 11. Right bottom. Ornate spiral torq from the Iron Age Snettisham hoard, UK. Probably dating from 75 BC. British Museum.

Plate 12. Reconstructions of Minoan Knossos in Crete.

Plate 13. Right. Helen of Troy, by Evelyn De Morgan.

Plate 14. Far right. Mary Magdalene, by Carlo Crivelli. Note that while the 'Virgin' Mary's traditional colours are blue and white, Mary Magdalene's are orange (red) and green.

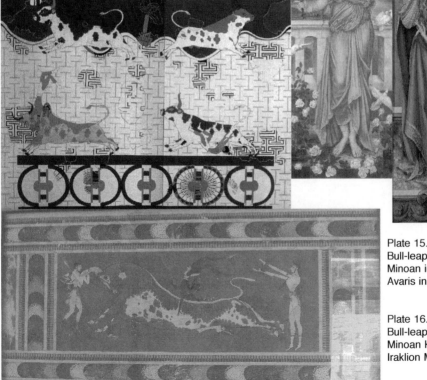

Plate 15. Lower left. Bull-leaping fresco, of Minoan inspiration, from Avaris in the Nile Delta.

Plate 16. Bottom left. Bull-leaping fresco from Minoan Knossos, Crete. Iraklion Museum.

Plate 19.   A truncated round-tower at Torello, Minorca.

Plate 17.   Top left.
The Mousa truncated round-tower (broch) on the Shetland Isles, Scotland.

Plate 18.   Middle left.
The Perets truncated round-tower, Santanyi, Mallorca. Both towers have raised doorways, and are situated in exposed and vulnerable positions.

Plate 20.   Top right.
Pillar room, Santanyi, Mallorca

Plate 21.   Middle right.
Pillar room, Phaestos, Crete.

Plate 22.
The Mound of Hostages; a part of the complex of tombs and henges at Tara, in the Boyne valley, Ireland.

Plate 23.
The truncated round-tower inside the Cahergall amphitheater, Ireland. Note the steps, picked out by the shadows, leading up to four levels of terraces. The photo does not show them very well, but each set of steps has a symmetric partner leading in the other direction, forming a 'V' shape.

Plate 24.   The Gallarus Ossuary near Dingle, Co Kerry, Ireland. This upturned boat design is identical to the navetas on Minorca, which demonstrates the close links that exist between these two cultures. The Scottish chronicles say that the descendants of Gaythelos and Scota travelled to Spain and Ireland, and so the mythology and the archaeology dovetail precisely.

Plate 25.   The Tudons Naveta, near Ciutadella, Minorca. Clearly, this design is the inspiration for the Irish navetas. The Scottish chronicles indicate that the Irish navetas would have been built one or two centuries after the Minorcan examples.

Plate 26. Top left.
The Rattoo round-tower, near Ballyduff, Co Kerry. The upper windows point to the cardinal points, and the doorway is raised above ground level.

Plate 27. Top right.
A traditional Celtic-Christian round-tower in Abernethy near Perth, Scotland.

Plate 28. Left.
Scota's grave, near Tralee, Co Kerry. Unfortunately, this is just a natural outcrop of rock and not a tomb of any kind.

Plate 29. Above.
North Molton necklace (top), containing lignite and faience beads from Egypt. Photo, Exeter Museum.
The similar Tara necklace (below), image finally received in early 2009. Photo, Dublin Museum.

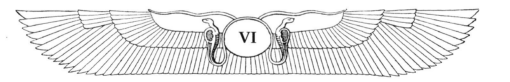

Evidence in Ireland & Scotland

Having landed in Ireland, these new immigrants from Iberia named their new homeland after their founding queen, Scota. And so the original name for Ireland was Scotia, as the following map confirms. This naming of a new land after a queen was not so unusual and it has occurred more than a few times in recent history. A later example occurred in about the sixth century BC, when the Babylonian king Nebuchadnezzar invaded both Judaea and lower Egypt. As is related in the book *Solomon*, a party of refugees from this invasion, under the command of Johanan and the guidance of the prophet Jeremiah, left the smouldering wreck of Jerusalem and went to the southern quarter of the Arabian peninsular. There, they set up a new nation that was called Saba, which was named after the long-since departed but greatly respected and deified Queen of Sheba (Saba).

Back in Ireland, an earlier queen was also conferring her name on a new nation. Although this association is sometimes disputed, it does seem likely that the original name for Ireland was Scotia, and that this title was derived from the name of the legendary exiled Egyptian queen who lived in Spain. Professor Watt, the translator of *Scotichronicon*, indicates that this royal name has been 'back engineered', and so John of Fordun or Walter Bower must have derived the queen's name from the Scottish nation, in order to weave their 'fictional' chronicle into the history of the land.

The evidence to demonstrate that this was not so is to be found in the other term that was applied to both Ireland and eventually Scotland: Hibernia, which is said to have been derived from Aye-Gaythelos and Scota's son, Hiber. Yet it is fairly certain that the ancient name for Spain,

Iberia, has the same epigraphic roots as Hibernia (and Hiber). But neither Fordun, Bower, nor any of the previous Scottish chroniclers could have 'back engineered' the original name for Spain into the history of Scotland, and so this name demonstrates a positive link between Spain and Ireland, and later Scotland.

Fig 42.   Map of Europe, by L Waddell 1929.

If there are known epigraphic links between Spain and Ireland there must have been a means of transference, and the obvious vehicle for this transference is clearly stated in the chronicle of Gaythelos and Scota. All we need to do is understand that this chronicle is more history than fiction. But if one name for a nation could have been transferred in this manner (Iberia-Hibernia), then why not two? Under the circumstances, the tradition of the name Scotia being derived from Queen Scota does not seem quite so fanciful.

If names can be transferred from one land to another, with the assistance of thousands of emigrants, then perhaps the same may be true for their customs and technology. If so, then further evidence for the *Scotichronicon* chronicle may be found in some of the traditions and archaeology of Ireland.

One of the enduring symbols of ancient Scotia (Ireland) is the frequent use of golden torqs, or necklaces, by the ancient Irish royalty. The Dublin Museum has a fine collection of these gold torqs, which all appear to have been made locally to a number of different designs. The majority of these torqs have been dated to the Iron Age, but since they were not discovered in clearly stratified locations, this date is based more upon guesswork than science. Similar torqs found on the British mainland, like the Snettisham hoard, are again said to date from the Iron Age. However, none of these have been discovered in reliably datable strata.

But where did the custom of wearing golden torqs ultimately come from? Examples of torqs appear in various locations all across northern Europe and similar designs in copper and bronze even turn up in the Baltic States. But the latter, especially, are quite obviously more recent examples of a much earlier tradition. To look for the origins of this type of artifact we really need to look south, towards the eastern Mediterranean, where the strongest candidate for the true origins of the golden torq is, of course, Egypt. It is in Egypt, and more specifically the Egypt of the Amarna era, that we find the earliest depictions of the golden torq.

Although none of these golden torqs appears to have survived in Egypt, the evidence for this custom can be seen in the tombs at Amarna. That we have this evidence at all is due, in no small part, to the less formal artistic style that pervaded the Amarna regime; and a good example of the new artistic style that had swept through Amarna during this period is to be found in the tomb of Aye [Gaythelos], which is the southernmost of the southern tombs at Amarna. Aye was in the process of excavating a grand tomb at Amarna that was to have had twenty-four pillars in its main hall, and an impressive array of wall paintings around the perimeter. Instead of the usual formalistic scenes of the deceased meeting the gods and being raised into the afterlife, we instead have a series of cartoon-like vignettes that portray the main events in the life of Aye-Gaythelos and the Amarna royalty.

One of these delightful depictions is of an award ceremony, where Aye and his first wife, Tiy, are shown being presented with a vast array of precious goods. Akhenaton and Nefertiti, who are giving out these awards, can be seen standing in the Window of Appearances along with three of their small daughters. As can be seen in the following

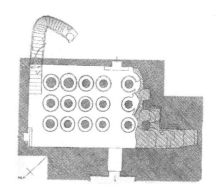

Fig 43. Plan of Aye's tomb at Amarna.

diagram, all of the royal family are depicted as being naked, which may seem odd for an award ceremony, but this is quite in line with Akhenaton's naturalistic views – views that also influenced the narrative in the Book of Genesis and the similar naturism of Adam and Eve. If one can imagine the scandal that would erupt if the British Royal Family all appeared on the balcony of Buckingham Palace completely naked, then the full impact of Akhenaton's religious reforms can perhaps be envisaged. Although the God's Wives of Egypt were invariably clad in long, revealing gowns, for the royal family to be completely naked was still a quantum leap in social etiquette.

In this particular scene, the royal couple and their children are all depicted in the act of giving out golden rewards to both Aye-Gaythelos and Tiy, and most of these happen to be in the form of gold torqs. Aye-Gaythelos

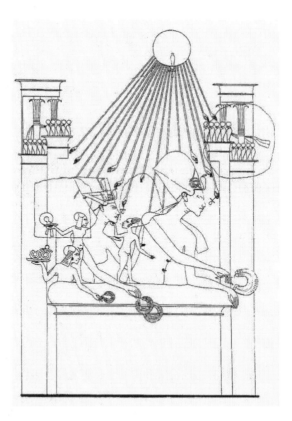

Fig 44. Akhenaton, Nefertiti and family giving golden torqs (necklaces) to Aye [Gaythelos] and his first wife Tiy. (Aye and Tiy are just out of view on this image.)

already has six torqs while his wife Tiy has five, and both are shown reaching out for yet more. This ceremony was obviously one of the highlights in Aye's career, for he is eventually shown with eighteen golden torqs and a host of other valuable goods. Since Aye could not possibly have worn quite so many necklaces, some of these torqs may have been used by Aye to reward a few of his favoured subordinates. Just as Akhenaton derived some of his status from the giving of these awards, so Aye in his turn would derive status if he could reward his favourite subordinates.

Whatever the final fate of these torqs, it is clear from this imagery that gold torqs were an important symbol of wealth and status in Amarna. So it is likely that Aye-Gaythelos would have recalled this event in later years, and perhaps recreated its potent symbolism during his own reign. This would not necessarily have been a ceremony in Amarna or Thebes, but a quieter event in the remoter periphery of the Mediterranean, at Brigantia in Iberia. No golden torqs have been discovered as yet in Catalonia, but since the prime location for the fortress-town of Brigantia has had no archaeological investigations, this is not so surprising. The descendants of Aye-Gaythelos moved on some generations later to Ireland, and it is here that many examples of this style of ornament are to be found. The cultural link here, between Amarna in Egypt and ancient Ireland, is unmistakable (see plates 9 & 10 for images of thes Irish torqs).

There is, however, one small mystery that remains, and that is the source of the gold used in the Irish torqs. Unfortunately, there is no evidence whatsoever for Bronze Age gold mining in Ireland. Gold-bearing seams are to be found in a range of hills that stretch from the Sperrin mountains in the north of the country through to Croagh Patrick in the central west. If anything, the composition of the gold in the Irish torqs is similar to the composition of the Croagh Patrick gold, but the comparison is not definite by any means. But the quantity of gold discovered in this sacred mountain of Ireland is minuscule and this, coupled with the lack of evidence for mining and smelting, has led many to speculate that the gold for the torqs must have been imported.

However, if this was all foreign gold, from where would the early Irish royalty have imported it? And with what would they have bartered for it? Since early Ireland was not known for its great wealth, the number of gold artifacts that have been discovered is both surprising and perplexing. One simple solution that would solve all these problems, would be the suggestion that the descendants of Aye-Gaythelos brought this gold with them. Although money was not used during the Egyptian eighteenth dynasty, gold was known for its intrinsic value and it was being demanded from Egyptian pharaohs by all the minor kingdoms that surrounded Egypt. In essence, golden artifacts or gold bullion was being used as money, even if this was not minted currency. Aye-Gaythelos and his advisors would have known the value of gold and would surely have taken as much of it with them as they could. Gold is of high value and easily transportable in ships, as it can be used as ballast in the hull. Kilos of gold could have been smuggled out of Amarna as the regime of Akhenaton collapsed, and similarly Aye-Gaythelos could have diverted much of the remaining national assets into his safekeeping before he was exiled.

We know that something like this was indeed happening at Amarna because a number of caches of gold bullion have been discovered in the remains of the city. But this was not the normal gold assets of the treasury, this was gold trinkets that had been hurriedly melted down and poured into small hollows in the sand to form very rough bars of gold. The hurried nature of this process has led to speculation that this gold represented emergency assets for a group that was making a quick getaway. And so the evidence suggests that Amarna was not just suffering a slow economic decline, because the center of power had shifted to Thebes. No, this was more like a population fleeing for their lives, for they even left behind some of the gold they had just smelted, in the small sand-depressions where they had just cast it.

While the evidence for the use of gold bullion at Amarna is compelling, even likely, the evidence in a later era in Israel is unmistakable. One of the most interesting of the Dead Sea Scroll finds was the Copper Scroll, which was not discovered until 1952. The Copper Scroll details the locations of 64 caches of gold and other precious objects, amounting to a staggering 4,630 talents of gold alone. Since a talent is supposed to weigh in at about 30 kg, this would equate to about 140 tonnes of gold. This just has to be in error, and so we have the same situation that has been discussed at length in the book *Solomon,* regarding the treasures of King Solomon. In this previous discussion, having looked at the Egyptian accounts in some detail, it was finally decided that the true weight of a talent had to be about 200 g, which would result in a total inventory for the Copper Scroll of about one tonne. While this is still a massive amount of gold, it is at least within the realms of possibility.

Debate still rages over when this hoard was buried and whether it is a true account or not. Some commentators regard it as an extension of the tales of treasure being buried just before the destruction of the first Temple of Jerusalem. However, as John Allegro pointed out, the Copper Scroll is not a story at all; just a list of locations and amounts buried, which had been recorded on an extremely expensive roll of pure copper. Having looked at all the arguments and counter-arguments, it would seem likely that this list was a real attempt to record the locations of treasures that were buried just prior to the destruction of Jerusalem by the Romans in AD 70. Indeed, these hidden caches of gold in Jerusalem may have been a part of what the Knights

Templar were looking for during the twelfth century AD. Had there been another copy of the Copper Scroll, which had been kept and handed down within one illustrious family, a thorough search of the newly captured city of Jerusalem may well have revealed a king's ransom in gold (plus some very interesting written accounts, histories and genealogies).

Whatever the case, all of this evidence points towards a long tradition of gold being buried or hidden away prior to an impending disaster, presumably to facilitate the founding of a new city and a new empire in the future. So despite the fact that the concept of tradeable money had not been established during the Amarna era, gold *was* being thought of and used as an asset. It may seem an obvious point that does not need labouring, but if a royal family was exiled from Egypt during the fourteenth century BC they are likely to have taken substantial amounts of gold with them, to assist with the purchase of materials from local tribes and to reward their own commanders and leaders.

If Aye-Gaythelos and Ankhesenamun-Scota did take a huge cache of gold from the Thebes or Memphis treasuries before departing to Brigantia, it may well be that much of this still remained some generations later when the subsequent move was made to Ireland. That Aye-Gaythelos would have had time to arrange all of this is implicit in the chronicle, which says of their journey:

> And as Gaythelos wandered through many provinces, stopping at various places which he considered suitable (along the North African and Eastern Iberian coastline) ... he knew that the people he led, burdened as they were with women, children and <u>much luggage</u>, were distressed beyond endurance. [SC1]

As we saw earlier, unlike the final flight from Amarna, this was no emergency evacuation from Egypt. Like the Hyksos-Israelites some centuries before, Aye-Gaythelos left Egypt on his own terms and in his own time; which was sufficient to allow for the collection of all their belongings and probably much else besides. All of these assets would have ended up in Brigantia, and at a later date some of these assets would naturally have been transferred to the new colony that was being established in Ireland, and it was this treasure and bullion that probably formed the basis of the Irish gold hoards. Much of this Egyptian gold may have been transported as ingots, and reworked into new forms to suit new fashions and tastes, but it is entirely possible that some of the torqs in the Dublin Museum may even represent original Amarna workmanship – one of the very golden torqs depicted in the tomb of Aye, perhaps.

Here we have a very plausible answer to a very intransigent problem. Ireland has produced a large number of finds of professionally made and intricately worked gold, and yet there is no evidence of gold mining or smelting in Ireland at this time. Conversely, we have a long tradition of gold being hoarded and used as emergency capital, or finance, during turbulent eras in Egypto-Israelite history. Similarly, we also have a persistent tradition that some of the ancient Egyptian royalty landed in Ireland and set up a colony there. The archaeological and literary evidence of Ireland seems to dovetail rather well, if only *Scotichronicon* is taken to be more history than mythology.

Tara prince

The same argument can also be made for the discovery of faience beads in a burial at Tara, north of Dublin. In the spring of 1955, a team of archaeologists led by Prof Sean O'Riordain discovered a burial at the ancient royal burial site at Tara. One of the skeletons uncovered in the upper levels of this cairn was rather interesting, as a Bronze Age dagger and pin were discovered in the grave and the skeleton of this young man still wore the remains of a bead necklace around its neck. The really interesting thing about this necklace was that it comprised alternate amber, jet, bronze and long, segmented faience beads. So unusual was this find that the skeleton became known as the Prince of Tara.[2]

Faience is not a natural mineral; instead, it is a man-made silicate material that is made in a similar fashion to glass manufacture, with a blue-green copper glaze on the surface of the bead. (In fact, the Tara beads are more glass than glazed.) Quite simply, this type of material had not been manufactured in Ireland in the Bronze Age, and the most likely source for these beads is Egypt or perhaps Minoan Crete. Dr J Stone, who led the examination of the faience beads, thought that the closest match to these beads was from finds that had been made in Abydos, Egypt and Tell Duweir in Israel.[3] Certainly, the considered opinion was that these beads were not of local manufacture and must have been imported. While the favoured argument was that these beads must have arrived in Ireland through a series of random trading links that stretched all the way across Europe, it is also possible that they arrived in the same flotilla that brought the descendants of Aye-Gaythelos and Scota to the shores of southern Ireland. These links to the Aye-Gaythelos exodus are further strengthened by some of the other artifacts that were discovered. Prof O'Riordain says of these:

> The occurrence of segmented bone objects similar to those in Iberia might be taken as indicating the route along which these trinkets came...[4]

And this was indeed the most probable route along which these faience beads travelled, because they were brought to Ireland by the descendants of Aye-Gaythelos, and the intermediate stop-off point for these exiles was on the river Ebro in Iberia. That these beads were considered to be highly valuable is perhaps confirmed by there only being four such beads on this necklace. Unlike Egyptian necklaces, which might have hundreds of faience beads on them, the Tara Prince could only afford four, and this is exactly what we might expect from the arrival of a flotilla that contained a limited amount of treasures.

Interestingly, from the burial artifacts that were discovered in this grave, the favoured date for this burial is the late fourteenth century BC; while the date of the Aye-Gaythelos exodus to Spain would also have been the late fourteenth century BC. Despite the exodus from Spain to Ireland occurring some generations after this period, the treasures that were carried onwards towards Ireland would have been the same late fourteenth century artifacts that had been taken from Egypt (if this was the necklace's true provenance), and so the burial of the Tara Prince would have appeared to have been late fourteenth century BC even if it actually took place several centuries later.

Incidentally, the passage grave that lay underneath this burial was excavated a year later, in 1956, and this turned out to contain a great hoard of some 250 assorted burials and cremations that had been interred there over a great span of time ranging from the Neolithic (c. 4000 - 2500 BC) to the early Bronze Age (c. 2500 - 1800 BC). Clearly, the Tara mound was a sacred site that contained the bones of many an early Irish leader or king, and it was no doubt for this reason that the Tara Prince was buried within the earth mound that covered this passage grave.

The subsequent history of this necklace is also interesting. During a visit to the Dublin Museum, which is a fine classical edifice modelled on the British Museum in London, I could not find this necklace anywhere. I was told that it was in storage, and I would need to contact the keeper of antiquities by post. Having done so, I was then told that no such necklace had ever been discovered in Ireland, let alone stored in the museum itself. After much searching on the internet, I eventually discovered a reference to the original excavations and asked again for a photo of the necklace; to which the reply was:

> Although this necklace was excavated in the 1950s, it has only recently come into our possession and has not, as yet, been photographed. [5]

Here we have one of the most interesting finds in Irish archaeology, and it appears to have been sidelined and ignored. This necklace is a dateable artifact that was important enough for the burial to have become known as the Tara Prince, and it is one of only two such artifacts that demonstrate that Ireland had trading links of some nature with the eastern Mediterranean during the Bronze Age. The other find of faience beads was at the Dundrum Sandhills, Co Down. Despite the importance of the find at Tara, it took the Dublin Museum fifty years to get a photograph of these beads! As the University of Dublin admits, in its newsletter of March 2006:

> The findings ranging from about 3500 BC were catalogued and stored at University College Dublin's School of Archaeology. And there they have rested, undisturbed for nearly 50 years, until Dr Muiris O'Sullivan and publisher Nick Maxwell took the initiative to share this treasure trove from the oldest visible monument on the Hill of Tara.[6]

My first request for a picture of the Tara necklace was made in 2005, and it was not until 2009 that the Dublin Museum could finally provide an image.

Luckily, while the reports and photos from the Tara excavation were dragging their collective heels, there was an excavation of a similar necklace in 1889 in North Molton, Exeter. This was a chance discovery of a Bronze Age tomb of a similar age to the Tara Prince. Once more, the burial goods associated with this tomb included a fine necklace containing lignite and faience beads, which were obviously not of local origin. One necklace might indeed be the result of fluke trading and bartering across the whole of Europe over many generations, with the necklace finally ending up in Tara, north of Dublin. However, two or three necklaces from the same era places a completely different perspective on these discoveries. That three necklaces have been discovered means that it likely that many more await discovery, and this proliferation of artifacts either means that there were good trading contacts between greater Britain and the eastern Mediterranean, or that an expedition from the east arrived in northwestern Europe with a hoard of jewellery on board.

The first option would mean that the Minoans, the Bronze Age's primary trading nation, were sailing regularly to Britain with supplies of gold and jewellery from the eastern Mediterranean; and possibly returning with copper mined at the huge Bronze Age copper mines near Llandudno, North Wales. While this would make some sense, there is no direct evidence for constant trade links with the eastern Mediterranean in this early era. Had this trade been this regular, with ships arriving every year perhaps, one would have thought that there would have been an abundance of Minoan, Mycenaean or Egyptian goods to be found in Britain. But there is not; there are odd finds from Egypt and Mycenae here and there, but there is no evidence of the abundance of goods and the kind of regular trade that was obviously present during the Roman era, for instance.

The first option also does not account for the surprising amount of trade that was conducted with Ireland, which appears to have received large amounts of gold (perhaps pre-manufactured torqs) and now also faience beads from the eastern Mediterranean. While North Wales had valuable copper to trade with any possible Minoan explorers, Ireland has always been short of valuable raw materials with which they could have traded for high-value Egyptian goods. So how, then, did Ireland receive all these luxury goods?

The alternative explanation is, of course, that all of these valuable goods arrived with Aye-Gaythelos and Scota – and so this was a limited, one-off arrival of gold and jewellery that had to last for many generations. Subsequent trading allowed some of this Egyptian jewellery to slip into England, but this would have been trading from an otherwise impoverished Ireland to wealthier England, and not *vice versa*.

Incidentally, an obvious Egyptian translation for the royal burial site at Tara would be Ta Ra ⌐⌐⌐ ⊙ meaning 'Land of Ra'. And while we are looking at epigraphic links with Egypt, it should also be noted that the primary goddess for Tara – who may also have been the wife of King Eremon, one of the first Milesian kings of Ireland – was called Tia or Tiye. Strange as it may seem, this Celtic name just happens to be the same as the names for the wife, sister and the mother of Aye [Gaythelos].[7] The second component to this title (sometimes said to be the name for the sister of Tia) was Tephi, and this may have been derived from *tepia* 🖺🏺 meaning 'noble ancestor'. Thus, the full title for Tia Tephi may well refer to 'Our Noble Ancestor, Tia'.

It is said that Queen Tia Tephi of Ireland came from the east, across the seas, and had she been a descendant of Tiye of Egypt then this ancestry would be absolutely correct. It is from this Celtic Queen Tia that the alternative Gaelic name for Tara, that of Tia-mair, was derived. But since Tia came from across the seas, this name may well have been derived from Tiye-Mer 𓇌𓈖𓏜 ⟤⟤ meaning 'Tia of the Sea'. This is a similar title to the one given to Mary [Magdalene] who was sometimes known as Marie Stella (Mary Celeste), or the Sea Star.

Gold cape

Another striking similarity between Egyptian and Celtic jewellery is the golden shoulder collar or cape. In 1833, workmen digging for stone in Mold, north Wales, uncovered an early Bronze Age grave containing a number of ornaments and artifacts. Among these was a crumpled sheet of gold which, when it was finally unfolded and restored, turned out to be a golden cape that covered the entire neck and shoulders. Arguments have raged as to how the cape should be worn, because it would radically restrict any arm movement, but the obvious solution to this is that the dead need no arm movement. In other words, the cape was designed and fabricated as a funerary artifact, to bejewel and glorify the dearly departed.

This type of funerary decoration is also to be found in Egypt. More specifically, a very good example of this type of cape can be found among the few remains of Queen Kiyah's burial goods. As has been suggested before, Kiyah and Akhenaton, the two naked lovebirds from the Book of Genesis, eloped to Avaris just prior to the fall of Amarna. This left unused a large number of grave goods, which had been destined for the royal couple's tomb; and so they were reworked and reused in other burials.

Queen Kiyah's Canopic jars, which would have held her internal organs after her death, had her name expunged from them and this left just her husband's name, Akhenaton, on them; which has caused an amount of confusion. They were then deposited – along with the mummy of an unknown male pharaoh, inside Kiyah's modified and reused coffin – in tomb KV55, and this chain of events has led some to claim that this burial was of Akhenaton himself. Unfortunately, although recent dental analysis has indicated a slightly older corpse than was previously thought, the general

Fig 45.   A funerary statuette of Kiyah, wearing a golden shoulder cape. See plate 7 for the gold cape from Mold.

opinion is that this mummy is still far too young to be that of Akhenaton, and so the most likely candidate has to be Smenkhkare.

Whoever this burial was eventually intended for, Kiyah's reused Canopic jars portray Akhenaton's favourite queen as being dressed for her future burial in a (golden) single-piece cape that covered the entire shoulder and upper torso. While some of these capes were made from a multi-coloured array of small beads, others were made of solid gold; as the capes worn by Tutankhamen's *ushabti* funerary figurines clearly demonstrate.

It has to be said that the similarity between this distinctive type of funerary decoration from Amarna and the Bronze Age example from North Wales is remarkable. (See the colour section for an image of the Mold cape.) Once again, this similarity demonstrates that there must have been close cultural or trading links between greater Britain and Egypt during the Amarna era – a link that is best explained by the *Scotichronicon* account.

Red hand

Another interesting symbol, which later became a prime emblem of Northern Ireland, is the red hand. Now this is a peculiar symbol that has only the most tenuous of myths associated with it, and these describe a race in which the first to reach land would win the throne of Ulster. A certain prince called O'Neil was losing the race but cut off his hand and threw it to the shore, ensuring that his hand touched land first.

This is supposed to explain the adoption of the red hand – and the drops of blood that are said to be dripping from its wrist – as an emblem of Ulster. But this kind of supernatural mythology is rarely even close to the truth and the true reasoning is likely to be more complex and have a much deeper symbology. Bearing in mind the strong possibility that the first Irish tribes may been the descendants of Aye-Gaythelos and Ankhesenamun-Scota, and that the biblical accounts were descended from the history of the Amarna regime, the true reason for the redness of this hand may lie in the Egypto-biblical accounts.

As has been pointed out in my previous works, there is a thread of redness that runs through the biblical narrative and many of the patriarchs and kings are said to be strangely red; including Adam, Esau and Kings David and Solomon. This red thread is quite literally expressed at the birth of Pharez and Zarah in the Book of Genesis:

> And it came to pass, when she gave birth, that the one (child) put out his hand: and the midwife took and bound upon his hand a scarlet thread, saying, This came out first. [B8]

Fig 46. Red hands (each with three drops of blood) on a bank in Bangor, N Ireland.

This strange propensity for redness is likely to be an oblique reference to the Hyksos-Israelite royalty, and the Red Crown of Lower Egypt. A similar explanation to this is sometimes given for the adoption of the red hand in Ulster symbolism, and the mythology in these alternative accounts indicates that Jacob's pillar (the Stone of Destiny) was taken into safekeeping by Jeremiah and that it somehow ended up in Ireland. This is how, so it is said, the Star of David ended up on the flag of Ulster. (I relate much of the history of Jeremiah in the book *Solomon*.) Another strand of the same mythology says that Pharaz and <u>Zarah</u> were exiled to Spain and founded the city of <u>Zara</u>goza, and at a later date their ancestors sailed to Ireland. Since Zaragoza lies on the river Ebro in Catalonia, this is a very similar story to the *Scotichronicon* account, and the symmetry between these two mythologies again links biblical and Egyptian history.

However, if the red hand of Ulster is somehow connected with Egypto-Hebrew culture and mythology, then this disembodied hand may be better explained as a component of the great Osirian myth. During a battle with his brother Seth, Osiris was killed and cut up into pieces, which were scattered around Egypt. Isis, Osiris' sister-wife, was said to have searched for these body parts and reassembled the late Osiris. However, the tradition of a dismembered Osiris and his various appendages being linked to each of the temples of Egypt, was still a strong part of this mythology. In other words, the presence of a dismembered holy relic does have a satisfactory explanation in Egyptian mythology. As with the later Catholic cathedrals, no temple of the gods was complete without a holy relic, which was often a body part of some saint or disciple. Likewise, no self-respecting Egyptian temple would be complete without a piece of Osiris, and perhaps the exiled Brigantians claimed to have one of his hands. This link with Osiris may not sit very well with the theology of Akhenaton, but in a similar fashion the story of Moses and Aaron's [TuthMoses and Akhenaton's] exodus from Egypt is littered with complaints about the people reverting to alternative belief systems.

Further evidence that this red hand may be a component of Osirian mythology may be seen in the three drops of 'blood' that sometimes issue from the wrist of this hand. The original symbol for Osiris in Egypt was the piece of flesh glyph , which spelt out the name Asar or Osiris.* So what we may be seeing here, on the red hand of Ulster, is a direct link to Osiris, and in the Ulster version his name was spelt as . The next chapter deals with this question in greater detail, and shows that this Osirian symbolism may well have travelled from Iberia to Ireland with the Pictish immigration.

Fig 47. Star of David on the flag of Ulster.

The other direct link between the red hand of Ulster and the Amarna dynasty in Egypt is to be seen in the symbolism of the red hand itself. If some of these Irish traditions were derived from Aye-Gaythelos and Scota, then one might expect to see some direct similarities between the Amarna royalty and the resulting society in Brigantia (Iberia) or Scotia (Ireland). Indeed, if Gaythelos were really Aye, then we might expect that this similarity would involve Aye himself. Strangely enough, one of the similarities we do see is the startling fact that Aye was the proud possessor of a pair of red leather gloves. They were presented to Aye-Gaythelos at

* Since Ast (Isis) used the egg glyph , a more logical explanation for the 'flesh' glyph used by Asar (Osiris) , is that it actually represented a drop of sperm. Thus the royal couple would have represented the totality of fertility by honouring the egg and sperm. This suggestion is reinforced by both the egg and sperm being pronounced *sa*, while *sa* also meant 'son'.

the same award ceremony that has just been discussed; but these particular gloves were obviously something rather special. As Professor Davies says:

> At any rate, the picture would lead us to think that Aye was intensely proud of this rare possession (the gloves). As soon as he is outside the gates of the palace he puts them on and exhibits them to his friends ... the bystanders press round to see and stroke them, lift up their arms in wild astonishment, and are ready to fall down and do homage to him and them (the gloves) indiscriminately. (Author's brackets.)[9]

Davies does not give the colour of these gloves in his report, but Professor Desroches-Noblecourt specifically states that they were coloured red on the tomb's wall-paintings.[10] Clearly, the special depiction and recording of this event demonstrates that this was not any old pair of red gloves. Aye-Gaythelos had just been given 18 gold *shebu* necklaces (torqs), 12 gold armlets, 11 semiprecious bead necklaces, 4 gold cups, 5 signet rings, 2 metal vases – indeed, everything bar a partridge in a pear tree. So great was his booty that the bottom of this particular tableau shows an excited courtier exclaiming, in the fashion of a modern cartoon, "Aye ... along with Tiy. They have been made people of gold!" Another bystander shouts, "Pharaoh has given Aye and Tiy millions of loads of gold and all manner of riches!" Indeed he had, but for some reason the item that most pleased Aye, in amongst all this bounteous treasure, was his pair of red gloves.

Aye's excited reaction to the presentation of these gloves is rather odd, for it is not as if gloves were an unknown commodity in Egypt; they were used by the royalty for horse-riding, and Tutankhamen owned several pairs. While it is true that Tutankhamen's tomb postdates Aye's Amarna tomb by a few years, are we to believe that these were the first pair of gloves that Egypt had ever seen? No, there must have been something especially symbolic about these gloves, and one is reminded of the similar fuss made about Moses' possible use of 'gloves':

> And god said unto him (Moses), Put now thy hand into thy bosom. And he put his hand into his bosom: and when he took it out, behold, his hand was leprous, as white as snow. And god said, Put thy hand into thy bosom again. And he put his hand into his bosom again; and when he took it out of his bosom, behold, it was turned back like his other flesh. [B12]

This strange display was intended as a symbol that would somehow impress the assembled priests of [Upper] Egypt, and place them in such awe of Moses' powers that the pharaoh would let the Hyksos-Israelites leave Egypt [on their own terms]. It is difficult to derive any real logic from this event, but the respective colours being used in these two 'glove' scenarios, that of red and white, are representative of the national colours of the Two Lands of Egypt. In which case, these 'gloves' may have been symbolic of the land and the nation of Egypt. They may have been similar, perhaps, to a modern-day high official being given the keys to a city. We know that Aye-Gaythelos was made vizier, or prime minister of Egypt, so were these gloves symbolic of his office in any way? Alternatively, since these gloves were often used for horse riding and Aye was also made Commander of the Horse, perhaps these gloves symbolised his position as supreme army commander.

Fig 48. Aye-Gaythelos showing off his red gloves.

One other possibility, is that the glove symbology was linked in some manner to the hands of the Aton. The Aton Sun-disk was always portrayed as having rays that ended in small hands, which caressed the royal couple or offered them the *ankh*, the symbol of life. It is entirely possible that this imagery turned the humble hand into a potent symbol of god, and the power of the gods to protect and give life. It may have been through this route that the symbol of a governor or army commander became linked to a glove; and the red colour used for these gloves no doubt reflected the redness that was always associated with the Lower Egyptian royalty.

Whatever these red gloves really symbolised, the fact of the matter is that a simple red glove could and did have a significant symbolic value within Egyptian culture, and especially within Amarna culture. Thus, it is likely that the descendants of Aye-Gaythelos would have likewise honoured this same symbology and made it an important component within their culture. This is exactly what we see in Ulster, where the red hand or glove and the Judaic Star of David have become fundamental symbols of the province and its people. Thus, both the golden torq and the red hand symbology appear to have made their way from Amarna to Ireland, a fact that strongly supports the Gaythelos and Scota story.

Round-tower

As we saw in an earlier chapter, one of the prime architectural forms to be seen in the Balearic Islands is the truncated *talayot* round-tower. It is likely that these Bronze Age towers were based upon earlier Minoan designs and so the cult of the round-tower could well have been brought to the Balearic Islands during the Aye-Gaythelos and Scota exodus. The Minoans were still the primary source of sea trading and ship design during this era, so it is likely that Aye-Gaythelos would have needed their expertise to organise and execute his exodus plans. It is also known that there were strong Minoan elements within the early Avaris and later Amarna eras of Egyptian history, and no doubt some of their theology and traditions could have been transported upon this same exodus. In addition, the Minoan cult of the round-tower could well have been a local version of the much earlier Benben tower veneration at Heliopolis, and so the round-tower monument would have already been familiar to most Egyptians.

It is not known exactly when the descendants of Aye-Gaythelos made their subsequent jump from Spain to Ireland, as the various chronicles give differing accounts, but at some point after the twelfth century BC a strategic move to Ireland was made. Along with the golden torqs, faience beads, bone artifacts and the red hand, any number of other traditions may well have been transported to Ireland, and one of these may have been the cult of the round-tower. Ireland has about seventy-three round-towers still standing, which were all associated with monastic centers, while Scotland has just two (see plates 26 & 27 for images of these towers). One of these Scottish examples is situated in the village of Abernethy, near Perth, and it demonstrates that these early Celto-Christian traditions spanned a vast tract of land from southern Ireland to eastern Scotland. These towers are variously described as being bell-towers, defensive positions or safe locations for valuables; however, these orthodox arguments have already been demolished in the book *Jesus*.

The general layout of these towers is for a tubular construction in stone and lime mortar, with walls that are battered (inclined and tapering) and a conical top. The upper windows, if they are present, are aligned with the cardinal points and not with topographical features or the adjoining monastery. One interesting aspect is that the towers' entrance doors are all situated above ground level, and wooden ladders were required to reach the entrance. It is said that this was for security, but in the majority of cases the first room in the tower was not tall enough to receive the ladder inside it. Thus, if a retreat to the 'safety' of the tower had ever been made, with enemies in hot pursuit, the ladder could not be drawn up into the tower. However, leaving your ladder up against the door rather defeats the strategic advantage of having an above-ground-level entrance. As has already been demonstrated, these towers were far from being places of refuge.

If these round-towers were not places of refuge, and if the windows at the top were often poorly suited to the ringing of bells,* then what was their function? Well, since they were all situated within monastic centers, they are likely to have had a religious function. Since the monastic traditions of Ireland are reputed to have been derived from Egyptian monastic customs, it is likely that the tradition of the round-tower also came from Egypt, either directly or through Iberia. In which case, these Celto-Christian round-towers would originally have been based upon the Benben tower at Heliopolis, and would have represented phallic symbols. The phallic Benben tower of Heliopolis was a Lower Egyptian complement to the feminine uterine temples of Upper Egypt. Likewise, the monastic towers of Ireland complemented the feminine uterine henges, like Newgrange and Knowth; the only problem with this argument being the differing eras for these structures. The henges of Ireland are said to be prehistoric, whereas the round-towers only date from the 6th

---

* The Rattoo round-tower in the colour section is a later example of these Irish designs, which dates from about the twelfth century AD. This round-tower has four windows at the top which face the cardinal points, as do many of these towers, a fact which may suggest that they were designed as bell-towers. However, other round-towers either have much smaller windows or none at all – as at Clonmacnoise, Co Offaly and Donaghmore, Co Meath – and so the generic function of these round-towers cannot be for bell-ringing.

century AD at the earliest.

One of the difficulties in dating these ancient sites is the long periods of time during which they were in use and during which time they may have been significantly modified. An obvious example of this possible modification lies in the significant difference between the megalithic circles and kerb stones at Newgrange, Knowth and Dowth, and the much smaller boulders and grass-turves that were used to construct the mounds themselves. Bearing in mind the open designs of Stonehenge and Avebury in England, it is not unreasonable to suppose that there were two building phases involved in the Irish henges. The earlier henge design may have resulted in an open area surrounded by megaliths, exactly as at Stonehenge and Avebury, and only in a much later era did the population decide to cover over this exposed area to properly imitate a uterine passageway. However, this second phase employed just small stones, earth and grass-turves; a technique which is significantly different to the earlier megalithic building phase.

Newgrange, Dowth and Knowth are said to be some 5,000 years old. However, since the carbon-dating for this assertion was conducted at a very early point in the development of this technique, these dates must be treated with caution, as the wide variation in the carbon dates for the Ferriby boats has clearly demonstrated. Even the modern dates for the Ferriby boats, using the latest carbon-dating techniques, were far earlier than the site archaeologists had predicted. However, the megalithic rings at Newgrange are certainly from the Stone Age and so I am fairly certain that none of the designs, technology and decoration used in the megalithic portions of the various henges in the Newgrange area had anything to do with an Egyptian influence. However, the mound and passageway was possibly a later construction, and whether this may have included some influence from the descendants of Aye-Gaythelos and Scota is open to speculation.

The next question is: could there possibly be any connection between these Celto-Christian round-towers and the truncated round-towers of Mallorca and Minorca or, indeed, the original towers at Knossos and Heliopolis? Although all the examples of round-towers in the Balearic Islands were most certainly truncated – and thus probably based upon the Minoan concept of a truncated tower and a sacred tree – it is said that some of the similar towers on Sardinia did once have conical tops, as do the Celto-Christian towers in Ireland and Scotland, and so may have been more influenced by the design of the Egyptian Benben tower. But there is still a large span of time between these Bronze Age Sardinian towers and the much later towers in Ireland and Scotland, which date from the sixth century AD. So were there any earlier Celtic round-towers that have not survived into the modern era?

Evidence for the possibility of earlier round-tower designs lies in the magnificent Iron Age 'fortresses' that appear along the western fringes of both Ireland and Scotland; a settlement pattern that strongly suggests that these people travelled up the western coastline by boat. It is thought that there were originally over 50,000 of these 'forts' in the western greater British Isles, but only a few of these remain standing to any degree. Remaining forts in Ireland include Grianan near Aileach, Co Donegal; plus Staigue near Catherdaniel; Cahergall near Cahirsiveen; and Navenooragh near Brandon Mountain, all of which are in Co Kerry.

In Scotland there are around fifty remaining examples of the larger *broch* designs scattered along the western coast and isles, including Borrafiach, Gearymore and Hallin, which reside along the Waternish peninsular on the Isle of Skye, and the magnificent Mousa Broch on the Shetland Isles. In addition, there are a vast number of smaller towers called *duns* all along the Western Isles. The larger of these 'fortresses' are essentially large, squat, truncated round-towers, and they appear to display all the features that were later absorbed into Celto-Christian round-tower construction. They are circular, with battered walls and a lintelled doorway. The only primary difference, one that may have limited these forts' girth and height, is that they were made from drystone walling.

However, as is usual with my lateral investigations into history, we have to question the established explanations given for these monuments. The traditional perception for the Irish examples is that these impressive constructions were forts, and the literature gives graphic illustrations of these massive forts containing a couple of mud huts: an image indicating that a fearful estate-owner had resorted to massive fortifications to protect his meagre possessions. On the surface this might seem like a reasonable view, but does it stand up to closer scrutiny?

While these monuments are large, they are certainly not big enough to contain a village. Conversely, these 'forts' appear to be much too large for a solitary fortified farmstead – these were definitely community construction projects that would have required a great deal of labour to build. What they look like is a castle-keep, or the motte from a Norman motte and bailey village fortification; the only trouble with this explanation being that we have a motte and no bailey: the castle-keep with no castle. So would a community build a keep for its valuables, and leave everything else – including the village – unprotected?

There is another problem with the castle-keep theory, and that is the internal design of these Irish 'forts'. Firstly, there is no evidence of hinge-points for a door at the entrance. Now the Gallarus Oratory, which will be mentioned later, had door hinges, so why not these 'forts'? Just how was the entrance closed? More alarmingly, there are a large number of stairways up and down the inner wall of the fortification (eighteen at Cahergall and

Fig 49. The Cahergall, Grianan and Staigue amphitheaters.

twenty at Staigue). But this is far too many to defend the fort, as any enemy who reached the top of the wall would have a very convenient choice of descent routes. A much more secure arrangement would be to have just three narrow stairways down from the upper walls, which could be defended with the minimum number of soldiers.

Finally, perhaps the primary reason why these monuments cannot be forts is that they all have the same internal dimensions. Now a fort would surely be tailored to suit the local topography and the community's budget, with more successful clans building huge forts and impoverished families building micro forts. Only a sacred precinct needs to be standardised in this fashion, especially if its dimensions conform to some kind of sacred metrology or numerology; a subject that we know was very important to many of these early religions. The sacredness of these monuments' metrology will be discussed at the end of this chapter.

So, if the fort explanation looks somewhat dubious, then what were these huge monuments built for? Well, the first time I stepped into one, I was immediately taken back to Rome and my recent tour of the Colosseum. All around the circumference of these 'forts' are staggered stairways leading to terrace after terrace, which are built into the sides of the walls. This terracing has no logical function, for a fort, but it makes every sense in terms of a stadium. Now while this terracing is rather precipitous, and would give a modern Health and Safety officer palpitations, there would have been no such qualms a few thousand years ago. Each and every terrace could have provided seating for scores of people, and the entire stadium could have seated several hundred people. This, I believe, was the true function of these monuments; and yet this simple observation changes our entire perception of these Irish communities. Out goes the image of a fearful, huddled population living behind vast fortifications due to rampant lawlessness throughout the land, and in comes the view of a confident and prosperous society that was able to entertain hundreds of people in some kind of social or spiritual celebration. This was the true function of these monuments and, after much research, I was at last able to find one author who might agree with this proposition. Jack Roberts, an author of Celtic mythology, says of these monuments:

> This type of enclosure is often misnamed a 'ring fort', but they were not defensive structures, their purpose being as places of assembly where people met for civil and religious purpose and to enact important ceremonies. [13]

Precisely. But what kind of shows would have been staged in these stadiums? Did the local population hope to see a Greek tragedy, or a religious rite? The answer to this lies at the Cahergall stadium, because upon entering its enclosure I received another shock. Inside this monument was not a large open-plan space resembling a circus arena, as I had expected; instead, there was a large truncated round-tower. This feature is not unique to Cahergall either, for the Navenooragh stadium sports exactly the same feature. But this revelation was a bit of a puzzle, for why should the standard Mallorcan or Minorcan round-tower have been placed inside a large stadium?

The answer to this was more than obvious on the respective days that I visited these monuments. In Mallorca and Minorca I was able to sit below the round-tower and consume a sandwich and a small beer while idly contemplating the size and form of the sacred tree that would have once erupted from the mouth of the tower. A priest, in ancient times, could easily have stood tens of meters away from me and explained in measured tones the function of his ritual. In great contrast to this, in Ireland I was only just able to stand up and could not even hear my own voice, let alone that of a distant priest. The wind howled, the rain skidded horizontally across the sodden turves, the windchill made it feel like -10°C, and it was all I could do to keep the camera steady. (I had to wait three hours for a break in the weather to take proper photos.) However, inside the stadium there was a small sanctuary of calm and normality. The air was relatively still and quiet, the temperature was almost tropical in comparison, and a voice echoed from wall to wall almost as well as in a Roman amphitheater.

Here, then, is the reason for the ancient traditions being modified and for the construction of great circular stadiums. In the Balearic Islands, the only problem was watering the sacred tree during the hot and dry summers. On the western fringes of Ireland, no self-respecting tree dares put a leaf above ground, and the foolhardy specimens that try are stunted, gnarled and blown into horizontal hedges. The cult of the sacred tree could not exist on the west coast of Ireland without some degree of protection and climate-control. In addition, the stadium allows for a large number of people to witness these sacred rituals in relative comfort. So, the Cahergall and Navenooragh forts are actually the Cahergall and Navenooragh amphitheaters.

The Scottish version of these stadiums, which are known locally as *brochs*, is very similar in design and usage to their Irish equivalents. Indeed, the Dun Beag *broch* on Skye is easily confused with the similarly named Dun Beag* stadium, which is located on the Dingle peninsular in Ireland. Despite their widely scattered locations, these Scottish *brochs* mostly follow a standard size and design, which bears more than a passing resemblance to the Mallorcan *nuraghi* and Irish stadiums. See plates 17 and 18 and figure 50 for a comparison.

---

* Dun Beag simply means 'little round hill'.

The Scottish *brochs* are somewhat smaller that the Irish stadiums, they usually have double-skinned walls, and once again they are said to be forts. Again, this assertion has to be doubted, for they are not always sited in the best defensive positions; they are too small to hold many people or valuables, the entrances are generally too small to allow a cow through (the cow being the standard measure of local wealth); and the entrance way is poorly defended. However, the final reason for these *brochs* not being forts is their dimensions for, just like their Irish cousins, most of these *brochs* appear to have identical dimensions, as will be discussed later. This metrological

Fig 50. The Cahergall amphitheater and the (Scottish) Dun Beag broch.

symmetry again indicates that these *brochs* were probably sacred precincts, rather than defensive positions; and this change in usage demands a familiar change in perception, for this again implies that the western fringes of Scotland were not lawless and heavily defended, but prosperous and pious.

There is one final problem to solve, for even when including these *brochs* and stadiums in the equation, there still remains a large expanse of time between the construction of the round-towers in the Balearic Islands and the Iron Age era of these circular Irish and Scottish stadiums or temples. However, there are so many similarities between these monuments, including their construction techniques, that it is likely that there is a common heritage here. The round-towers in Ireland, Scotland, Mallorca and Minorca all sport a truncated, circular layout; they all have battered walls and a lintelled doorway; they are all drystone constructions, and the Scottish, Mallorcan and Minorcan towers even show evidence of the raised doorway design which is such a common feature of the later and slimmer Celto-Christian round-towers. In the Balearic design, the raised doorway was sometimes accessed by an inclined ramp, but was often suspended in midair – just as we see with the later, slimmer Celto-Christian round-towers and the Egyptian pyramids.

So can this difference in dating between the Balearic and the Celtic truncated round-towers be overcome in any way? Well, as ever with these monuments, stone cannot be dated and so the age of these constructions can only be implied by other artifacts on the site. But if the site has no occupation stratification, which is a common feature of religious monuments rather than domestic settlements, the dating of the site becomes more problematic. Thus Brian Lalor, an author on the history of Irish round-towers, describes the Grianan amphitheater as being 'variously dated'. In other words, nobody can give a precise date for these monuments and the dates we are presented with are based upon pure guesswork. The earliest suggested date I have seen in a historical text is 500 BC for the Irish stadiums and 700 BC for the Scottish *brochs*; however, the tourist guide to western Ireland says that the stadiums date from 1400 BC. Indeed, the fact that these stadiums and *brochs* have so little in the way of stratification and other artifacts with which to date them, again strongly suggests that these constructions were religious temples (stadiums) and not secular forts. Sacred temples are kept spotlessly clean, while forts and settlements accumulate the detritus of everyday life.

Given the uncertainty within *Scotichronicon* regarding the date of the subsequent exodus to Ireland, and the uncertainly regarding the construction date of these amphitheaters and *brochs*, I think there is enough slack within these uncertainties to allow them to meet at some point in the distant past. In which case, the later, slimmer Celto-Christian round-towers of Ireland may well have been influenced by the design of the earlier stadiums and *brochs* and the internal round-towers that they sometimes contained – with this religious symbolism being transported across the Mediterranean by the descendants of the various Hyksos-Israelite refugees, following their unfortunate but numerous forced evacuations from Egypt. See Appendix 1 for a flowchart of these various migrations.

Navetas

The final piece of synergy between Ireland and the Balearic Islands is perhaps the most convincing of all, and it virtually proves beyond doubt that there were direct cultural links between the communities on these distant islands. As has already been mentioned, Minorca is also home to a Bronze Age monument known locally as a *naveta*. These large stone monuments resemble an upturned boat that has been cut in half, with a door placed in the opened section of the 'boat'. They appear to be tombs, but have been more accurately identified as ossuaries; or places where bodies are allowed to rot

Fig 51. The statue of Imhotep discovered on Minorca.

away and where the remaining bare bones can be stored (the bones may have been stored in the 'loft' or upper chamber). These *navetas* are thought to date from the fourteenth century BC, the same date as the Scota exodus, and their shape indicates that the builders of these monuments were seafarers who most probably came to the Balearics from the east. Since the doorway of the Tudons Naveta measures exactly 52 cm across, and since this length equates to exactly one Thoth cubit (one Egyptian Royal cubit), it is highly likely that these seafarers had strong links with Egypt, as I have suspected. See the end of this chapter for further details on the metrology of these sites.

Further links to Egypt were found at the *talayotic* site of Torralba d'en Salord. There were several finds made at this site, which included some Amarna blue glassware, several scarabs and a small statue of Imhotep. The statue is seated and on its lap is a scroll that reads 'Imhotep, son of Ra-Ptah'. This type of statue was common in Egypt during the sixth century BC, which is much later than the construction of the site at Torralba, but it does indicate that this sacred precinct may still have been in use at this time and that its custodians or visitors had strong links to Egypt.

Thus, the possibility exists that the people who built these *navetas* originally came from Egypt at the same time as the Scota exodus; but where may they have travelled to in future generations? Well, since these boat-shaped *naveta* monuments are more unique than the ubiquitous *talayot* or *nuraghi* towers, it is entirely possible that they can be used as a geographical marker, through which the migrations of this particular nation or culture can be traced. So are there any other locations in which these *navetas* and *talayots* can be found together? Surprisingly, there is.

I stumbled upon the Irish versions of a *naveta* while thumbing through a book on Irish archaeology in the Tralee library; a book that I very nearly dropped in surprise. For there, on the pages in front of me, were a pair of Minorcan *navetas* that were situated in southwest Ireland. It was a site that I had to see as soon as possible. The journey out to the end of the Dingle peninsular was made with great anticipation, and I was not to be disappointed. There, in a small enclosure, was the Gallarus Oratory, a perfect copy of a Minorcan *naveta* (see the colour section for a comparison).

The literature indicates that this structure is actually a boat-shaped Christian church, which dates from the sixth century AD. However, once more we find that there is nothing within this structure that can be dated, and so this presumed Christian identity and sixth century date is simply based upon a Romanesque arch to the rear window. However, even this observation creates its own chronological problems because the Roman arch did not arrive in Ireland until the twelfth century AD, and yet the construction techniques used on the Gallarus Oratory show it to be much older than this. The answer to these inconsistencies, in my estimation, is that this window has been re-carved into a Roman arch in a later era – for the keystones that form the arch are dangerously thin and are unlikely to have been designed in this fashion, while the arch itself displays evidence of post-installation cutting. In fact, the rear window may have originally mimicked the inverted boat-shape of the building itself, before it was re-carved in the twelfth century to suit later fashions.

Having taken the rear window out of the equation, the date and function of this structure becomes entirely fluid. It could be Iron Age, it could be Bronze Age. It could be a church, it could be a tomb or an ossuary. Indeed, since the *naveta* ossuaries on Minorca are said to date from 1400 BC, it is entirely reasonable to suppose that the identical Irish *navetas* date from the same kind of era. Thus the Gallarus Oratory could be up to 2,000 years older than is currently thought.

While it is true that the Gallarus Oratory looks better constructed and substantially younger than the Minorcan equivalents, that may simply be due to the fact that the Dingle peninsular is made from a tough gritstone that has been naturally stratified. This means that very hard but roughly flat and angular stones were available to the architects in the west of Ireland, for very little cost in labour. In contrast, the Minorcan *navetas* are made of limestone, a rock which has to be labouriously shaped by hand and yet weathers easily. In addition, the Minorcan masons have used surface limestone instead of deep-quarry limestone, and so the blocks they selected had already been naturally weathered over the preceding millennia – just as the limestone pavements of Yorkshire are similarly weathered today. Thus, although they may superficially look to be of differing ages, the Irish and Minorcan *navetas* may share a common construction era and thus a common heritage. So, the Gallarus Oratory was probably designed as the Gallarus Ossuary, a boat-shaped chamber to contain the bones of the dead.

Once again we see a dramatic similarity between the cultures of the Balearic Islands and Ireland, and once again we need to find a cultural conduit that would allow for this fusion in beliefs, technology and architecture between these two widely separated islands. Once again we already have literary evidence for that conduit, provided for us by the accounts of the Irish and Scottish chronicles. But these chronicles attach certain dates to these migrations between Egypt, the Balearic Islands, and Ireland. Thus we can say with some confidence that the Balearic *navetas* were actually constructed in about 1300 BC, while the later migration to Ireland occurred a few generations later (say within two hundred years), and so the Irish *navetas* (and amphitheaters) would have been constructed in about 1150 BC. The migration to Scotland occurred a few generations later still, perhaps in 1000 BC (alternatively, the Pictish migration to Scotland might suggest a date as late as 700 BC).

Sacred metrology

It is a fact that many of the ancient religions of the world incorporated an element of sacred metrology, or sacred measurement systems. I discuss many of the metrological curiosities that can be found in the megalithic monuments of the world in the book *Thoth*, and from these deliberations it is clear that mathematical formulae like Pi and the Pythagorean theorems were deliberately incorporated into the dimensions of the pyramids of Giza and the henges of England. A cursory glance at the Book of Exodus will also confirm that the Hyksos-Israelite people had more than a passing interest in measurements.

What, then, of the ancient monuments scattered across the Balearic Islands and the western fringes of greater Britain? What can the dimensions of these constructions tell us about the beliefs and migrations of the people who built them?

Balearic navetas

Many of the monuments in the Balearic Islands were not manufactured to very high tolerances, and so it is difficult to say with any certainty what the units of measure were. However, a few elements of their designs, like the doorways, had a great deal more care and attention applied to them, and these betray the repetitive usage of certain measurements. The most common of these are 52 cm and 76 cm, with the former of these equating to one Egyptian Thoth (Royal) cubit (tc). However, when looking at the external dimensions of these same monuments, these units of length often result in fractional dimensions, and it is unlikely that any prestigious monument would have been designed using fractions.

This inconsistency might be solved by looking instead at the dimensions of the T-shaped *taule* monuments that are dotted all across Minorca (see the colour section in the book *Jesus* for an example). These are finely cut megalithic monuments dating from the same era as the *navetas* and *talayots* and a probable subunit used in their construction measures about 14 cm. Multiplying this unit upwards by four, to derive a more manageable length, would result in a unit measuring 56 cm. As it happens, the Tudons *naveta*, when measured in units of 56.4 cm, has dimensions of 10 x 24 of these units – 10 x 24 Tudons yards (ty). This is a rather satisfying deduction, which suggests that the primary measurement unit in use in Minorca was 56.4 cm long.

The only problem with this proposed measurement system being that the Rubi *navetas* do not appear to have used the Tudons yard at all; although it should be pointed out that differing units of measure will shortly be demonstrated to have been a feature of Celtic architecture too. With the Rubi *navetas*, the units of length that give whole number results for both of these constructions measure about 83 cm and 93 cm. The first of these measurement systems would give dimensions of 8 x 14 units and 9 x 15.5 units for the two *navetas* at Rubi, while the second would give 7 x 12.5 units and 8 x 14 units. These units of measurement may also have been used in the Celtic round-towers, as we shall see later.

Irish navetas

The lesser known Irish *navetas* (ossuaries) at Kilmakedar and Ballymorereagh (Manachain) have exactly the same length, 715 cm, and so it seemed likely that this unit was a whole-number multiple of the measurement system used at these two sites. If these *navetas* were presumed to be 10 units long, then this new unit would measure 71.5 cm in length; a unit that I shall call the Kilmakedar yard (ky). Sure enough, a unit of 71.5 cm divided very nicely into all the other measurements on these sites. Thus these Irish *navetas* measure:

Naveta	External	Internal	Door	
Kilmakedar	7 x 10	$4 \times 7\,^2/_6$	$1 \times 1\,^5/_6 \times\,^5/_6$	(ky)
Manachain	9 x 10	$4\,^4/_6 \times 6$	$1 \times 2 \times\,^4/_6$	(ky)

However, the Gallarus Naveta (Oratory), which happens to be the finest of all the remaining Irish *navetas*, does not result in a tidy arrangement of whole numbers when using the Kilmakedar yard, and so another unit of measure must have been in use here. To resolve this issue, and taking the Tudons Naveta as my cue (for both of these *navetas* have the same width), I presumed once more that the unit of measure in use here had a length of 56.5 cm. In other words, the proposed Gallarus yard (gy) measures almost exactly the same as the Tudons yard (ty). The Gallarus and Tudons *navetas*, when measured in this new yard length, become:

Naveta	External	Internal	Height	Door height	
Gallarus (Ireland)	10 x 12	$5\,^3/_6 \times 8\,^2/_6$	9	3	(gy)
Tudons (Minorca)	10 x 24			$1\,^2/_6$	(gy)

I think it can be seen that sufficient measurements at the Gallarus Naveta have resolved into whole numbers, to declare that the Gallarus yard is a real unit of length.

In the colour section, readers will have already seen the uncanny similarity between the Gallarus and Tudons *navetas*. They not only look as if they have come from the drawing board of the same designer, they are also similarly orientated towards the northwest and the summer sunset. However, it can now be seen that these two monuments were also using a unit of measurement that was, to all intents and purposes, exactly the same. How much more evidence do we need to prove that, at some point in the remote past, the people of the Balearic Islands migrated to Ireland and Scotland?

Scottish brochs

Despite these Scottish *brochs* being scattered all across the Western Isles, a great number of them seem to have been constructed with the same dimensions, namely an external diameter of 17.5 m and an internal diameter of 10 m. Like their Irish equivalents, a fort would surely be tailored to suit the local topography and the community's budget, and only a sacred precinct needs to be standardised in this fashion. So what is so special about this dimension that it needed setting in stone for future generations?

The answer to this takes us back to the Great Pyramid at Giza, which I have already demonstrated to have been a forty-times copy of the Pi fraction of 22:7. To achieve this fraction with a pyramidal structure is reasonably complex, but to do the same with a circular monument is simplicity itself: for all you need is a monument with a diameter that is a multiple of seven. The evidence that these *brochs* were indeed sacred precincts, designed around the Pi fraction of 22:7, can be seen in the dimensions of many of the doorways and also in one abnormally large block of stone in the Borrafiach *broch*, which measures 83 cm across. This unit of 83 cm is not only a component of the Rubi *navetas* of Minorca, it is also a well-known unit of measure in Britain, for it is one Megalithic yard (my). This was the unit of measure derived by Alexander Thom in the 1960s, and he comprehensively demonstrated that it had been used in many of Britain's megalithic structures.

Fig 52. *Carloway broch, Lewis.*

Looking at these *brochs* again, when using a Megalithic yard of 83 cm, it can be seen that the external diameter of the majority of these *brochs* measures 21 my and, when using a Pi fraction of 22:7, the circumference of these circular constructions will therefore become 66 my. But this process of initiation can continue further, for it is likely that there was also a larger unit of measure in use in Scotland, which is known as a Megalithic rod (mr), and this comprised three Megalithic yards. If we measure these *brochs* using this rod unit, it can be seen that many of them appear to have a diameter of 7 mr and a circumference of 22 mr. In other words, these *brochs* hold within their dimensions the secrets of the Pi fractional of 22:7.* Thus they were indeed sacred precincts, perhaps designed for the circumperambulations of a masonic-type sect, as well as being a repository of sacred metrology. Since sacred metrology was an established part of Egyptian theology, with the mathematical constant Pi being similarly woven into the design and fabric of the Great Pyramid itself, it is highly likely that the concepts that lay behind the design of these *brochs* had an Egyptian heritage.

Irish stadiums

In a similar fashion to the Scottish *brochs*, the internal dimensions of many of the Irish stadiums are the same, with the Navenooragh, Cahergall and Staigue stadiums all measuring 25.7 m internally. Again, it is unlikely in the extreme that a fort would require identical dimensions in varying locations across Ireland. Thus it seemed likely that these were sacred sites once more, and that the units of measure would again be derived from the Pi fractional of 22:7.

However, the results of this investigation were initially a little confusing, because many of the measurement lengths that we have already looked at seemed to fit the diameter of these stadiums and returned whole-number results. The various units of measure that we have looked at are shown in the following table:

Measurement unit	Stadium internal diameter	Stadium internal circumference
Metric (100 cm)	25.7 m	80.8 m
Megalithic yd (83 cm)	31 my	97.5 my
Kilmakedar yd (71.5 cm)	36 ky	113.1 ky
Rubi yd (93 cm)	28 ry ?	88 ry ?
Thoth cubit (52.5 cm)	49 tc	154 tc

* A table of measurements for the Scottish *brochs* follows (measurements are of external and internal diameters in meters, and only to the nearest 0.2 m due to the scale of the plans used):

Dun Osdale	16.8	x	9.6	Dun Boreaig	17.6 x 10
Dun Colbost	17.4	x	10.4	Dun Fiadhairt	16.4 x 9.6
Dun Hallin	15.5	x	10.2	Dun Borrafiach	16.4 x 10
Gearymore	16.4	x	10	Edinbain	17.5 x 10
Flashader	17.5	x	10	Suledale	17.5 x 12.4
Kingsburgh	16.8	x	9.5	Floddigay	17.5 x 11
Greanan	16	x	10.5	Sabhail	17.5 x 10.4
Arkaig	16.8	x	9.2	Dun Beag	17.5 x 10.4
Garsin	16	x	9.2		

A dimension of 17.5 x 10 m would translate as 21 x 12 my.

So which of these was the real unit of measure that was in use at these sites? Part of the answer can be seen in the circumference measurements, where only two of these measurement systems result in whole numbers for both the internal diameter and the internal circumference of the stadium. This is due to the measurements of 88:28 and 154:49 being a simple four and seven times multiple of the 22:7 Pi ratio respectively, and surely any competent designer would prefer whole numbers in both the diameter and circumference of their construction. This observation would knock out most of the other measurement systems from this competition. Furthermore, the 93 cm unit of length does not quite fit, as it would actually have to be more like 92 cm to derive whole-number answers.

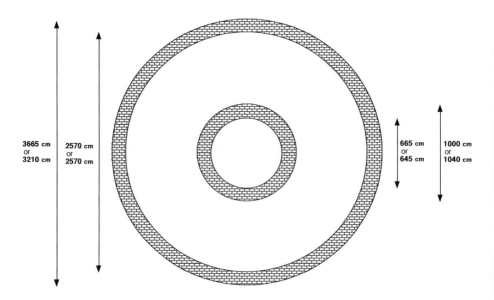

| 3665 cm or 3210 cm | 2570 cm or 2570 cm | | 665 cm or 645 cm | 1000 cm or 1040 cm |

Fig 53.   Dimensions of the Cahergall temple or stadium (upper figures)
*and Navenooragh temple or stadium (lower figures).**

Thus it would seem likely that the true measurement unit in use at most of these Irish stadiums was the Egyptian Thoth cubit, measuring 52.5 cm in length. This suggestion is greatly reinforced by the fact that the entrance

---

* The other dimensions of these two stadiums appear to be simple multiples of the internal diameter of the internal truncated round-tower.

passageways and other dimensions of these stadiums were also constructed using the Thoth cubit. The entrance of the Navenooragh stadium is exactly 3 tc wide, while the Cahergall entrance measures 4 tc at the base and $3^3/_7$ at the top (the hand unit of the Thoth cubit being $^1/_7$ th of a cubit). Furthermore, the terraces for the audience, which once filled these giant stadiums, are also exactly 52 cm, or 1 tc, in depth.

In using these precise lengths, the architect is clearly stating that this construction was designed and fabricated in units of the Egyptian Thoth cubit, and so these stadiums are actually a sevenfold celebration of the Pi fractional of 22:7. Thus we have not only discovered a metrological link that leads from Ireland directly back to the Balearic Islands, through the boat-shaped *naveta* monuments, we now also have a direct link back to Egypt and the measurement units that were used in the Great Pyramid itself. A similar argument will be made in a later chapter regarding the round-tower at the center of the Church of the Holy Sepulchre in Jerusalem.

Maritime units

The design of the *naveta* ossuaries in Minorca and Ireland may also give us some further information about the design of the boats used by Aye-Gaythelos and Scota during their various migrations. These monuments were obviously modelled upon the form of an upturned boat, as the literature readily acknowledges, and the reason for this symbolism is fairly obvious. Having arrived in a new land, these people would have needed shelter fairly quickly. The plebeians would have to fend for themselves, but the easiest method for constructing a reasonably palatial abode for the aristocracy or a temple for the priesthood would be to select the worst of the boats in the fleet, cut them in half, and turn them upside down. Within a day or so, each boat could provide two houses or temples for the leaders and priests of the exiled population. These prefabricated constructions could have lasted for at least a generation, and so the society would have been very used to associating religion and privilege with a boat-shaped building. It would not take much of a leap in imagination to transfer this same shape to a house, temple or tomb, constructed in more durable corbelled stonework.

Both the Tudons Naveta in Minorca and the Gallarus Naveta in Ireland measure about 5.65 m across. If these *naveta* monuments had been designed to mimic the original boats that comprised the Scotian's fleet in every detail, then we might speculate that their boats also measured about 5.65 m (10 ty or gy) in breadth. If we were to apply the standard 7:1 length-to-breadth ratio that was discussed in Chapter V, then these same vessels would have measured some 39.5 m (70 ty or gy) in length – dimensions that are similar to the reconstructed Athenian vessel called Olympias.

Finally, it is probably worth mentioning that it was this direct association between Minorcan theological architecture and the sea that convinced archaeologists in Spain that the Minorcan people came from across the seas, presumably from the east. It is this same direct association between Celtic theological architecture and the sea that should likewise convince historians in Ireland that these early Celtic leaders (and many of their people) also came from across the seas. Since *Scotichronicon* clearly states that these people came from Spain and Egypt, an assertion that the design and metrology of these *navetas* positively confirms, it is highly likely that the Scottish and Irish chronicles are based upon historical facts rather than unreliable mythology.

Norman Towers

The cult of the round-tower was not simply a Bronze Age phenomena, of course, and we have already seen evidence that it continued through the Iron Age at least until the beginning of the second millennium AD in Ireland. But that was not the end of the round-tower by any means, as the tradition flowed into the Medieval period and it may well have been through this ancient usage of circular round-tower temples and amphitheaters that the designs of circular Templar churches evolved.

Conversely, it is often asserted that the design of Templar churches and some preceptories was derived from the circular form of the Dome of the Rock* and thus from the earlier Church of the Holy Sepulchre, which both reside in Jerusalem. So were these later, Templar round-tower designs more influenced by the architecture of the Celtic north west, or the Judaeo-Arabic south east?

One of the noble houses that went on the first crusade to Jerusalem was that of the Scottish Sinclairs, with Henry de St Clair departing for the Holy Land in AD 1095 and being at the fall of Jerusalem in the following year. Upon the return of these intrepid crusaders from the far reaches of Christendom, the Sinclairs built a 'castle' in their former homelands of Normandy. Today it sits among cornfields just outside the village of St Clair sur Epte, near Gisors. In actual fact, the building has been constructed upon the traditional planform of a Norman motte and bailey, and so it may initially seem obvious that the round-tower of this Sinclair 'castle', and its associated curtain wall, have been built primarily as a fortified village rather than as a

---

* The exterior of the Dome of the Rock is octagonal, but the cupola is a hemisphere and rests on a cylindrical drum.

religious structure. However, the exposed locations of these towers and their small and cramped design still leads to doubts. Christopher Gravett, in his chronology of Norman castles, says:

> It is by no means clear exactly what function the earliest stone towers were designed to fulfil. Some of them were cramped and lacking in charm...[1]

Which is very true, for the tower at St Clair sur Epte could hardly be described as comfortable accommodation for a lord of the manor. An alternative option may be that the lord lived in a large manor house in the bailey, as the present farmer does, while the tower performed a more esoteric role, with defence only being a secondary consideration. However, this design would have left any associated village for the estate workers outside the fortification, and completely undefended.

A nearby 'castle' at Bezu, which lies even closer to Gisors, was built at the same time by Henry I of England. The Bezu 'castle' has an identical motte and bailey layout to the 'castle' at St Clair, although little remains today of the curtain wall that surrounded the bailey. Since both of these fortifications reside upon the same topographical feature, it would appear that we have here two links in a chain of early Anglo-Norman fortresses that once stretched along the north bank of the river Epte in Normandy. This explanation would again imply that these towers were fortifications, and nothing more – or were they?

Fig 7.1. The design of a motte and bailey. Note, however, that this 'village' can only hold three or four families, and this hardly represents a viable village. The St Clair motte and bailey is very similar to this artist's impression, and the entire bailey

enclosure now contains just one farm and one family. It is likely that these motte and bailey fortifications were just for the family of the lord of the manor and his key possessions, including his workshops and stables, while the common people resided outside the bailey in a few mud huts. This would allow the round-tower to be used for the safe storage of foodstuffs, as a last salient of defence, and for ritual purposes.

As just mentioned, Andrew Sinclair, who is a direct descendant of the

Fig 61.   The St Clair round-tower (top) and the Bezu round tower (bottom). Both are situated near Gisors, Normandy.

ancient Sinclair family, has stated in a recent documentary that the circular layout of the round-tower attached to this Sinclair 'castle' in Normandy was derived from the circular layout of the Church of the Holy Sepulchre, which the Sinclairs had obviously visited during the crusades. In other words, the form of this fortification was actually based upon the design of a sacred church in Jerusalem, and so again the design may actually perform a sacred role, with any secular defensive considerations being secondary.

However, the motte and bailey design of both of these fortifications would initially suggest a purely defensive role for the round-tower. The motte and bailey design was the standard form of defence for the Normans in Britain, after the invasion by William the Conqueror in 1066, and literally hundreds of these fortifications were built across greater Britain; there being over seventy in Herefordshire alone. Most of these fortifications started as simple earth banks with wooden defences, but were later rebuilt in stone.

Many of these forts had a traditional Norman square-tower placed upon the motte, but some sported round-towers, just as the examples in Normandy do. Examples of motte and bailey forts in Britain include Hen Domen near Montgomery, and Berkhamstead and Longtown in Herefordshire – even the massive Conisborough and Windsor Castles are simply elaborate motte and bailey designs. But many of these English and Welsh fortifications were constructed well before the first of the crusades to the Holy Land, and so the influence of the Church of the Holy Sepulchre on their design may have been negligible or nonexistent. So did the St Clair and Bezu round-towers acquire their inspiration from Jerusalem, or from elsewhere?

Sepulchre

Incidentally, the dimensions of the Dome of the Rock are rather interesting, for it seems obvious that this sacred Islamic monument is simply an Islamic copy of the Church of the Holy Sepulchre. Just as the majority of Islamic mosques copy the architecture of the Christian Aye Sophia cathedral in Istanbul, so the Dome of the Rock copied the nearby Christian cathedral. Since the Church of the Sepulchre was built in AD 335 and the Dome of the Rock in AD 690, it is quite certain that the Dome was aping the Sepulchre.

However, the architects of the Dome were obviously not fully conversant with all of the sacred metrology used in the Sepulchre, as their copy came out a few centimeters too small, and they had not realised that the original design for both of these temples was firmly rooted in Egyptian theology. Like the beautiful Pantheon in Rome, the cupolas of the Dome and the Sepulchre were constructed so that the internal height of the dome equalled half of its diameter. In other words, if the curve of the dome were to be continued downwards, a perfect sphere would result. In the example of the Pantheon, this imaginary sphere was also designed so that it would just touch the ground; and so elegant was this design that it has inspired the design of the Jefferson Memorial in Washington, which appears to be almost an exact replica of the Pantheon.

Clearly, these cupolas were designed to imitate the hemispherical vault of the heavens or, as I pointed out in the book *Tempest*, they may have invoked the spherical shape of the Earth itself. Actually, the distinction is of little consequence, because if one knows that the vault of the heavens is hemispherical then surely the Earth must be hemispherical to match it. As the spheres of the Earth and the heavens on the top of the pillars at the Temple of Solomon clearly demonstrated, the spherical form of the Earth was well-known in the centuries BC and AD.

But what of the original dimensions for these Earth-like cupola-spheres in Jerusalem? Well, the cupola of the Sepulchre measures some 20.90 m in diameter and its full spherical height would be 21.05 m, and so it seems likely that the architect was aiming at a measurement of about 20.95 m.* As it happens, this translates into exactly 40 Thoth cubits (tc). This fortuitous arrangement is highly likely to have been a part of the original design, because not only is the number 40 central to many of the biblical story-lines, as has been mentioned previously, but the Great Pyramid itself is a 40-times copy of the Pi fractional of 22:7, when measured in Thoth cubits. Thus any adept who had been initiated into the secrets of the Sepulchre, would have been acutely aware of the sacred nature of the dome's measurements and its intimate links with the Egyptian's ancient 'masonic' style of theology; a central component of which involved sacred measurements and sacred mathematical formulae.

Sinclair and Rollo

It would appear, therefore, that the churches or mosques of the east may have been infused with sacred mathematical and metrological dimensions. However, it has already been argued that the Irish amphitheaters and Scottish *brochs* were similarly infused with sacred metrology and may also have used the Thoth cubit in their design. In other words, the towers in the east and

---

* The cupola has been destroyed and rebuilt on a few occasions, but it has been rebuilt upon the original rotunda underneath, and so the current dimensions should be the same as in the original fourth century design. The Thoth cubit is the Royal cubit of Egypt: the unit of measure that was used in the designs of the Giza pyramids.

the northwest were both sacred monuments and both were basically round-towers, so which of these traditions was the primary influence on the early Medieval and later Templar designs?

Being Normans, the Sinclair clan had arrived in England and then Scotland with the Norman invasion at the Battle of Hastings, in 1066. They quickly (re)established themselves, before the turn of that same century, as lairds of Scotland, with lands in the far north and on Orkney. But it is on the islands of the Hebrides, Orkney and Shetland that the majority of the Scottish *brochs* reside. The wonderful Mousa *broch* on the Shetland Islands stands almost fully preserved to this day, and so it is highly likely that many more *brochs* were preserved in the years before the first crusade. So on their return from Jerusalem, did the Sinclairs and Templars build copies of the Church of the Holy Sepulchre, or copies of the Mousa Broch?

A significant factor in this argument has to be the origins of the

Fig 62. Statue of Rollo in Falaise, Normandy.

Normans, and thus the origins of the Sinclairs, of King Henry I, and of the later Plantagenet kings of England. Strangely enough, the Normans were not French (Gauls) at all, but hailed from Scandinavia instead. During the Viking raids on greater Britain and the north French coast, these people from the north began to settle in many coastal lands, and so these new settlers became known as the North-men, Norse-men, or Normans. But of all the settlements and minor kingdoms that were established around the coasts of the North and Irish Seas, there was one particularly influential princeling who left his indelible mark on history. I refer to the infamous Rollo (Rollon), and his history is highly significant because it is from Rollo that the Sinclairs were descended.

The early history of Rollo is complex and rather uncertain, as there are few surviving records of this family prior to their arrival in France, but since much of English royal history is descended from Rollo it is a subject worth pursuing. Since the history of Rollo is fragmentary and many families have claimed relations to and descent from this legendary figure, I have taken the Icelandic Sagas as my primary source. These sagas were written in a very early period, from AD 1200, and so represent one of the closest sources to these events in both time and place.

Once upon a time, then, there was a minor king living in Norway by the name of Harald Harfager. Harald was an aggressive monarch and expanded his small empire out to encompass all of modern Norway and much of modern Sweden too. In doing so, he had encountered the wrath of several minor lords and kings of Scandinavia, one of whom was Rolf Ganger, son of Ragnvald of More. Rolf was a strapping lad and apparently so tall he was forced to walk everywhere, presumably because northern horses in this era were mere ponies by modern standards (Shetland ponies are still smaller than usual ponies); and so Rolf was given the nickname of Ganger (from the Norse and Saxon *ganger* meaning 'walk', and from which we derive the English 'gangway' or 'gangplank'). Rolf Ganger was a swashbuckling Viking adventurer who had plundered many lands and was growing rich and influential, but in doing so he had crossed the path of King Harald once too often. Rolf was forced to flee from Norway and take refuge in his half-brother's lands of Shetland and Orkney, and parts of northern Scotland. But Rolf was an ambitious princeling and the Scottish islands were never going to be big enough or rich enough for his aspirations, and so he sailed south, to pastures new.

Rolf arrived in northern France (Normandy) in about AD 910, and immediately fell on his feet. In France, Rolf became known as Rollo (Rollon), and King Charles the Simple of northern France offered Rollo extensive lands around Rouen and the hand of his daughter in marriage, if he stopped raiding his lands. Rollo accepted, and the treaty was signed in AD 912 at St Clair sur Epte, the very place where the Sinclairs' later thirteenth century round-tower was built.

Moreover, Rollo decided to convert to Christianity, and so he was introduced to a hermit called St Clair, who lived in this very same location and after whom the town (and later the 'castle') was named. Following his conversion, Rollo surnamed all of his sons 'Saint Clair' (or 'Sinclair'), and it was the descendants of these sons who accompanied William the Conqueror on his invasion of England in 1066. Indeed, the Icelandic Sagas indicate that William the Conqueror himself was directly descended from Rollo, as the family tree in fig 63 demonstrates.

In a similar fashion, the ancestry of King Canute and his son King Harold I - the eleventh century kings of England - goes back to Harthacnut and Gorm, who were kings of Denmark. But it would seem that Harthacnut was not Danish himself, but had invaded Denmark from Norway in about

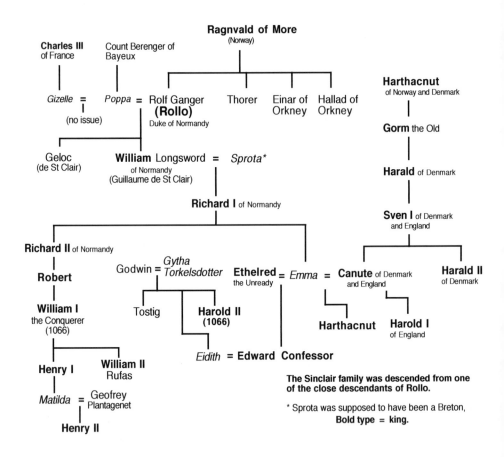

Fig 63. Family tree of Rollo (Rolf), as given by the Icelandic Sagas.

AD 880. The exact ancestry of Harthacnut is unknown, but it happens that this is the same era during which Harald Harfager of Norway was expanding his empire, and princelings like Rolf (Rollo) were being exiled from Scandinavia. King Harold II of England, who defended England against William of Normandy in 1066, was similarly related to this Daneo-Scandinavian royal line, as his mother, Gytha Torkelsdotter, was a Danish aristocrat or princess. Thus it would appear that by invading England, William of Normandy (William the Conqueror) was simply continuing a Daneo-Scandinavian royal feud that had festered for many generations.

The original provenance of this aggressively successful, redheaded

Scandinavian monarchy, which suddenly propelled itself onto the central European stage is, of course, unknown. However, had they been descended from the (redheaded?)* Hyksos-Israelite Scotan refugees from Egypt and Iberia, this would give a degree of extra impetus to the plans for the Crusades. The Normans of France, Scotland and Italy were heavily represented on the first Crusade and English Normans like Richard I (the Lionheart) were similarly represented on later crusades. Had they been aware of their Judaeo-Egyptian ancestry, an expedition to that region would have been rather inviting for these monarchs.

Whatever their ancestry, it was from these influential Rollo-St Clair invaders who arrived with William the Conqueror in 1066 that the Sinclair clan of Scotland was descended. However, in truth the Sinclairs had only 'returned' to Scotland, as the brothers of Rollo, Einar and Hallad, had ruled Orkney, Shetland and some of northern Scotland back in the tenth century AD. The prodigal son (or descendant of the son) had at last returned.

Having been through this long history of England and France, and demonstrated the Scandinavian ancestry of the English and Scottish nobles and kings, perhaps we are now in a better position to analyse the design of the motte and bailey fortification, and the accompanying round-tower that often sat upon the motte (a term derived from the Old French *mote* meaning 'mound').

It seems clear that the motte and bailey was not simply a fortification, there was much more to it than that. While the motte and its tower is clearly a defensive position, to have it situated at the extremity of the enclosure means that it can be easily attacked. Later castles, like Dover, Dinefwr and Pembroke, have the motte and its tower *inside* the outer castle wall, which is clearly a better design. But for some reason the original design persisted and, where there was obviously less of a military threat, later motte and bailey designs have the round-tower standing on flat ground and separated from the fortified manor. Clearly, this kind of round-tower is no longer a simple fortification, and good examples of this type are to be found at Vernon,

---

* The Norman and English monarchs who were descended from Rollo were known for their red hair. These include William the Conqueror himself and his son William Rufus (the red), Richard I and II, Edward I, II and III, Edward the Black Prince, nearly all of the Henrys through to Henry VIII (courtesy of the redheaded couple, Matildan and Geofrey of Anjou) and, of course, the fiery-red Elizabeth I. This should not be so surprising, since all these related royal families were descended in some manner from typical Scandinavian redheads: namely Rollo of Normandy and successive Scandio-Norman princes.[2] As a reminder, the Bible likewise insists that many of the Judaic leaders and kings, from Adam and Esau through to King David, were of similarly ruddy complexion.

Verneuil sur Avre, Falaise and possibly at Gisors too. At Vernon the round-tower has been joined onto the town wall at a later date, but the stone fabric of the tower is completely separate from the wall itself and this demonstrates that the tower was originally freestanding. In which case, the upper door of the tower must once have been accessed by ladder or drawbridge, just as the round-towers in Ireland were. The doorway on the Falaise round-tower is similarly accessed by a suspended walkway.

Third Reich

The Greek explorer and geographer Pytheas mentions a mysterious land in the far north of Europe called Ultima Thule. While Thule has been linked at some point with all the northern European islands or peninsulars, the Sinclair website indicates that it referred to Shetland. The connection between a Greek explorer and the current discussion on round-towers comes from the nineteenth century occult German organisation known as the Thule Society, a mystic organisation that was based upon the legends of Ultima Thule.

This occult society was officially suppressed under Nazism, but elements of the beliefs and rituals are thought to have been taken up by Heinrich Himmler, who was overtly interested in many forms of occult mysticism. In 1934, Himmler commandeered Wewelsburg Castle for the ritual headquarters of his SS troops, and immediately began a reconstruction of the north tower. What Himmler constructed, as an ill-fitting appendage to a Renaissance castle, was a large, truncated

Fig 64. Round tower at Vernon, on the river Seine. Note the suspended upper door, a feature that is also to be found on Irish round-towers.

round-tower. The tower bears a distinct resemblance to many of the round towers we have looked at and, just like the motte and bailey towers of the early Sinclairs, it sits as an odd-looking appendage to a fortress – the only prime difference being that the Sinclair tower contained an internal octagon (8 sides), while Himmler's tower had an internal dodecagon (12 sides).

On the floor of Himmler's tower there is an inlayed 12-limbed swastika Sun-wheel - the *Schwarze Sonne* or Black Sun, from which some say that the SS name and insignia were derived. Significantly, at the end of the war, an unsuccessful attempt was made to destroy this same north tower; and so its urgent construction and its equally urgent destruction indicate it held some particular significance for Himmler.

Thus, it would appear that we again have the same dual usage for a round-tower. In eras before the invention of cannons and howitzers, the newly constructed north tower of Wewelsburg Castle would indeed have been an impregnable strong point. However, that was not its true function, for both the history of the tower and its interior design confirm that its primary purpose was as a spiritual assembly room for the twelve highest ranking SS officers; plus Himmler as the pseudo-Arthurian or pseudo-Jesusian thirteenth.*

It is indisputable that round-towers may have been used as a refuge on occasions, just as villagers have often flocked to the safety of their church when under attack. But that defensive reaction is only due to the church (or tower) being the town's most sturdy stone construction, and it does not imply that a church is a castle.

But if the motte and round-tower are not ideal for defence, then why was this design adopted by the Norman Vikings and used so widely? The answer, I think, is to be found in the Western Isles of greater Britain. In Ireland and Scotland we have seen truncated round-towers that held some kind of sacred function, but were not associated with artificial mounds in any way. The Normans were descended from Rollo who was, of course, of Norwegian descent, but had spent a number of years on the Scottish isles and would have been very familiar with these sacred towers and their sacred functions. In addition, the leaders on the Isle of Man used an artificial mound, Tynwald, as their parliament, and so a mound may well have been regarded as a central component in the governance of the people. But Rollo would not have had to travel to the Isle of Man to see a mound of this nature, for there is one just down the road from Stockholm's Arlanda airport. In fact, this artificial mound looks exactly like a half-sized Silbury Hill, and it is associated with a large necropolis which makes it appear like a motte and bailey for the dead.

Here, then, may be the origins of the motte and bailey design. The motte, the mound, was an elevated position from which the leaders of the society could address the public, and it was closely associated with death and spirituality. Conversely, the sacred round-tower was a central theological feature of the lands occupied by the Norsemen, as they ventured across the North Sea (and also a feature of Iberia, Jerusalem, Sardinia, Crete and Saba). Both the mound and the tower were spiritual sites and centers of leadership for the aristocracy, and perhaps it was noticed that an amalgamation of both forms produced a passible fortification too. In effect, the Bezu and St Clair towers are simply a Silbury Hill with a Mousa Broch on its summit.

In fact, if one looks closely at the sites of the Gearymore and Borrafiach *brochs* on Skye, a walled enclosure to the west of the round-tower can be seen in both cases. Although these walls are too low and flimsy to have ever been defensive structures, what we seem to have in both cases is the plan and outline of a round-tower with a walled garden or village on one side. In other words, Gearymore and Borrafiach are proto-motte and baileys, which were constructed in the ancestral lands of the Rollo-Sinclairs some 1800 years before the St Clair and Bezu motte and bailey 'castles' in Normandy. So the prototype of the ubiquitous motte and bailey fortification,

---

* As was pointed out in Chapter I, Arthur may have been a later pseudonym for Jesus. Hence we see this similar symbology in the twelve disciples and the twelve knights of the Round Table (the Last Supper table). See *King Jesus* for further details.

which were constructed all across Normandy and greater Britain, can still be seen along the Waternish peninsular on Skye.

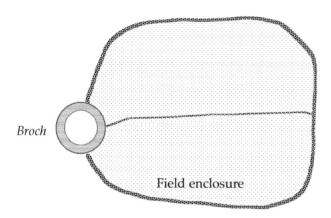

Fig 66. Rough sketch of Borrafiach broch and its walled enclosure. The function of the enclosure is uncertain; if it contained a field it was very small, while if it contained a village the boundary wall was certainly not defensive against a military force.

Thus, the original design for the Norman (Scandio-Scottish) motte and bailey was born on the barren slopes of the Scottish Isles. But the round-towers in the Scottish Isles are not fortifications and nor are they habitations, and so the only real alternative is that these were temples (a sacred round-tower) together with its small (village?) enclosure. But the usage of this somewhat exposed round-tower as a pure fortification, in Normandy and Britain, was always compromised and so their construction only lasted a few generations until the much more secure 'castle and central keep' design was adopted.

In conclusion, these round-towers were originally conceived as sacred monuments, which were invariably situated at the extremity of an enclosure, and we see that same type of layout in diverse locations from Crete to Sardinia, to Mallorca and Minorca, Ireland and Scotland, and finally to France and England. The evidence seems to suggest that Prince Rollo took this design from Scotland to Normandy, and so one might suspect that a similar historical character took this same design from the Balearic Islands to Ireland and Scotland. In other words, the motte and bailey design once again supports the theory of a migration from Crete to Mallorca and thence to the north-western fringes of Europe.

Scota's Tomb

According to local legends, the final piece of evidence that Queen Scota came to Ireland is the presence of her tomb, which lies in a valley just south of Tralee in Co Kerry. Of course, in my slightly revised version of this same mythology, this tomb would have been for a descendant of Queen Scota-Ankhesenamun, and not the queen herself. Nevertheless, it is entirely probable that Queen Scota's great-great-granddaughter carried the same name and rank as the founding monarch, and so it is entirely possible that a new Queen Scota migrated to Ireland around the tenth century BC.

Unfortunately, the local tourist office in Tralee was not sure where Scota's tomb was, and so I was directed towards the library. Eamon, the very helpful librarian, was a mine of information, and I soon had a pile of maps and old history books that showed exactly where her tomb lay. The data looked promising as the tomb was located up a steep-sided gorge to the south of town and this kind of topography was remarkably similar to the tombs in the Valley of the Kings and the royal tombs at Amarna. With the descendants of Scota having been denied their rightful resting place in the royal valley at Amarna, what better than to find an identical burial site in this foreign land?

The mythology indicated that the Scotian people landed along the Dingle and Iveragh peninsulars, which are located in Co Kerry in the southwest of Ireland. This did seem to be an unlikely location for the Scotians to make landfall as mariners in this early era preferred to hug the coastline. This kind of navigational technique may well have resulted in a colony being located near Wexford or Dublin, which lie to the southeast and east of Ireland respectively, but not in Kerry. However, in mitigation the myths do say that Scota's fleet was scattered during a storm, and so perhaps only a few lost ships found the rugged inlets of Kerry. The majority of the fleet may well have sailed on to Dublin, and thus we now see similar legends that emanate from opposite sides of the country.

But the landing in Kerry was not unopposed and a battle is reputed to have ensued with the local tribes, during which Queen Scota and Princess Uin were killed. It may be worth recalling at this point that the throne name of Pharaoh Akhenaton was Uin-Ra (see fig 2 for a larger version of this cartouche). According to legend, Queen Scota was laid in a tomb in the small valley that runs up to Mount Knockawaddra, where it lies to this day. It is also said that there was originally an Ogham inscription on the grave; Ogham being an old Celtic script of uncertain age and provenance. The inscription read 'Leacht Scoihin', or 'Tomb of Scothin'. However, upon translation it was decided that this inscription was a recent addition to the tomb.

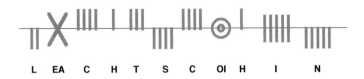

Fig 68.   The Ogham inscription on the Tomb of Scota.

I set off the next day, following the path of the stream up into the hill-country above the town. The path wound its way through a 'magical' forest of gnarled beech and holly trees covered with hanging moss, a scene that would have befitted a scene in Lord of the Rings. Finally, there by the stream, I recognised the stone slab that marked Scota's tomb.

Unfortunately, this was not a tomb. This rough and misshapen slab of stone that lay beside the stream was merely an outcrop of natural rock, which thrust its way out of the vegetation that grew all around it. This location had never been the tomb of anyone, let alone an Egypto-Celtic queen named Scota. In addition, there was so much graffiti carved upon the surface of the slab that any Ogham inscription – had there ever been such a thing – had been completely obliterated. It was a disappointing end to a promising avenue of research.

All one can say is that there is a strong association, which has been passed down through the ages in local folklore, between a Queen Scota (a later Queen Scota) and this particular valley. But the underlying rocks in this valley are of a hard gritstone, and so a deep burial or an elaborate tomb is highly unlikely here. Perhaps there may still be a small cairn lying undiscovered in this fairly remote and undisturbed valley, which might contain a burial of some description, but any more than this is extremely unlikely.

This disappointing result does question the whole association between Scota and this region of Ireland. However, the Cahergall, Navenooragh and Staigue amphitheaters plus the Gallarus, Kilmakedar and Manchain *navetas* are all located upon the Kerry peninsulas, so there is a definite historical link between the Balearic Islands and the southwest of Ireland. Likewise, one of the earliest maps we have of this region, the second century Claudius Ptolemaeus, calls the Kerry peninsular 'Hiberni'; and this is a clear indication that this part of Ireland is linked in some manner to Hibernia and thence to Iberia (through the son of Scota called Hiber).

To trace the extent of the Roman Empire, one only needs to plot the locations of their ubiquitous triumphal arches on a map.* Likewise, in order to trace the migrations of the Scotian people, we only need to follow the trail of their round-tower temples, their boat-shaped *naveta* tombs and the measurement systems that they preserved in stone. Surprisingly, these same monuments litter the Kerry peninsular.

Thus it is highly likely that some enterprising individuals from the Balearic Islands must have travelled up the Atlantic coastline and landed in Kerry, and some may even have settled and been buried there; but whether this cultural link also includes the location of a tomb for a queen called Scota is anyone's guess. Perhaps, in this case, the last words in this short chapter should be left to a seventeenth century Kerry poet:

> In yon cool glen, beside the mount, close by the wave, fell Scotia while pursuing the enemy across the hills.

---

* The first Roman triumphal arch to be built in Britain is located at Richborough in Kent, the site of the Roman landing. Unfortunately, only the concrete foundations of this huge structure remain.

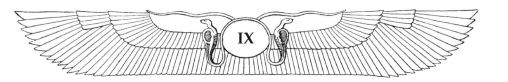

Pharaoh Plunket

Within later explanations of *Scotichronicon*, and indeed within the chronicle itself, there is an amount of confusion about the era in which this exodus to Ireland actually occurred, and the geographical area that it originated from. It seems likely that this confusion has arisen because there were actually two immigration events that have, in some of these accounts, been telescoped together.

It would appear to be more than likely that the first wave of immigrants to Ireland came from Brigantia and Mallorca, and they set sail only four or so generations after Aye-Gaythelos and Ankhesenamun-Scota landed in Spain. This was the major exodus event that the chronicle relates. However, there was a further, and smaller, wave of immigrants that came from another location in a later era. Geoffrey of Monmouth, in his *History of the Britons*, says of this later wave of immigrants:

> Gurgant Bartrud, king of the Britons, was sailing back home through the Orkney Islands ... he came upon thirty ships full of men and women, and when he enquired the reasons for their arrival, their leader ... said that he had been driven out of a region of Spain ... he asked for a small portion of Britain to settle in ... So when Gurgant learned that they had come from Spain and were called Basques and understood what their request was, he sent them to the island of Ireland. [SC1]

This passage is initially being presented as yet another story about Aye-Gaythelos. But even as Bower quotes this passage in *Scotichronicon*, he also points out its discrepancies. The leader of these wandering tribes was called

Partholomus, the great-great-grandson of Aye-Gaythelos; and yet the British king called Gurgant supposedly lived in the sixth century BC, which is many centuries after the voyages of Aye-Gaythelos and Scota. So how does this story fit into the saga of Aye-Gaythelos and his peoples? The answer may lie in the history of those people who chose to stay behind in Brigantia, instead of sailing off to Ireland in about the eleventh century BC:

> For about 240 years they stayed, poorly fed and meanly clad, among the Spaniards who attacked them ceaselessly. The desolate wastes and forest of the Pyrenees were entirely handed over to them by the Spaniards, so that they were scarcely able to survive, supporting life on goat's milk and wild honey. [SC2]

There is another obvious allusion here to the biblical exodus of Moses and Aaron [TuthMoses and Akhenaton], whose destination was also said to be a land of 'milk and honey'; although the biblical account makes this prospect sound much more inviting than this account of the high Pyrenees.

Anyway, had Brigantia been located on the river Ebro, and had the people there either been driven out or voluntarily migrated to new lands, an obvious choice would have been to retrace the flow of the Ebro. This river was reliable and fertile, and no doubt its headwaters would be equally so; as are the upper reaches of the Nile. However, had these people been driven onwards and northwards, past the city of Zaragoza, rather further than they had intended, then they would indeed have found themselves up in the high Pyrenees – a land which becomes increasing cooler and less fertile. In fact, they would have found themselves exiled to the source of the Ebro at Naverra, which is the Basque homeland.

Although it is possible that the Brigantians (Scotians) had influenced and infiltrated the Basques, it is not really possible for them to be the Basques themselves. The Basque nation appears to be a separate culture from much or all of Europe, be that genetically, culturally or linguistically. Little, if anything, within Basque culture can be traced back to Aye-Gaythelos and the wider Egypto-Hyksos-Israelite nations around the Mediterranean; and so if there were Brigantian influences upon the Basques, they must have been quite subtle.

The only element that was readily visible, during my research, was their national emblem which is composed of four teardrops and known as a *lauburu*. In essence, this is a variation on the traditional four-legged swastika, which is known to be a Sun-symbol of great antiquity. However, the curved design of the Basque symbol is very similar to the legendary Irish four-leafed shamrock or clover, which is a symbol of luck.

The *lauburu* also bears a passable resemblance to the three-legged *triskelion* symbol, which adorns the Isle of Man flag (the Isle of Man being the site of the world's oldest parliament). This three-legged emblem is also thought to have been a derivation of the ancient Sun wheel; a swastika with three legs rather than four. But this particular symbol is not thought to have originated in the Isle of Man, for it has a much more ancient pedigree on the isle of Sicily, where examples go back to the fifth century BC. The question, of course, is how this symbol found its way from the toe of Italy to a small island in the Irish Sea. It has been speculated that the Vikings brought the symbol in the eleventh century AD, following their expeditions through the Mediterranean, as the earliest Man emblems only date from the thirteenth century AD. However, there is nothing to preclude the *triskelion* and the *lauburu* having a much older heritage in these northern islands, and having links directly back to the early eras of the Basques and Phoenicians.

Sicilian triskelion

Isle of Man triskelion

Fig 70.   Basque lauburu

Irish four-leafed shamrock.

As was mentioned earlier, the *lauburu* is said to be a Sun symbol, like the swastika. However, since this emblem has a distinctive curved design, there is another possibility for its design. The original symbol for Osiris in Egypt was the 'piece of flesh glyph' (the drop of 'sperm glyph'), which spelt out the name Asar (Osiris), as we have already seen. But on occasions, the sperm glyph can be displayed as a line of three 'sperm' glyphs, which is yet closer to the *lauburu* symbol. Only in the nineteenth dynasty, probably after Akhenaton's iconoclastic reforms, was this sperm glyph changed to the egg glyph ◌ , which was also the symbol of Osiris' sister-wife, Est (Isis).

Back in Eustar Dinau, the local name for the Basque country, the god-name that is given to the four-lobed *lauburu* is Ostri, which sounds a great deal like a combination of Asar and Ast (Osiris and Isis):

> **Ostri:** The Sky in Basque mythology, he later became an equivalent of Heaven. This god is often represented by the *lauburu* (literally, 'four heads', like a swastika). [3]

It would seem that here, deep in the Basque country, we have a symbol of Osiris being venerated, and perhaps we can also speculate that this belief system was brought to this region by the bands of impoverished Brigantians who were migrating up the Ebro river system into the high Pyrenees. In a similar fashion, some versions of the *Scotichronicon* epic named the primary hero as Gaythelos Glas, or Gaythelos the Green. The *Labor Gabala* works this odd colouration into the tradition of there being no snakes in Ireland; however, a simpler explanation is that Osiris was the green god of Egypt and Aye-Gaythelos was

Fig 71. The Green Man, Nantwich, UK.

being identified with Osiris. Since Aye-Gaythelos was no longer a devout Atonist, it would be natural for him to be depicted as Osiris upon his death, as all pharaohs were, and this is probably the origin of the title 'Glas'. This Osirian image survived through to mediaeval times, where it manifested itself in churches and cathedrals all over Europe as the ubiquitous Green Man.

Thus, according to Geoffrey of Monmouth and others, it would appear that in the sixth century BC some of these people from the Basque region of Spain set off for Ireland. Perhaps they had heard how well the Scotians were doing there, and sought to ape their success. Having sailed to Ireland and been given lands to settle in Scotland instead (as we shall see shortly), these people became known as the Picts. This is perhaps confirmed by another chronicle that says:

> After a long time had passed in which the Scots (the Irish) had lived in peaceful and quiet prosperity (in Ireland), a certain unknown people, later called the Picts, appeared from the lands of Aquitania and landed on the Irish shores. (Author's brackets.) [SC4]

As mentioned in Chapter I, the southern lands of Aquitaine lie against the Pyrenees, deep in Basque country, and so there was a long tradition that the Scottish Picts arrived from this region on the borders of Spain and France – the Basque country. The full title for the region just to the north of the western Pyrenees was originally Aquitania Novempopulana, or 'Aquitaine of the Nine People'. Since Osiris has already been identified in Basque culture, there is an outside possibility that the 'nine' may refer to the Egyptian Paut, the company of the nine great gods (or laws).*

It is because of these many connections and traditions that it is thought by some researchers that the Pictish language may have been related to Basque; although because Pictish culture and language died out completely, this is far from certain:

> Of the non-Celtic element in Pictish, the best conclusion is that it is a remnant of one of the languages prevalent in Europe before the spread of the Indo-European language family. Basque is the only remnant of this type surviving today ... For this reason, some writers relate Pictish to Basque directly. [5]

So the Scottish Picts may have come from the Pyrenean Basque country. Whilst not mentioning the Basques, the venerable Bede says of this same event:

> ... it happened that the people of the Picts ... reached Ireland and landed on its northern shores. There they found the race of the Scots (the Irish) and asked for places to settle in ... The Scots replied that their island (Ireland) was not big enough for both peoples (and advised they should go to Scotland) ... The Scots (the Irish) agreed to give them some wives on condition that (they should choose the royal secession) from the female line. [SC6] (Author's brackets.)

It should be noted that the royal succession through the female line is an

---

* The Paut of Hermopolis (City of Thoth) were:
  Atum, Kek and Keket, Heh and Hehet, Nun and Nunit, Amen and Amenet.

  The Paut of Heliopolis were:
  Shu and Tefnut, Geb and Nut, Asar (Osiris) and Ast (Isis), Seth and Neb-het (Nepthys), and Heru (Horus).

Egypto-Israelite tradition, and so this agreement is exactly what one might expect if the Scotians had an Egyptian ancestry. This new Pictish settlement on the west coast of what is now Scotland became quite successful, and so wave after wave of Scotians from Ireland voluntarily decided to follow their Pictish partners to this new land. The Picts were unimpressed by this sudden influx of Scotians from Ireland, as an oracle had prophesied their extinction at the hands of the Scotians – and so it eventually proved to be.

It was through this later wave of migration, from Scotia (Ireland) to the northern half of greater Britain, that this land inherited the title that had originally been bestowed upon Ireland. The Scotians called their new land Scotland, and as the new colony grew and prospered, the usage of this same name declined in Ireland. They also called this new land Hibernia, after Hiber, the son of Aye-Gaythelos, and it is through this process that Spain and Scotland now share a common name.

Language

One of the biggest problems in the whole of this revisionist history of Ireland and Scotland is the fact that no Egyptian hieroglyphs have been discovered in all the diverse places that these Egyptian refugees were supposed to have landed. How could a nation have forgotten such a fundamental aspect of their culture so quickly?

To be more accurate, there are virtually no inscriptions on these monuments whatsoever, which might tend to suggest that these Bronze Age cultures were in a pre-literate phase of their development. But this is not necessarily so, as we might say much the same of the early Irish monasteries. The Rattoo Abbey, for instance, was founded in the highly literate thirteenth century AD, and yet not one letter of script or one idolatrous image remains within the present-day ruins of the abbey. It is likely that any imagery was inscribed onto plasterwork, which has long since fallen away, but the end result is a ruin that is completely devoid of inscriptions.

Another reason for the lack of Egyptian hieroglyphics in western Europe may lie in the fact that the Hyksos-Israelites, who were the ancestors of the Amarna regime, had many trading contacts around the eastern Mediterranean. These contacts would have been reinforced by their many exiles in foreign lands, so that the Hyksos-Israelites became recognisably separate from Upper Egyptian culture. It is likely that through these many contacts with neighbouring civilisations, the Hyksos-Israelites would have come into contact with alternative alphabets and languages that were substantially easier to learn and use. Indeed, it is likely that the Hyksos-Israelites, being the dominant party in these contacts and trading links, influenced the development of these alternate scripts; and with the Hyksos preferring the cursive demotic script, rather than the archaic hieroglyphic system employed in Thebes, the former is thought by some to be the original foundation for the abstract Mediterranean scripts.

As it happens, *Scotichronicon* makes this very same point about Aye-Gaythelos. The chronicle states that at the time of Jacob there was contact between King Phoroneus of Greece and the Egyptians, and a prince of Greece sailed to Egypt and was worshipped as a 'god'. This is interesting as it conforms to the biblical history that I outlined in the book *Jesus*. There, I stated that the (first) great exodus occurred during the time of the biblical Jacob, and that this incident was one and the same as the great Hyksos exodus from Egypt. So, Jacob may well have been the Hyksos monarch who is known to history as Pharaoh Jacoba (𓀀𓏤𓈖𓊃) , and many of the (biblical) Hyksos-Israelites may well have been scattered all over the Mediterranean at this time (c. 1600 BC). King Phoroneus' name is likely to have been a corruption of the Egyptian term *per-aa* 𓉐𓉻 , meaning 'pharaoh'.

In which case, the story about a prince of King Phoroneus sailing (back?) to Egypt and being worshipped as a 'god', would equate very well with the biblical story of Joseph, one of the twelve sons of Jacob. Joseph was the famous, favourite son, who had a coat of many colours (a priest's cope or cloak). Joseph is said to have gone down (back?) to Egypt, and there he is said to have become vizier or prime minister of Egypt, and founded a highly successful dynasty. This is what I believe the chronicle is trying to describe, but it is using historical data rather than biblical data, and the chronicler has either not seen or did not want to see the obvious comparison between the two accounts.

The outcome of this similarity is that it is likely that during the first biblical Hyksos-Israelite exodus, some of the Hyksos-Israelite refugees from Lower Egypt ended up in Greece instead of Jerusalem. There, they became influential in the region and set up their own royal dynasty, but perhaps more importantly, they also influenced the local script and some components of the local language. Thus when Joseph came [back] to Egypt and became vizier, he already knew of and perhaps taught this new, simpler script to his immediate followers. It is possibly due to this royal cross-fertilisation that *Scotichronicon* claims that the Greeks and the Egyptians followed the same laws at this time. The chronicle says of this:

> Gaythelos, bearing in mind ... the laws which King Phoroneus had entrusted to the Greeks and which were still used by the Egyptians in Gaythelos' time, imbued the people who followed him in these same laws ... Hence it is the proud boast of our nation, the Scots, that they still use these same laws up to the present day. SC7

The claim here is that the laws (and the script?) that Aye-Gaythelos took with him on the exodus to Brigantia were not pure Egyptian; rather, they were Hyksos-Egyptian-Israelite laws that had been incubated in Minoan Crete and Mycenaean Greece for more than two centuries, before being brought back to Egypt [by Joseph and Aye-Gaythelos] and then transported on the exodus to Brigantia. Had Aye-Gaythelos spent a number of years in exile in Greece, as seems likely, it would have been readily apparent to him that their early Paleo-Phoenician script – which had been developed from the Egyptian demotic script and was spreading its way across the Mediterranean – was far easier to use. The chronicle alludes to this when it says:

> Gaythelos ... became highly skilled in a variety of languages. Because of his skill the pharaoh [posthumously Akhenaton] gave him (Gaythelos) his daughter and heir Scota as his wife. So since the Hibernians are descended from Gaythelos and Scota they are named Gaitheli (Gaels) and Scoti (Scots). Gaythelos, so they say, invented the Hibernian language which is also called Gaelic. (Author's brackets.) SC8

In fact, it is said that Aye-Gaythelos knew 72 languages, but this specific and rather implausible number is simply another of the coded messages that are frequently woven into biblical-type stories. A reference to the number 72, which occurs in many ancient texts and may have also influenced the name for the Septuagint Bible itself, simply means that the individual in question has been initiated into the cult of the 'Watchers' or 'Guardians'. The Watchers were the astronomer-priests of Egypt, and one of their primary tasks was counting off the astrological millennia. (The purpose for this laborious task is given in *Eden in Egypt*.) The Earth, in its orbit, precesses through all of the constellations of the zodiac in about 25,750 years. Thus one degree of precession (or one precessional 'day') equates to 72 Earth years.

Therefore, the period of 72 years was an important element of the Watcher's ritual calendar, and hence this number has been implausibly forced into many odd locations to indicate the arcane knowledge of certain individuals. For instance, there are 72 angels of the Cabalah zodiac, while in a similar fashion in Luke 10:1 and 10:17 Jesus appointed another 72 disciples.* Since Jesus' original 12 disciples were obviously representative of the zodiac, the additional 72 disciples conform precisely with Cabalistic astrological teaching. That this same number should also have been associated with Aye-

---

* There is a discrepancy in translation within the available Bibles. Bibles taken from the Greek say seventy disciples, while Bibles taken from the Latin say seventy two. I would suggest a look at the Vulgate, Douay Rheims and Rotherham for clarification.

Gaythelos again demonstrates that he must have been allied in some manner to the Hyksos-Egyptian priesthood.

Notwithstanding this, it may well be that Aye-Gaythelos was also an accomplished linguist, and so he would have been in a position to teach his people a variety of scripts and languages. Since the main allies of the exiled Aye-Gaythelos were now in Greece, Crete and Israel, rather than in Upper Egypt, a move towards their language(s) and script(s) would not be so surprising.

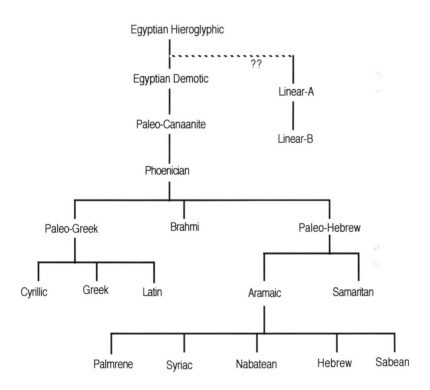

Fig 72. Chronology of Mediterranean scripts.

The early Minoan language, known as Eteocretan, used the Linear-A script, and both this language and its script have never been deciphered. Professor Cyrus Gordon has argued that Eteocretan was a Semitic language related to Phoenician, but this has never been proven – although it has to be said that such a heritage would make a great deal of sense. However, as was indicated in Chapter V, it is likely that this Minoan language did spread to Mycenaean Greece during the early part of the second millennium BC. This is a distinct possibility because the later Mycenaean (and Greek) language used the pictorial Minoan Linear-B script, which was a derivative of the pictorial Minoan Linear-A script and was not related to the later abstract Phoenicio-Greek script.

This chronology means that the Greeks must have swapped scripts from Linear-B to the Phoenician alphabet around the ninth century BC, presumably because the latter was either easier to use or because it had a wider usage around the Mediterranean. This change in national script is similar to the wide-ranging reforms of Kemal Ataturk who, in 1928, changed the alphabet of Turkey from Arabic to Latin almost overnight. The Turkish language is still unintelligible to most Europeans, but the change in alphabet signalled a significant political leaning towards the West. The only real advantage of this change, to visiting Westerners, is that Turkish signposts and shop prices are now much easier to read.

Aye-Gaythelos was also related to the Hyksos-Israelites, and so an alternative language and script that may have influenced him is Hebrew itself. This language was most certainly based upon the Egyptian language, as has been demonstrated in the book *Eden*, so it is more than likely that Aye-Gaythelos spoke a Paleo-Hebrew language as well as pure Egyptian itself. Just as with the later Greek script, the alphabet that the early Israelites used was and is demonstrably based upon the Phoenician script, and not the pictorial Minoan Linear-A or -B alphabets. Yet the Phoenician script is thought to have been strongly influenced by Egyptian hieroglyphs, and may have been a derivative of the cursive Egyptian demotic script, which would not be surprising considering the many other cultural and artistic Egyptian influences upon the Phoenician people. Whatever its source, the adoption of the Phoenician alphabet by both the Israelites and the Greeks in the eleventh and ninth centuries BC is certain.

In the following table, take a look at the Phoenician and Hebrew letters denoting the Latin z, k, l, m, p, ts and sh, and a direct comparison will be immediately apparent between the two scripts. Likewise, take a look at the Phoenician and Greek letters for a, b, g, d, e, u, th, k, m, o, q, p and sh, and the similarities will again be obvious.

Further evidence for the common ancestry of the Greek and Hebrew scripts can be seen in the common name for their alphabets. The Hebrew word for this list of letters is the *alef-bet* אלף־בית, which was derived from the first two letters of the Hebrew alphabet: the *aleph* א and the *bet* ב. Similarly, the Greek name for their alphabet is the *alpha-beta* αλπηα-βετα, which was again derived from the first two letters of their alphabet: the *alpha* α and *beta* β. This common heritage demonstrates that the Phoenicians were very influential throughout the Mediterranean, and that many nations and city states saw the potential of using this new, simplified alphabet.

Phoenician alphabet	Phoenician meaning	Latin	Hebrew	Greek	Cryillic
𐤀	ox	a	א	Aα	А
𐤁	house	b	ב	Bβ	Б
𐤂	throw-stick	g	ג	Γγ	Г
𐤃	door	d	ד	Δδ	Д
𐤄	window	he	ה	Eε	E
𐤅	hook	w, u	ו	Υυ	У
𐤆	weapon	z	ז	Zζ	З
𐤇	fence	h	ח	Hη	Ч
𐤈	wheel	th	ט	Θθ	Ф(f)
𐤉	arm	y	י	Iι	И
𐤊	palm	k	כ	Kκ	К
𐤋	goad	l	ל	Λλ	Л
𐤌	water	m	מ	Mμ	M
𐤍	fish	n	נ	Nν	H
𐤏	eye	o	ע	Oo	O
𐤐	mouth	p	פ	Ππ	П
𐤑	papyrus	ts, z	צ	Σσ	Ц
𐤒	monkey	q	ק	Ψψ	
𐤓	head	r	ר	Pρ	P
𐤔	tooth	sh	ש	Σσ	С,Ш
𐤕	mark	t	ת	Tτ	Т

Pronunciation, especially with the pseudo-vowels, is approximate.

Fig 73. Evolution of the Phoenician alphabet. In chronological order, the Phoenician script evolved into the Hebrew, Greek and Latin scripts.

Although the Phoenician script is not thought to have been created until about the twelfth century BC, had an earlier Paleo-Phoenician script been in use at the time of the Aye-Gaythelos' exodus from Egypt (in the 1320s BC), it is highly likely that Aye-Gaythelos would have been familiar with it and used it in preference to the cumbersome hieroglyphic script. It is known that the Hyksos-Israelites did indeed get expelled from Egypt on at least two major exoduses, which spread far and wide across the Mediterranean and the Arabias, and nowhere do we see a concerted effort to retain the hieroglyphic script. It was obviously not a well-liked system of writing and preference was given to simpler cursive demotic scripts.

Thus, the most likely script that Aye-Gaythelos might have used is an early Paleo-Phoenician alphabet, combined with a Paleo-Hebrew-Egyptian language that had long been in use in the Nile Delta among the Hyksos-Israelites. Thus, it may well be that the exodus of Aye-Gaythelos and Ankhesenamun-Scota did not spread the usage of the cumbersome Egyptian hieroglyphic script around Western Europe, but an early version of the simpler Phoenician alphabet instead.

Beliefs

Another potential stumbling-block in this new history of Western Europe, is the apparent lack of commonality between the theology of Egypt and the theology of Spain and Ireland. But, as with my analysis of early Judaism in the book *Cleopatra*, it rather depends on what 'Egyptian' religion we are expecting to find. A cursory glance at Egyptian theology might convince us that we should be looking for pyramids, uterine temples, megalithic architecture and the standard pantheon of Egyptian gods.

However, these emigrés to the western fringes of Europe would have been impoverished, and unable to perform great feats of architecture. In addition, the bulk of these exiles to Spain and Ireland would have been from Lower Egypt (descendants of the Hyksos), and in the north of Egypt they had their own, idiosyncratic forms of belief. A typical example of this was arboreal veneration, a cult that was well established in Avaris in the Nile Delta and became a central component of early Judaism. In this arboreal creed we can see great similarities between Egypt, Israel, Crete, the Balearic Islands and Ireland; as was demonstrated in the chapters that referred to truncated round-towers.

Even today in Ireland, isolated *sceach* trees, as they are known, are deemed to be sacred: as they are said to be the portal into other worlds for the leprechauns, or little people. Indeed as recently as 1999 the Latoon *sceach* held up the construction of a new road to Shannon airport, as its potential destruction was declared to be unlucky. (The image of a windblown *sceach* was also adopted as a symbol of the Irish famine.)

Another similarity between Egyptian and Irish theology may be bull-worship. The Minoans were great followers of the original Apis-bull cult of Egypt, and if a large number of the sailors on this voyage were Minoan, this alternative cult may also have established itself along the western fringes of Europe. That a bull-cult was established in Spain needs no further explanation, but the evidence for a bull-cult in Ireland is perhaps more subtle. To uncover the Irish bull-cult we again need to look at the early manuscripts, and there we find the *Lebor na Huidre* (the *Book of the Dun Cow*). This is a twelfth century manuscript that was copied from much older texts and in part it relates a mythical tale known as the *Tain bo Cuailnge* (the *Cattle Raid of Cooley*). This is a semi-mythological tale about a battle to possess the most perfect cow in all of Ireland. There were two contenders for this title: the White-cow and the Dun-cow (Dark-cow), and the two animals finish the story in a great mythological fight to the death, which was won by the Dun-cow.

There is an amount of synergy between this Irish story and the cult of the Apis-bull. Unusually for Egyptian theology, the Apis was a real animal; the most perfect black bull in all Egypt, with a white star on its forehead (a motif that was to be repeated in Anna Sewell's novel, *Black Beauty*). Like the Irish Dun-cow, the Egyptian Apis-bull was to be coveted and venerated as a symbol of power, and so it is not unreasonable to see a tentative cultural and theological link within these ancient tales.

More importantly, perhaps, this exodus was the exile of Aye-Gaythelos and Ankhesenamun-Scota of the Amarna regime, and so it is likely that the religion they would have taken with them was substantially Atonist – the original monotheistic belief system. Since I have already demonstrated that Atonism was an early form of Judaism, much of the theology of these first settlers in Ireland may have been largely indistinguishable from the Christianity that arrived many centuries later. Indeed, this could be one reason why Christianity was accepted so readily in Ireland, as it was simply a variation on an already established creed.

Lost pharaoh

While the golden torqs, faience beads, red hands, boat-tombs, round-towers and the epigraphic evidence from Ireland strongly hint at ancient cultural links with Bronze Age Iberian and Egyptian cultures, none of these items can be seen as being derived unambiguously from the Egyptian Amarna era. Nevertheless, having followed the trail of the descendants of Pharaoh Aye-Gaythelos and Queen Ankhesenamun-Scota all the way from Amarna, through Brigantia in Iberia and on to the 'Emerald Isle' of Hibernia or Scotia (Ireland), it would have been nice to have discovered an artifact that came directly from Egypt. One might have hoped that the descendants of Aye-Gaythelos had followed the Egyptian custom of elaborate funerary rituals and ancestor veneration, which have provided such rich archaeological treasures in Egypt. Were it not for the funerary rituals of the Egyptian royalty, we would have very little information on the true history of Egypt.

While it is true that a forced colony like Brigantia would have been relatively poor, and unable to afford great tombs; nevertheless, such an ingrained, ancient tradition should still have resulted in small tombs containing a few hand-me-down items of jewellery taken from Egypt. The evidence from Thebes and Tanis even hints at the possibility that these burials would not necessarily have been left in Brigantia when the move to Ireland was made. In Tanis, some of the earlier royal burials in this region were moved into the tomb of Psusennes II. Their original burial location is not known, but it appears that they were exhumed and moved to Tanis when this new city was constructed. Likewise in Thebes, when the systematic looting of the tombs in the Valley of the Kings was in progress, nearly all the royal mummies were salvaged and relocated in a secret location behind the temple of Queen Hatchepsut.

Thus, the tradition seems to be that the burials of ancestors would, if possible, be moved with the people rather than leaving them to be pillaged by strangers. So it would have been nice to have ended this investigation with the remains of a mummy, which may be linked in some way to the Amarna era: a discovery something like the burial at Tara with its necklace of Egyptian faience beads, the Tara Prince, but with a mummified body too.

Strange as it may seem, in actual fact the head of a mummy can be found in this very same part of Ireland, and it resides in the Catholic cathedral of St Peter's at Drogheda, which lies just a few kilometers from Newgrange. I was introduced to this odd feature of Irish history by Andrew Power, the author of *Ireland, Land of the Pharaohs*. This mummified head is supposed to be that of Oliver Plunket, the seventeenth century archbishop of Armagh who was executed in London in 1681 – but the reason for this head's strange state of preservation remains a complete mystery. Frank Donnelly, the author of a booklet on the mummified head, says:

> Although some of the features of the preservation of St Oliver's remains are strange and difficult to explain in scientific terms, it is not at all claimed here that there has been any miraculous intervention.[9]

'Difficult to explain' is an understatement. The unfortunate Oliver Plunket was said to have been hung, drawn and quartered at Tyburn, London, for the crime of being an agent of the Pope and plotting rebellion in Ireland. His severed head is said to have been placed in a tin and kept at the church of

IX   Pharaoh Plunket

St Giles. However, the dark, dank recesses of a London church are hardly conducive to any form of natural mummification. Let's put this claim into its proper perspective; of the millions of people who have died and been buried in northwest Europe, absolutely none of these corpses have spontaneously embalmed themselves. Each and every one of them has rotted and decayed within a very short period of time, and left very little in the archaeological record. Miracles aside, which is a possibility that I dismiss out of hand, no corpse is going to mummify itself in the northern European climate (unless it is dropped into a peat-bog). It is impossible, therefore, for this to be the true history of the head that lies in Drogheda cathedral. Either Oliver Plunket had had a remarkably effective form of preservation and storage applied to his corpse, or this is not the head of Archbishop Plunket.

Even if we allow the former possibility to be true, I still wonder about the state of preservation that has been achieved here. Britain was not exactly at the forefront of the world's embalming industry, especially in the seventeenth century AD. If the head of Oliver Plunket really has been embalmed by an undertaker in London, then this is a remarkable and absolutely unique example of their work. Unlike Egyptian embalming, 'modern' techniques have revolved around pumping preservative fluids through the blood system, a technique which was discovered by William Harvey in 1628. The far more superior formaldehyde preservation was not discovered until 1868, by the German chemist William Hoffman. But even with these advanced techniques, the British Institute of Embalmers only admits to:

> The treatment of a dead human body in order to achieve an aseptic condition, temporary preservation and a pre-mortem appearance. [10]

Note the word 'temporary' in this quotation. But the embalming of Plunket's head is far from temporary, having already lasted for over 300 years. In fact, the very look of this head, in both colour and texture, is wholly reminiscent of the mummies that still lie in the Cairo museum, and which have remained in that state for 3,000 years or more. Like the Egyptian mummies, Plunket's head is on the small side, with a light blonde-ginger stubble to both scalp and chin.* The skin appears to have been desiccated and treated with resins, while

---

* Many of the Egyptian aristocracy, priesthood and royalty had shaven heads, presumably for health reasons, and so their mummies only sport a light stubble. Many of the Amarna royalty appear to have had reddish hair, while the mummy of Ramesses the Great has blonde hair. There is some uncertainty as to how much influence the mummification process has had in this colouration.

the flattened ears and rucked skin show that the head has been wrapped with cloth at some point in time. But perhaps the most telling similarity to the Egyptian equivalents, is the mention of the head being 'sweet smelling'.

As far as the head of an Egyptian mummy is concerned, the full mummification process involved the removal of the brain through the nose, the drying out of the external tissues with natron (a natural salt), and then the filling of the brain cavity with resins. The resins used in this process differed, with some mummies having bitumen applied; but for royal burials, the resins were often frankincense and myrrh – the expensive and aromatic resins that were said to have been brought by the Magi to the infant Jesus. There is no natural reason for this aroma emanating from the head at Drogheda, but had the head been mummified in the Egyptian fashion then it is entirely possible that a skull full of frankincense and myrrh would still emit a faintly sweet aroma after 3,000 or so years.

It would seem likely that the head of Oliver Plunket may have an alternative history to the one advertised. Orthodox history claims that his head led a charmed life, as it was sent from London to Rome where it spent some forty years. Then, resplendent in a new casket, the head made its way back to Drogheda, where it spent some 200 years in the care of the Dominican nuns at the Siena Convent. In 1921 it was then transferred to the Catholic St Peter's Church in Drogheda, which was built as the Oliver Plunket Memorial Church.

Could this 'new' church, and the head it contains, be a central component in a much greater historical mystery? Well, despite the Catholic cathedral of St Peter's being highly orthodox, this edifice is not without an element of covert symbolism. Like many Catholic churches around the globe, St Peter's contains a scene of the Last Supper; which was beautifully carved in milky white marble by the late Victorian sculptor, Edmund Sharp. However, as in Leonardo da Vinci's version of the Last Supper in the refectory of Santa Maria delle Grazie in Milan, the disciple on the right of Jesus is clearly a woman (who looks remarkably like the late Diana, Princess of Wales; see fig 74). Now this in itself is not so unusual, as at least half the Last Supper scenes I have investigated do indeed depict a woman on the right-hand side of Jesus. But these female 'St Johns' generally reside in the great stately homes of Britain, and not in the Catholic churches of Ireland. That this overt representation of Mary Magdalene, the sister-wife of Jesus, should reside in the midst of a Catholic church in the devout heartland of southern Ireland is quite remarkable.

This controversial depiction of the Last Supper would suggest that the Catholic Church is not always as orthodox as one might imagine, and there may be characters behind the scenes who know rather more than they would ever admit to. So could there be another mystery concealed under the

Fig 74. The Last Supper carving in St Peter's (Catholic) Church, Drogheda. The disciple to the right of Jesus is clearly a woman and so this is an overt portrayal of Mary Magdalene, the sister-wife of Jesus.

soaring vaults of St Peter's in Drogheda? Could this head be a central component in the story of Aye-Gaythelos and Scota?

Well, without an examination of the condition of this mummified head's nasal bone and the content of the skull cavity, to see if the head was really mummified in the Egyptian fashion, this proposal will no doubt remain a intriguing mystery. While some readers might scoff at the proposition that this head was mummified in the Egyptian fashion by immigrants who came to Ireland from Egypt, this suggestion is no more fanciful than the present claim that Oliver Plunket's head managed to mummify itself through some unspecified but semi-miraculous process. Given a straight choice between the two possible histories that have been outlined here, I myself would definitely opt for the Egyptian heritage.

Coda

Unfortunately, this is the end of the trail for research into Gaythelos and Scota.

While much of the information presented in this book may be considered to be circumstantial, there is a growing body of evidence that points towards a historical basis for the various chronicles of the Irish and Scots. But if this is so, then this would mean that both Ireland and Scotland were seeded during the Bronze Age with much of the high culture and civilisation of Egypt.

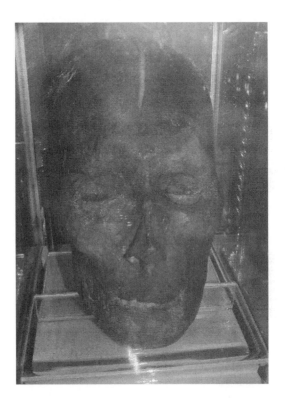

Fig 75. The mummified head claimed to be that of Oliver Plunket.

That this implantation did not immediately result in a flourishing advanced culture in greater Britain, as was the result of similar contacts in Greece, may be due to the harsher climatic conditions in northwest Europe; which demanded a greater expenditure of energy just to survive. Nevertheless, an echo of that advanced culture may well have rippled down through the millennia, for it was Britain that eventually shrugged off the oppression of the Catholic Church and ushered in the Enlightenment Era; and it was this Age of Reason that formed the foundations upon which the mighty edifice of the Industrial Revolution was based. It would be pleasing to think that our modern technological world was, in some small part, a by-product of Gaythelos and Scota's arduous journey to the Emerald Isle many millennia ago.

✠✠✠   End   ✠✠✠

Appendix

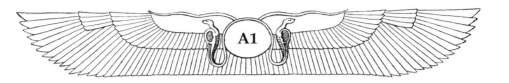

Exodus Timeline

This revised history of the Egypto-Israelite nation has highlighted a number of exoduses to and from Egypt. The complexity of this history has probably generated an amount of confusion, and so the diagram overleaf attempts to portray these migrations graphically, in order to clarify the situation as much as is possible. The top of the chart gives the names of the pharaohs of Egypt for each significant era, while the lower register gives the equivalent Old Testament patriarch who lived in that same era.

A1 Exodus Timeline

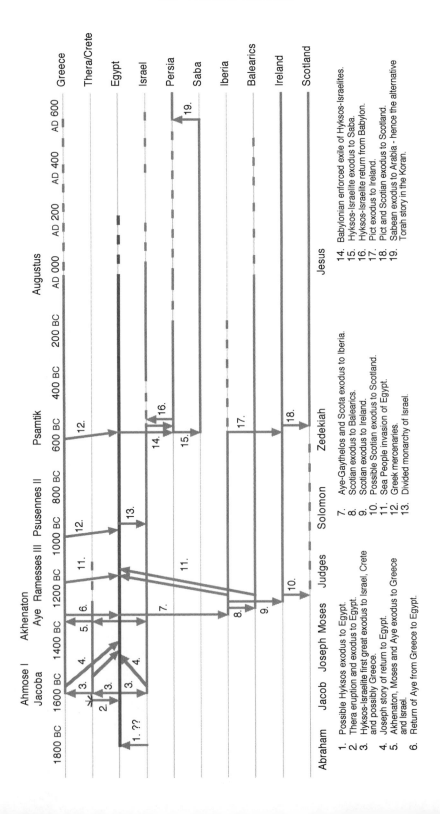

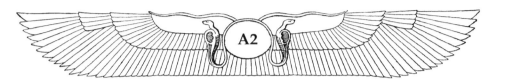

Four-room House

In my previous books I have made a reasoned case for the Israelite exiles in Judaea being the Hyksos people from Lower Egypt. This idea has, of course, been vigorously denied by the academic establishment. One of the arguments devised to prove that I was wrong, was the 'fact' that the thirteenth century Israelite housing in Judaea is unique to the Israelites. So why would the Hyksos people, upon being exiled to Judaea, suddenly begin building a completely new type of domestic housing? Ergo, the Israelites cannot have been the Hyksos.

However, this supposed 'demolition' of my thesis does not stand up to closer scrutiny. The Israelite houses in Judaea are frequently designed around a standard 'four-room' layout. It has often been said that there is no antecedent for this design within Egypt; but in actual fact this confident assertion is wrong, for there *is* an Egyptian predecessor to the four-room house. In fact, the design came from the standard Hyksos mortuary chapel, which had exactly the same layout as the Israelite house design. But it is the Hyksos mortuary chapel that predates the Israelite house by a considerable margin, and so it is likely that Israelites inherited this design from Hyksos at Avaris – because they were one and the same people.

The eminent Egyptologist, Manfred Bietak, also discovered the four-room house on the west bank at Karnak. He says of this discovery:

> Huts more than 3,000 years old belonging to workers – perhaps slaves – and with the same floor plan as ancient Israelite four-room houses have been identified at Medinet Habu, opposite Luxor in Egypt. These reed huts may represent extra-Biblical evidence of Israel in Egypt.

If true, Israelite or proto-Israelite workers were in Egypt in the second half of the 12th century BC, more than half a century later than has previously been thought. This evidence, in turn, would have important implications for the historicity of the Biblical narrative. [1]

Interestingly, these huts were found inside the temple of Pharaoh Aye on the west bank at Karnak. Professor Bietak dates them to the post-Amarna era, but whatever their exact age it is certain that they were in use at a date that is very close to the emergence of the four-room house design in Israel. Bietak is excited because this provides evidence that the Israelites were resident in Egypt at a similar time to the biblical exodus; but he then manages to reverse the exodus, using a logic that completely escapes me, by indicating that the Israelites were exiled from Canaan to Egypt and not *vice versa!*

In short, Bietak's arguments do not use all the evidence available and are therefore incorrect. The Avaris (Hyksos) chapels are much earlier than the Karnak houses, as they date from the seventeenth dynasty and it was not for several centuries that these same designs subsequently appeared in Israel and Karnak as domestic dwellings. Contrary to Bietak's theory, what these four-room house layouts really indicate is that this design was an ancient and well-established component of Hyksos culture long before the Israelites inherited it, and so it is highly likely that the Israelites were indeed the descendants of the Hyksos.

Strangely enough, although Bietak was keen to highlight his four-room house discovery in Karnak – which he instantly linked with itinerant Israelite workers slaving for the pharaoh in an appropriately biblical fashion – he makes no mention of the strikingly similar design of the Hyksos chapels in Avaris. This is doubly strange when one realizes that the excavation of the chapels at Avaris were performed by one Manfred Bietak. [2] It's amazing how far a (religious) preconception will go to maintain the status quo.

A2 Four-room House

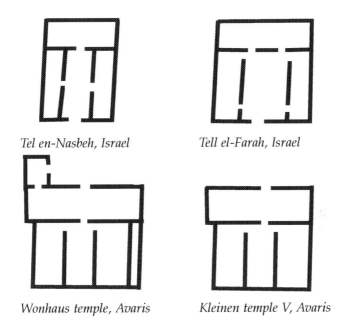

Tel en-Nasbeh, Israel   Tell el-Farah, Israel

Wonhaus temple, Avaris   Kleinen temple V, Avaris

Fig 78.   Four-room houses of Israel and four-room temples of Avaris.

List of diagrams

List of diagrams

Photo credits

Plate 1.   View from the El Maestrat mountains in Catalonia - Ralph Ellis.
Plate 2.   Satellite image of the Ebro Delta, Earth Data Analysis Center.
Plate 3.   A reconstruction of the Dover boat - Ralph Ellis.
Plate 4.   The Dover boat - Ralph Ellis.
Plate 5.   Model of the Ferriby boat - Ralph Ellis.
Plate 6.   Bronze Age cartwheel from Dublin - Ralph Ellis.
Plate 7.   Solid gold cape, discovered at Mold, Flintshire - Ralph Ellis.
Plate 8.   The Ring of Minos, from Minoan Crete - Ralph Ellis.
Plate 9-10. Two golden torqs from the Dublin museum - Ralph Ellis.
Plate 11.   Ornate spiral torq from the Iron Age Snettisham hoard - Ralph Ellis.
Plate 12.   Partial reconstructions of Minoan Knossos in Crete - Ralph Ellis.
Plate 13.   Helen of Troy, by Evelyn De Morgan.
Plate 14.   Mary Magdalene, by Carlo Crivelli, Rijksmuseum, Amsterdam.
Plate 15.   Bull-leaping fresco, of Minoan inspiration, from Avaris, Vivian Davies.
Plate 16.   Bull-leaping fresco from Minoan Knossos, Crete - Ralph Ellis.
Plate 17.   Truncated round-tower of Mousa broch, Shetland - Ralph Ellis.
Plate 18.   Truncated round-tower near Santanyi, Mallorca - Ralph Ellis.
Plate 19.   Truncated round-tower at Torello, Mallorca - Ralph Ellis.
Plate 20.   Pillar room, Santanyi, Mallorca - Ralph Ellis.
Plate 21.   Pillar room, Phaestos, Crete - Ralph Ellis.
Plate 22.   The Mount of Hostages, at Tara in the Boyne valley - Ralph Ellis.
Plate 23.   Truncated round-tower inside the Cahergall amphitheater - Ralph Ellis.
Plate 24.   The Gallarus Ossuary near Dingle, Co Kerry, Ireland - Ralph Ellis.
Plate 25.   The Tudons Naveta, near Ciutadella, Minorca - Ralph Ellis.
Plate 26.   Rattoo round-tower, near Ballyduff, Co Kerry - Ralph Ellis.
Plate 27.   Abernethy tower near Perth - Steven.
Plate 28.   Scota's grave, near Tralee, Co Kerry - Ralph Ellis..
Plate 29.   North Molton necklace, photo - Exeter Museum.

Notes & references

Bible: All references taken from the King James edition, although the text is often modernised for clarity.

Josephus: AA = Against Apion, Ant = Antiquities, JW = Jewish war, L = Life.

Page references are to the Loeb Classical Library system. Quotes taken from William Whiston's translation, which was first published in 1736; some references are from the Penguin Classics edition by G. Williamson, first published 1959.

Manetho   All page numbers are taken from the LCL edition, editor G. Goold.

Within the referencing system in this book, some of the reference numbers are prefixed with letters. This is to give the reader an idea of the source of the reference, without having to look up that particular reference. This only applies to the more popular reference works, and the following have been prefixed:

B = Bible, M = Manetho, J = Josephus, H = Herodotus,
T = Talmud, KN = Kebra Nagast, K = Koran, S = Strabo
SC = Scotichronicon.

All references to Egyptian words are taken from:

An Egyptian Hieroglyphic Dictionary, E A Wallis Budge, Dover Publications. The entries in the dictionary are substantially in alphabetical (glyph) order, and so the references are easy to find and have not been listed in the references by their page number.

Abbreviations:

ECIiAT	=	Egypt, Canaan and Israel in Ancient Times, Donald Redford.
TTIPiE	=	The Third Intermediate Period in Egypt, Kenneth Kitchen.
EotP	=	Egypt of the Pharaohs, Alan Gardiner.
ARoE	=	Ancient Records of Egypt, James Breasted.
K. Nagast	=	Translation taken from 'Queen of Sheba', W Budge.

Notes & References

Introduction

1. http://albanach.org/kilt.html

Chapter I

1. A history book for Scots (A selection from Scotichronicon) Donald Watt; Scotichronicon, Donald Watt, vol 1 pxv.
2. Veue of the present state of Irelande [1596].
3. Scotichronicon, W Bower bk 1 ch 10.

Chapter II

1. Ian Shaw, Oxford History of Ancient Egypt.
2. Scotichronicon, Walter Bower bk 1 ch12.
3. http://www.saxakali.com/suzar/madonna.htm
4. Scotichronicon, Walter Bower bk 1 ch 9.
5. Ibid bk 1 ch 9.
6. Manetho, Aegyptica Fr 50, Fr 53.
7. Hughes, Dictionary of Islam.
8. Bible Est 1:19.
9. James Pritchard, Ancient Near-Eastern Texts. Hieroglyphic Dictionary, W Budge.
10. Scotichronicon, Walter Bower.
11. Scotichronicon, Walter Bower bk 1 ch 9.
12. Bible I Maccabee 12:20-21.
13. The Greek Myths, Robert Graves bk 60.
14. The Greek Myths, Robert Graves bk 60.
15. Scotichronicon, Walter Bower bk 1 ch12.
16. She was the Amity Brig, Les Johnson.
17. Lebor Gabala Erein, The Book of Invasions.

Chapter III

1. Bible Ex 3:14.
2. Bible Ex 3:11-14.
3. Bible Ex 24:12.
4. Strabo 5.2.40, quoting Euripides.
5. Rock tombs of Amarna, N Davies vol 6.
6. Akhenaton, C Aldred.
7. Akhenaton, C Aldred p289.
8. Scotichronicon, Walter Bower bk 1 ch 9.

9.   Bible Num 12:1.
10.   Josephus Ant 2:238-253.
11.   Scotichronicon, Walter Bower bk 1 ch 11.

Chapter IV

1.   Scotichronicon, Walter Bower bk 1 ch 13.
2.   Ibid bk 1 ch 15.
3.   Ibid bk 1 ch 17.
4.   Ibid bk 1 ch 16.
5.   Ibid bk 1 ch 18.
6.   Scotichronicon, notes by Prof D Watt, p121.
7.   The Classical Gazetteer, William Hazlit (1851).
8.   The Classical Gazetteer, William Hazlit (1851).
9.   Scotichronicon, Walter Bower bk 1 ch 16.
12.   Ibid bk 1 ch 18.
13.   Ibid bk 1 ch 22.

Chapter V

1.   http://touregypt.net/featurestories/tt56.htm
2.   Helen of Troy, Bettany Hughes p59.
3.   Connections between Egypt and the Minoan world, Manfred Bietak.
4.   Minoan Painting and Egypt, Lyvia Morgan Quoted in: Egypt, the Aegean
      and the Levant, Vivian Davies.
5.   Ibid.
6.   Histories, Tacitus bk 5. (The Works of Tacitus in Four Volumes,
      Liberty Library)
7.   Peter Warren, Minoan Crete and Pharaonic Egypt.
8.   Minoan Painting and Egypt, Lyvia Morgan Quoted in: Egypt, the Aegean
      and the Levant, Vivian Davies.
9.   The Decipherment of Linear B, J Chadwick.
10.   The Decipherment of Linear B, J Chadwick
11.   Kebra Negast Wallis Budge xii.
12.   www.phoenicians.org
13.   Biblical Concordance.
14.   The World of the Phoenicians, Sabatino Moscati.
15.   The World of the Phoenicians, Sabatino Moscati.
16.   Aegeanet, Maria C. Shaw, ('Murex', May 13, 1999).
17.   Palmer, Leonard R. (1963), The Interpretation of Mycenaean Greek Texts.
18.   Bible Zech 5:1.
19.   Bible 2 Ki 23:13.
20.   Minoan Painting and Egypt, Lyvia Morgan Quoted in: Egypt, the Aegean

and the Levant, Vivian Davies.

22. www.phoenician.org.
23. http://www.ekathimerini.com/4dcgi/_w_articles_politics_598535_03/10/
      2003_34767
24. Odyssey, Homer 5:227-261.
25. Coventry Boat-builders and Chandlery.
      Gloucester Street, Spon End, Coventry CV1 3BZ, U K.
26. The Athenian Trireme, J Morrison.
27. http://www.ferribyboats.co.uk
28. Murano Magic, the history of Murano glass, Carl Gable.
29. The Greek Myths, Robert Graves bk1-60.
30. Model Ships and Boats, G Reisner.
32. Gallic War, Julius Caesar 3:13.
33. Geography, Strabo 4:4:1.

Chapter VI

1.   Scotichronicon, W Bower, bk 1 Ch 13.
2.   A burial with faience beads at Tara, Prof Sean O'Riordain.
3.   Ibid.
4.   Ibid.
5.   Letter from the Assistant Keeper of Irish Antiquities, National Museum of
      Ireland.
6.   http://www.ucd.ie/news/mar06/030306_mound_of_the_hostages.htm
7.   Sacred Mythological Centers of Ireland, J Roberts.
      Aye's mother's name can be pronounced as Tuyu or Tiyu.
8.   Bible Gen 38:28.
9.   Rock tombs of Amarna, N Davies vol VI.
10. Tutankhamen, Christine Desroches-Noblecourt, p144.
12. Bible, Exodus 4:6-7.
13. Sacred Mythological Centers of Ireland, Jack Roberts.

Chapter VII

1.   Norman Stone Castles (vol 2), Chris Gravett.
2.   http://en.wikipedia.org/wiki/List_of_redheads.

Chapter IX

1.   Scotichronicon, W Bower, bk 1 ch 23.
2.   Scotichronicon, W Bower, bk 1 ch 21.
3.   Basque Mythology, Olga Gomez http://www.pantheon.org/areas/mythology
      /europe/basque/article

4. Scotichronicon, W Bower   bk 1 ch 30.
5. Pict resources. http://www.tylwytheg.com
6. Scotichronicon, W Bower, bk 1 ch 31.
7. Scotichronicon, W Bower, bk 1 ch 20.
8. Scotichronicon, W Bower, bk 1 ch 20.
9. Until the Storm Passes, Frank Donnelly.
10. http://www.bioe.co.uk/history.asp

Appendix 2

1. http://www.institutoestudiosantiguoegipto.com/bietak_I.htm
2. Biblical Archaeological Review.
   Avaris, the Capital of the Hyksos, by Manfred Bietak.
   British Museum Press. Research by Robert Giles, Arizona.

Index.

Symbols

22 : 7 ~ 169, 170, 171, 172, 173, 181.

A

Aaron ~ 51, 70, 72, 73.
Abernethy ~ 157.
Abraham ~ 44.
Abydos ~ 146.
Acencheres ~ 17.
Acencris ~ 11.
Achaemenid dynasty ~ 28.
Achen ~ 16.
Achencheres ~ 11, 12, 15.
Acherres ~ 11.
Achilles ~ 96.
Achorisis ~ 11.
Adam ~ 185.
Adam and Eve ~ 142, 151.
Adhon ~ 112, 117. *See also* Aton.
Adonis ~ 117.
Aegyptus ~ 45.
Aeria ~ 6.
Agamede ~ 96.
Age of Reason ~ 210.
Ahmos ~ 12.
Ahmose I ~ 12, 94, 97, 98, 100.
  Avaris ~ 100.
Aileach ~ 159.
Akhenaton ~ xiv, 7, 9, 10, 11, 12, 16, 17,
      18, 22, 24, 34, 35, 40, 41, 42, 46,
      47, 51, 53, 55, 56, 57, 59, 60, 64,
      65, 66, 68, 69, 70, 71, 72, 73, 74,
      76, 94, 98, 101, 102, 112, 116, 117,
      141, 142, 150, 153, 190, 198, 202.
  artwork ~ 98, 100.
  Aye ~ 46, 53, 72, 141, 202.
  daughters ~ 18, 35, 202.
  death ~ 69.
  exile ~ 47, 56, 65, 66, 68, 69, 94, 101.
  Hymn to the Aten ~ 116.
  Minoans ~ 101.

Moses ~ 11, 55, 57, 68, 71, 72.
Mutnodjmet ~ 60, 64.
name ~ 190.
Osiris ~ 198.
palm frond ~ 112.
Phoenicians ~ 117.
Scota ~ 9, 16, 17, 22.
torqs ~ 142.
Tuankhamen ~ 65.
wives ~ 40, 59, 60.
Akhetaton ~ 22. *See also* Amarna.
Akrotiri ~ 95, 97, 118.
Albany ~ 50.
Aldred, C ~ 63, 65.
Alexander the Great ~ 32, 105.
Allegro, J ~ 144.
alphabet ~ 204.
Amarna ~ 7, 9, 10, 15, 16, 18, 22, 23,
      27, 28, 34, 35, 38, 40, 43, 46, 48,
      53, 54, 56, 60, 61, 62, 67, 68, 72,
      73, 74, 101, 105, 107, 113, 141,
      143, 144, 145, 150, 153, 156, 189.
  artwork ~ 101.
  Aton ~ 16.
  bull-worship ~ 101.
  exile ~ 54, 56, 73, 74.
  family tree ~ 39.
  gold ~ 145.
  Minoans ~ 107, 156.
  Phoenicians ~ 113.
  quarry ~ 68.
  red hand ~ 153, 156.
  Thera ~ 105.
  tombs ~ 46.
  torqs ~ 141, 143, 144.
Amen ~ 61.
Amenhotep I ~ 12.
Amenhotep II ~ 12, 66, 95.
Amenhotep III ~ 11, 12, 13, 40, 64.
Amenhotep IV ~ 101. *See*
      also Akhenaton.
Amenophath ~ 13.

Index

Index

Index

Index

Printed in Great Britain
by Amazon